Workshop on Computational Models of Reference, Anaphora and Coreference 2018

New Orleans, Louisiana, USA
6 June 2018

ISBN: 978-1-5108-6356-9

NAACL HLT 2018

**Computational Models of
Reference, Anaphora and Coreference**

Proceedings of the Workshop

June 6, 2018
New Orleans, Louisiana

Introduction

There has been a lot of research activity in anaphora / coreference resolution in recent years, but once the DAARC series ended, there have been no events in Computational Linguistics entirely dedicated to this type of research. The Coreference Beyond Ontonotes (CORBON) workshops held in 2016 (with NAACL) and 2017 (with EACL) partially addressed this need, but their focus was primarily on under-investigated coreference phenomena. This 2018 workshop on Computational Models of Reference, Anaphora and Coreference aims to be the first of a series of workshops with a broader focus, aiming to attract the entire anaphora / coreference / reference community. Our intention is for these workshops to provide a forum where work on all aspects of computational work on anaphora resolution and annotation can be presented, including both research on coreference and research on types of anaphora such as bridging references resolution and discourse deixis. We also hope to attract research on closely related topics such as psycholinguistic models of anaphoric interpretation and computational models of reference–e.g., research on deictical reference to objects displayed in a multimodal interface.

This year's workshop attracted 16 submissions. 11 were accepted, for an acceptance rate of 68%. The accepted papers cover work on anaphora annotation or resolution in 6 different languages. As traditional in this series of workshops, a number of papers focus on less-studied aspects of anaphora resolution such as bridging reference resolution or discourse deixis resolution, but many papers study coreference as well. The genres are also varied, ranging from news to social media and dialogue.

The workshop was again associated with a Shared Task. This year's Shared Task, co-chaired by Yulia Grishina and Massimo Poesio, was on anaphora resolution in the ARRAU corpus, an anaphorically annotated corpus of English that contains documents covering both written text and spoken dialogue, and annotated for identity anaphora, bridging reference and discourse deixis. Two of the papers in the workshop, by Poesio *et al* and by Roesiger, describe work related to the Shared Task.

To conclude, we wish to thank the Program Committee, who did an excellent job at choosing papers in a very short time, and the organizers of the Shared Task. And we're looking forward to meeting the authors and the other participants to the workshop in New Orleans.

Massimo Poesio, Vincent Ng, and Maciej Ogrodniczuk

Organizers:

Massimo Poesio, Queen Mary University of London (UK)
Vincent Ng, University of Texas at Dallas (USA)
Maciej Ogrodniczuk, Institute of Computer Science, Polish Academy of Sciences (Poland)

Program Committee:

Anders Bjorkelund, University of Stuttgart (Germany)
Antonio Branco, University of Lisbon (Portugal)
Dan Cristea, A. I. Cuza University of Iasi (Romania)
Pascal Denis, MAGNET, INRIA Lille Nord-Europe (France)
Sobha Lalitha Devi, AU-KBC Research Center, Anna University of Chennai (India)
Yulia Grishina, University of Potsdam (Germany)
Veronique Hoste, Ghent University (Belgium)
Ryu Iida, National Institute of Information and Communications Technology (NICT), Kyoto (Japan)
Varada Kolhatkar, Simon Fraser University (Canada)
Katja Markert, Heidelberg University (Germany)
Costanza Navaretta, University of Copenhagen (Denmark)
Anna Nedoluzhko, Charles University in Prague (Czech Republic)
Michal Novak, Charles University in Prague (Czech Republic)
Simone Paolo Ponzetto, University of Mannheim (Germany)
Sameer Pradhan, cemantix.org and Boulder Learning Inc. (USA)
Marta Recasens, Google Inc. (USA)
Dan Roth, University of Pennsylvania (USA)
Veselin Stoyanov, Facebook (USA)
Olga Uryupina, University of Trento (Italy)
Yannick Versley, IBM (Germany)
Sam Wiseman, Harvard University (USA)
Heike Zinsmeister, University of Hamburg (Germany)

Invited Speaker:

Ana Marasovic, Institut für Computerlinguistik, Universität Heidelberg (Germany)

Shared Task Organizers:

Yulia Grishina, University of Potsdam (Germany) (chair)
Varada Kolhatkar, Simon Fraser University (Canada)
Anna Nedoluzhko, Charles University in Prague (Czech Republic)
Massimo Poesio, Queen Mary University of London (UK)
Adam Roussel, University of the Ruhr at Bochum (Germany)
Fabian Simonjetz, University of the Ruhr at Bochum (Germany)
Olga Uryupina, University of Trento (Italy)
Heike Zinsmeister, University of Hamburg (Germany)

Table of Contents

Workshop Program

Wednesday June 6 2018

09:00–10:30   **Session 1**

09:00–09:10   *Welcome*
Massimo Poesio, Vincent Ng, Maciej Ogrodniczuk

09:10–10:00   *Invited Talk*
Ana Marasovic

10:00–10:30   *Anaphora Resolution for Twitter Conversations: An Exploratory Study*
Berfin Aktaş, Tatjana Scheffler and Manfred Stede

10:30–11:00   **Break**

11:00–12:30   **Session 2: Shared Task, Plural Reference**

11:00–11:30   *Anaphora Resolution with the ARRAU Corpus*
Massimo Poesio, Yulia Grishina, Varada Kolhatkar, Nafise Moosavi, Ina Roesiger, Adam Roussel, Fabian Simonjetz, Alexandra Uma, Olga Uryupina, Juntao Yu and Heike Zinsmeister

11:30–12:00   *Rule- and Learning-based Methods for Bridging Resolution in the ARRAU Corpus*
Ina Roesiger

12:00–12:30   *A Predictive Model for Notional Anaphora in English*
Amir Zeldes

Wednesday June 6 2018 (continued)

12:30–14:00   Lunch

14:00–15:30   Session 3: Bridging, Discourse deixis, Anaphora in German, Corpus annotation 1

14:00–14:20   *Integrating Predictions from Neural-Network Relation Classifiers into Coreference and Bridging Resolution*
Ina Roesiger, Maximilian Köper, Kim Anh Nguyen and Sabine Schulte im Walde

14:20–14:50   *Towards Bridging Resolution in German: Data Analysis and Rule-based Experiments*
Janis Pagel and Ina Roesiger

14:50–15:10   *Detecting and Resolving Shell Nouns in German*
Adam Roussel

15:10–15:30   *PAWS: A Multi-lingual Parallel Treebank with Anaphoric Relations*
Anna Nedoluzhko, Michal Novák and Maciej Ogrodniczuk

15:30–16:00   Break

16:00–17:30   Session 4: Corpus Annotation 2, Cognitive Models

16:00–16:30   *A Fine-grained Large-scale Analysis of Coreference Projection*
Michal Novák

16:30–17:00   *Modeling Brain Activity Associated with Pronoun Resolution in English and Chinese*
Jixing Li, Murielle Fabre, Wen-Ming Luh and John Hale

17:00–17:30   *Event versus entity co-reference: Effects of context and form of referring expression*
Sharid Loáiciga, Luca Bevacqua, Hannah Rohde and Christian Hardmeier

Anaphora Resolution for Twitter Conversations: An Exploratory Study

Berfin Aktaş   **Tatjana Scheffler**   **Manfred Stede**

`firstname.lastname@uni-potsdam.de`

SFB 1287
Research Focus Cognitive Sciences
University of Potsdam
Germany

Abstract

We present a corpus study of pronominal anaphora on Twitter conversations. After outlining the specific features of this genre, with respect to reference resolution, we explain the construction of our corpus and the annotation steps. From this we derive a list of phenomena that need to be considered when performing anaphora resolution on this type of data. Finally, we test the performance of an off-the-shelf resolution system, and provide some qualitative error analysis.

1 Introduction

We are interested in the task of pronominal anaphora resolution for conversations in Twitter, which to our knowledge has not been addressed so far. By 'conversation', we mean tree structures originating from the `reply-to` relation; when using replies, people often (though not always) interact with each other across several turns.[1] Hence, anaphora resolution needs to attend both to the general and well-known problems of handling Twitter language, and potentially to aspects of conversation structure.

In order to study the properties of coreference relations in these conversations, we built a corpus that is designed to represent a number of different relevant phenomena, which we selected carefully. We annotated pronouns and their antecedents, so that the data can be used for systematically testing anaphora resolvers, and we conducted experiments with the Stanford system (Clark and Manning, 2015).

The paper is structured as follows: Section 2 introduces general phenomena found in Twitter conversations and describes earlier research. Section 3 discusses our approach to corpus construction and annotation. Section 4 shows in detail which "non-standard" phenomena we encountered in annotating the Twitter conversations in our corpus, and which need to be tackled by a coreference resolver. Section 5 outlines our experiments with the Stanford resolver and presents the results; finally we draw some conclusions in Section 6.

2 Overview of the Task and Related Work

In this section, we provide an overview of research that has addressed anaphora resolution specifically in the context of dialogue, multilogue, or social media. There we encounter the following phenomena that are potentially relevant for our scenario of Twitter conversations (and which are largely not present in monologue and hence in the "standard" work on anaphora resolution):

1. Pronouns referring to speakers

2. Other exophoric reference

3. Conversation structure as a factor for antecedent selection

4. Phenomena specific to spoken conversation

5. Phenomena specific to social media text

Obviously, not all of these phenomena are equally relevant in all interactive dialogue settings — in fact, certain settings basically do not require attending to such phenomena. For instance, the early work on TRAINS/TRIPS (Tetreault and Allen, 2004) emphasized the role of semantic features for pronoun resolution, while the factor of conversation structure was not so relevant, as the human-machine dialogues were relatively simple. Likewise, early work by Strube and Müller (2003) on the Switchboard corpus demonstrated that existing approaches to statistical pronoun resolution

---

[1] For an overview of constructing corpora of this kind and some annotation tasks, see (Scheffler, 2017).

Proceedings of the Workshop on Computational Models of Reference, Anaphora and Coreference, pages 1–10
New Orleans, Louisiana, June 6, 2018. ©2018 Association for Computational Linguistics

could carry over to conversational data, but the authors focused on non-nominal antecedents and did not emphasize the need for using additional interaction features.

2.1 Reference to Speakers

In addition to using proper names, speakers can refer to one another using pronouns, and several early systems implemented simple rules for resolving *I* and *you* (e.g., (Jain et al., 2004)). In multilogue, it is also possible that third-person pronouns *he/she* refer to conversation participants; we are not aware of systems addressing this.

2.2 Other exophoric reference

This phenomenon was already prominent in TRAINS (see above), but largely handled by using semantic type constraints. It also occurs in Maptask dialogue and similar task-solving interactions like the Pentomino puzzle studied by Schlangen et al. (2009). Why is it potentially relevant for Twitter conversations? Because messages may contain embedded images, and speakers occasionally refer directly to entities therein. This is also possible with URLs and prominent objects present in the target page.

2.3 Conversation structure

The role of the turn structure in dialogue has received a lot of attention for anaphora resolution. Both (Poesio et al., 2006) and (Stent and Bangalore, 2010) were interested in the relative performance of specific dialogue structure models (the Grosz/Sidner stack model and Walker's cache model). Luo et al. (2009) worked with the mixed-genre ACE 2007 data and showed that features capturing the identity of the speaker and the same/different turn distinction can be very helpful for anaphora resolution, yielding an improvement of 4.6 points for telephone conversations. In contrast, Désoyer et al. (2016) used French spoken dialogues and could not find improvements when using information on speaker identity and the distance measured in number of intervening turns.

Niraula and Rus (2014) conducted a thorough analysis on the influence of turn structure for anaphora resolution in tutoring system dialogues. Following their corpus analysis, they implemented a single "discourse" feature, viz. the location of the antecedent candidate on the dialogue stack; this turned out to be one of the most predictive features in their classifier.

2.4 Spoken conversation

Not much work has been done on speech-specific features for anaphora resolution; we mention here the influence of hesitations that Schlangen et al. (2009) studied for referring to Pentomino pieces. The potential connection to Twitter is the fact that Twitter users often borrow from speech, for example emphasis markers such as vowel lengthening (*honeyyyy*) and hesitation markers (*hmm*).

2.5 Social media text

The need for pre-processing Twitter text is widely known and not specific to anaphora resolution. As just one example, Ritter et al. (2011) worked on Named-Entity Recognition on Tweets. They show that performance can be significantly improved when a dedicated preprocessing pipeline is employed. But we are not aware of Twitter-specific work on coreference or anaphora.

Finally, we mention an early study on threaded data, as found for instance in email, blogs or forums. (Hendrickx and Hoste, 2009) studied the performance of coreference resolution (implemented following the mention-pair model) when moving from standard newspaper text to online news and their comments, and to blogs. They found performance drops of roughly 50% and 40%, respectively.

3 Corpus

3.1 Collecting Twitter Threads

We used *twarc*[2] to collect English-language tweets from the Twitter stream on several (non-adjacent) days in December, 2017. We did not filter for hashtags or topics in any way, since that is not a concern for this corpus. Instead, our aim was to collect threads (conversations) by recursively retrieving parent tweets, whose IDs are taken from the `in_reply_to_id` field. We then used a script from (Scheffler, 2017), which constructs the conversational full tree structure for any tweet that generated replies. Now, a single *thread* (in our terminology) is a path from the root to a leaf node of that tree. For the purposes of this paper, we were not interested in alternative replies and other aspects of the tree structure; so we kept only one of the longest threads (path) from each tree and discarded everything else. Therefore, the data set does not contain any overlaps in tweet sequences.

---

[2]`https://github.com/DocNow/twarc`

thread length	3	4-10	11-50	51-78
number of threads	20	120	43	2
pronouns per thread (avg.)	4	5	19	55

Table 1: Distribution of thread length and 3rd person pronoun frequency in the annotated corpus

We decided to start our study on 3rd person sg. pronouns, as these are the most relevant for anaphora resolution. Hence we leave the handling of first and second person pronouns (which are usually deictic, i.e., depending on who is replying to whom in the conversation structure) as well as plural pronouns for future work. To ensure a minimum conversation complexity, we selected only threads containing at least three tweets; the additional selection criterion is that the thread has at least one instance of one of the pronouns *he, him, his, himself, she, her, herself, it, its, itself.*

For the manual annotation of pronouns and antecedents, we randomly selected 161 threads containing *he, she* or inflected forms, and 24 threads with *it* or inflection. In this set, the length of threads varies between three and 78, with the average being 10 and median being 7. Table 1 gives more information on the distribution of thread length and pronoun frequency.

Finally, we note that 77 root tweets contain visual data (pictures, videos etc.), and 20 contain a quoted tweet[3]. Both of these aspects may potentially affect pronominal reference, as mentioned in the previous section.

3.2 Data Preparation

It is well known that tokenization is a crucial preparatory step for doing any kind of NLP on tweets. We experimented with two different tokenizers: the Stanford *PTBTokenizer* (Manning et al., 2014) and *Twokenizer* (Gimpel et al., 2011). It turned out that these systems have different strengths in handling the variety of challenges, such as:

- PTBTokenizer decides whether to split at apostrophes (whereas Twokenizer does not). For example:

O'neill $\rightarrow$ O'neill
d'Orsay $\rightarrow$ d'Orsay
aren't $\rightarrow$ are, n't
London's $\rightarrow$ London, 's
The final example demonstrates the relevance of this feature for anaphora (or general reference) resolution.

- Twokenizer recognizes punctuation symbols such as sentence final full stop, question mark, exclamation mark, and also social media signs such as emoticons even if they are not surrounded by white space. PTBTokenizer was not designed to do this.

U.S. $\rightarrow$ U.S.
e.g., i.e. $\rightarrow$ e.g., i.e.
here.Because $\rightarrow$ here, ., Because
here:)Because $\rightarrow$ here, :), Because

We thus decided to use both systems: the output of Twokenizer is sent as input to the PTBTokenizer. One drawback of this approach might be duplicating over-tokenization errors. For instance, some URL forms such as *ftp://xxx.yyy* are considered as URL in Twokenizer, hence recognized as one token. But PTBTokenizer is not recognizing them as URLs and, therefore, divides them into smaller tokens. However, for our purposes, over-tokenization (i.e., producing too many tokens) is preferred to insufficient generation of token boundaries, because annotation tools (see below) can handle markables containing more than one token, but they do not allow for selecting a substring of a token as a markable.

3.3 Annotation

In our annotation scheme, we so far consider only the *identity* relation. With tweets being structurally relatively simple, we were interested in lean annotation guidelines, and followed the strategy defined in (Grishina and Stede, 2015), with some modifications in the treatment of predicative nouns and appositives. In our scheme, predicative nouns and appositions are considered as markables indicating reference identity. We defined additional attributes to differentiate these markables (i.e., copula constructions and appositives) from the other mentions. Also, we annotate the structural relation (anaphora, cataphora and exophora) of the pronouns, in order to cover the phenomena we will explain in Section 4. For exophora, additional more fine-grained categories are used:

3

Threads:	185
Coreference chains:	278
Annotated mentions:	1438
Annotated pronouns:	853
Annotated predicative NPs:	65
Length of longest coreference chain:	56
Average length of coreference chains:	5
Median length of coreference chains:	3
Intra-tweet coreference chains:	100
Inter-tweet coreference chains:	178
Threads with username or hashtag ref.:	43

Table 2: Descriptive statistics of annotations in the corpus

whether the antecedent is in the attached picture, quoted tweet, embedded link, or can be inferred by world knowledge.

Due to the data selection criteria, every thread contains at least one chain involving one or more 3rd person singular pronoun. For each pronoun, we annotated the complete reference chain (i.e., not just its antecedent). Hence, a chain can also include proper names and full NPs. The annotation tool is MMAX2 (Müller and Strube, 2006). Since it is important to know the authors of the tweets being annotated, both the user and the textual content of the tweet are shown together in the annotation window. Regarding the mention span, we do not allow discontinuous markables.

Since the annotation guidelines of (Grishina and Stede, 2015), on which ours are based, have already been evaluated with an inter-annotator agreement study (see that publication), we did not conduct one here. Our approach to quality control was that two annotators worked on separate files, but all chains marked by one annotator have been reviewed by the other, and were adjudicated when necessary. In a few cases (around 5), this did not lead to agreement; those threads were removed from the dataset. Altogether, our initial dataset of 225 threads shrank to the final size of 185 that we stated above. The majority of removed tweets were just incomprehensible or contained large portions of non-English content.

Table 2 gives an overview of the size of the annotations in the corpus. Also, to (partially) estimate the difficulty of the resolution problem, we calculated the distance for each consecutive pair of mentions in the coreference chains, in terms of the number of intervening turns. Figure 1 shows

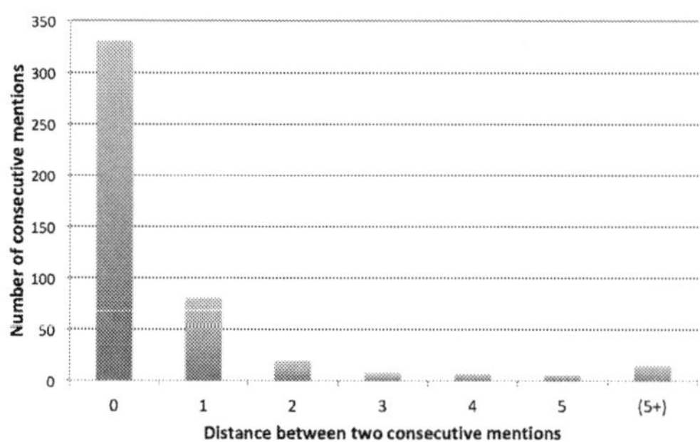

Figure 1: Distribution of distance between two consecutive items in reference chains

this information. Distance 0 means that the mentions are in the same tweet; 1 means they are in adjacent tweets, and so on. The longest distance values between a markable and its antecedent are 53, 37 and 19. In these chains the referring mention is either a definite NP or a named entity:

- Referring mention is a definite NP[4]:
  1:@10DowningStreet:*[The Prime Minister]$_i$ has started a refreh of [her]$_i$ ministerial team - updates will follow #CabinetReshuffle*

  ..

  54:@10DowningStreet:*[The PM]$_i$ with [her]$_i$ newest appointments to the Government Whips ' Office in Number 10 this afternoon #Reshuffle https://t.co/vgu9ioueu3*

- Referring mention is a named entity:
  17:@AustraliaToon1:*@cbokhove @oldandrewuk @Samfr @mikercameron I disagree with your analysis of [Andrew]$_i$'s form of arguing. ..*

  ..

  54:@littlewoodben:*@mikercameron @oldandrewuk .. What I find shocking , really shocking , is how [Andrew]$_i$ defends a man with a prolific history of odious misogynistic remarks. ..*

4 Pronominal anaphora in Twitter: Phenomena

Non-aligning replies A potential complication in any approach to analyzing Twitter conversations from a discourse perspective is possible mismatches between the `reply-to` ID and the

---

[4]If the conversational structure is important for demonstrating the phenomena, the examples are organized as follows: Tweet_order_in_thread:Username:Tweet_content

actual relation based on the contents of the tweets: In certain Twitter UIs, it may well happen that a user reads a sequence of related tweets, hits "reply" to tweet X, but then in fact responds to a different tweet Y in the neighborhood of X. We encountered a few clear cases in our threads. In general, they can obviously be hard to detect automatically, and it is not possible to estimate the frequency of the problem just on the basis of our relatively small sample. Hence we leave a deeper investigation for future work.

Hashtags In contrast to other social media conversations, Twitter offers the instrument of hashtags, which users employ gladly and frequently. Thus it is not surprising that hashtags can also work as referring expressions and hence as antecedents to pronouns. We distinguish two cases:

- Hashtag syntactically integrated:

  [# Oprah]$_i$ will be my favorite in 2020 selections. I will vote for [her]$_i$.

- Hashtag is not integrated:

  [She]$_i$ should be our president on 2020. [#Oprah]$_i$

The non-integrated case is challenging for annotation and automatic resolution, as this phenomenon is unknown from standard text. We decided to treat it on a par with cataphora (instead of looking for an antecedent in a previous tweet), assuming that hashtags at the beginning and end of tweets are textually-prominent entities.

Furthermore, we occasionally find references to substrings of hashtags, again with or without syntactic integration:

- *Let's #findClara, I hope she is safe.*

- *#findClara Our little girl is still missing. Please help us to find her.*

As we are doing a token based annotation and the hashtags are considered as single tokens in our scheme, we do not annotate these cases.

Usernames and display names These can act as referring expressions, too. Again, we find them both integrated in the syntax and disintegrated. The following example demonstrates how the username can become part of the syntax:
2:@Karen_LHL: *[@DannyZuker]$_i$ is funny*
3:@JanettheIntern: *@Karen_LHL Got [him]$_i$* !

Notice that in Twitter, the username of the replied tweet's writer is automatically added to the content of the reply message. Since this is not part of the text written by the user who is replying, we consider such usernames as part of the metadata of the tweet and outside the realm of reference annotation.

Multi-user conversations When more than two users are involved in a thread, 3rd person pronouns can refer to authors of previous messages. In those cases, we annotate the first occurrence of the username for the user being referred to as the referent for the pronouns. Then, the first (I), second (you) and third (he, she) person pronouns may refer to the same entity as indicated in section 2.1:
1: @realDonaldTrump: *[I]$_i$ 've had to put up with the Fake News from the first day [I]$_i$ announced that [I]$_i$ would be running for President. Now [I]$_i$ have to put up with a Fake Book, written by a totally discredited author. Ronald Reagan had the same problem and handled it well. So will [I]]$_i$!*
2: @shannao29522001: *[@realDonaldTrump]]$_i$ Stay strong. [You]$_i$ are our hero. I'm so proud to call [you]$_i$ MY president. As an educated female, I would be the first to stand up for [you]$_i$. I'm so tired of the fake news.. [..]*
3:@Lisaword7: *@shannao29522001 @realDonaldTrump [He]$_i$ can quote things out [his]$_i$ mouth and you hear [him]$_i$. Come back two days later and say, fake news. [His]$_i$ base will agree with [him]$_i$.[..]*

As a complication, (part of) a Twitter username and (part of) a display name can be used interchangeably to refer to the same entity. For example:
@CBudurescu: *I have seen @[EdsonBarbozaJR]$_i$ fight and I have seen [@TheNotoriousMMA]$_j$ fight. I am pretty sure [Edson]$_i$ whoops [Conor]$_j$. Thats what @TeamKhabib meant when he said there are many fighters in lightweight division who would beat [Conor]$_j$. [Barboza]$_i$ is for sure one of them.*

In chain i, the display name of user @EdsonBarbozaJR is "Edson Barboza"; the parsing of either the display name or the username gives the relevant information that "Edson" refers to "Barboza".

In chain j, the display name of user @TheNo-

Antecedent in the attached media (threads):	12
Antecedent in the quoted tweet (threads):	3
Antecedent in the attached link (threads):	2

Table 3: Exophoric reference statistics

toriousMMA is "Conor McGregor". Here, unless we know what the display name is, it is not possible to relate @TheNotoriousMMA with "Conor", as the username itself gives no hint about this.

Exophoric reference On the one hand, this concerns the use of 1st and 2nd person pronouns as also mentioned as a natural result of multi-user conversations above:
1:@user1: *[[my]$_a$ aunt]$_i$ won't eat anything.*
2:@user2: *@user1 [[my]$_b$ aunt]$_j$ eats everything.*
3:@user3: *@user1 @user2 hope [[your$_{a/b?}$ Auntie]$_{i/j?}$ picks up soon.*

Resolving such coreference chains requires knowledge of tweet authors and of the *reply-to* structure.

On the other hand, as mentioned earlier, Twitter allows users to insert images, videos and URLs into their tweets. It is also possible to quote (embed) a previous tweet and comment on it.

For anaphora, this means that antecedents can be entities found in embedded images, videos, and even material somewhere in a referred URL or an embedded tweet, or its author. We annotate these anaphors where the antecedent is out of the current linguistic domain (i.e., the text of the tweet or its preceding tweets) as exophora, using the categories given in Table 3. As the numbers in the table show, in most cases of exophora the antecedents can be found in the attached pictures, as in the following example:
1:@LondonCouple2:*Few more of me on the way to work had to get the Train into day as Toms car in the Garage so he had to take mine did I sit opposite you today on the train if I did did u notice my stocking Xxx PICTURE_URL*
..
4:@cheknitallout:*@LondonCouple2 i know i would have enjoyed the view ! make eye contact , gesture her to show me more*

A final category of exophoric reference results from Twitter's listing the top keywords or hashtags being currently discussed ("trending topics") in the UI. For example, this a tweet that appeared after the 2017 Golden Globe awards:
Come onn! How can she be a president?!
Most probably, *she* refers to Oprah Winfrey, as her possible presidential candidacy was a trending topic emerging from the ceremony. In such cases, We annotate *she* as an exophoric type of pronoun and assign the attribute "antecedent can be inferred by world knowledge" (cf. Section 3.3).

There are cases where the antecedent of the pronoun is to be found in the text but it is ambiguous. In the example below, the ambiguity can be resolved only by inference:
1:@jessphilips:*Watching [@lilyallen]$_i$ and @stellacreasy stand their ground for last few days is inspiring for those who need resilience. Oh for the days of reasonable discourse where issues could be explored.*
2:@CorrectMorally: *@jessphillips @lilyallen @stellacreasy It started when [she]$_i$ insinuated Maggie Oliver was part of a right wing agenda to make Labour look bad. I couldn't let that go unchallenged, I'm surprised that you find [her]$_i$ stance so admirable, some of the things [she]$_i$ has said about the victims have been vile,*

The pronouns *she* and *her* in the second tweet are ambiguous as they can both refer to @lilyallen and to @stellacreasy. Knowing that @lilyallen's comments on some victims of a well known incident are criticized on the date of conversation and the second tweet has a reference to *victims*, the feminine 3rd person pronouns are inferred as referring to @lilyallen instead of @stellacreasy. This example is illustrating that all the participants are aware of the relevant discussions, so there is – presumably – no ambiguity in resolving the pronouns for them.

General Twitter challenges Finally, we mention some of the phenomena that are well-known problems in Twitter language, focusing here on those that can have ramifications for reference resolution.

- Typos affecting referring expressions: *@kennisgoodman: @Karnythia @TheRealRodneyF She not qualified to **he** president why?*

- Name abbreviations are frequent. E.g., *Barack Obama* can be referred to as *BO, O.,* etc.

6

- Missing apostrophe in contracted copula:
  Hes my best.

- Intentional misspellings:
  *Its **himmm** who does it.*

- Frequent elision, e.g., of subjects

5 Experiments

5.1 Setting

As a starting point for performing automatic anaphora resolution on the data set described above, we decided to test the performance of an off-the-shelf system. Thus we compared the output of the Stanford statistical coreference resolution system (Clark and Manning, 2015) with our manually annotated data. The input to the system was in an XML format that includes information on speakers and turns for each tweet.[5]

The Stanford resolver does not produce singletons in the output, and therefore, we also removed all singletons from our annotated data for this evaluation process. Further, we noted above that in our data we only annotated the coreference chains including 3rd person singular pronouns; other chains are left out of the scope of the annotation. In contrast, automatic resolution systems extract all the coreference chains in the input text. In order to make the Stanford resolver's output comparable to our annotations, we therefore needed to filter out some coreference chains in the resolver's output (viz. the chains with no 3rd person pronouns and the chains belonging to different entities than we annotated). Thus we extracted the coreference chains with the 3rd person singular pronouns and also the chains with at least one overlapping item with our mentions from the Stanford resolver's output and used only those chains for the evaluation.

5.2 Evaluation

In our experiments, the resolver's algorithm option is set to the value of "clustering". There is also an option for activating the "conll" settings in the Stanford resolver. When this setting is on, the resolver does not mark the predicative nominals and appositives, because in the CoNLL 11/12 shared tasks, these were not treated as markables[6]. We

Metric	Recall	Precision	F1
MUC	58.24	48.97	53.21
BCUBED	45.8	40.75	43.13
CEAFE	52.57	47.69	50.01

Table 4: Evaluation results with speaker and turn info included in the input data (CONLL 2012 scorer)

Category	Count	%
Wrong/missing items in chain:	279	60
Missing chains:	55	12
Incorrect mention spans:	130	28
Total error count :	464	100

Table 5: Statistical information on error categories

preferred to keep that setting off, as our dataset is annotated for those mentions.

The metric scores are calculated using the reference implementation of the CoNLL scorer (Pradhan et al., 2014). The results are given in Table 4. It is difficult to compare them to results published on standard monologue text datasets, due to our selecting only a subset of the output chains. The scorer considers a mention to be correct only if it matches the exact same span in the manual gold annotations. The partial match scoring (e.g. checking the matching of heads for each phrase) might be more insightful for our data as the impact of differences in annotation schemes will be reduced by this way. The comparison of the metric results with each other may create more understanding on the strong and the weak aspects of the resolver on Twitter conversations. We leave the partial matching scoring and analysis of the differences in metric results as future work. However, for the present study, we made a qualitative analysis of the errors existing in the automated results and present them in the next section.

5.3 Error Analysis

We classified the errors in the automatically created coreference chains into 3 categories for which general statistical information can be found in Table 5.

5.3.1 Wrong items or missed references in the chain

1. Wrong or missing antecedent in the chain:

   This error classification indicates that the pronouns are captured correctly in the chain

---

[5]We also conducted experiments with the raw input text (i.e., with no speaker or turn info provided), but it is ongoing work to interpret the difference in the results we found.

[6]http://conll.cemantix.org/2012/task-description.html

but a wrong antecedent is assigned to them or no antecedent at all exists in a chain. This is a generic classification, there could be different reasons for these mismatches but as we didn't observe any clear pattern for the reasons of these wrong/missing assignments, we decided to present them in a generic classification.

We observed that 39% of the errors in this category are of this type.

2. Missing matches due to lack of world knowledge:

In the following thread, "Hillary Clinton" and "The Secretary of States" are referring to the same person, but this chain could not be captured correctly by the automated system due to the lack of knowledge that "Hillary Clinton" was "The Secretary of States".
1:@TheRealJulian: *The only Russia collusion occurred when* **Hillary Clinton** *conspired to sell US Uranium to a Russian oligarch* [..] 12:@jolyeaker: **The Secretary of States** *should* [..]

We observed that 23% of errors in this category are of this type.

3. First, second and third person pronouns corefer:

Occasionally, first, second and third person pronouns are erroneously put in the same chains. Although coversation structure may in principle allow all these pronouns to refer to the same entity as indicated in Section 4, the chains we inspected do not seem to follow a logical selection mechanism on the input structure. A representative example is the one below, where the first person pronouns are put in the same chain with *@EricTrump* who is obviously not one of the conversation participants.
1:@ALT_uscis:*[@EricTrump]$_i$, [his]$_i$ wife/guests wore sombreros during [his]$_i$ . . wait for it ... Mexican themed birthday party , while [his]$_i$ dad is DEPORTING THEM and wants to build a WALL on the border . ..*
2:@ActualEPAFacts: *@ALT_uscis @EricTrump So , the irony [I]$_i$* get. [I]$_i$* am a 45 year old man whose family frequents a TexMex restaurant in DC . On my birthday , I have worn a sombrero a few times . It isn't*

unusual.

We observed that 15% of errors in this category are of this type.

4. Missing matches due to hashtags and at-sign:

"#Borisjohnson", "@Borisjohnson" and "Boris" were not recognized as the same entity below:
3:@angelneptustar:*To B sure* **#Borisjohnson** *held 4 huge consultations*

..

7:@angelneptustar:*... But sadly a raving anti semite , totally divisive.* **@Borisjohnson** *'s biggest achievement , he united London.*
8:@WMDivision:*.. given* **Boris** *has published articles brimming ..*

We observed that 7% of errors in this category are of this type.

5. Missing matches due to case sensitivity:

The usage of upper and lower case in Twitter posts deviates from conventional usage in many forms. The resolver makes case-sensitive decisions, but the problems can lead to missing matches, such as in the next case where "LINDA SARSOUR" and "Linda Sarsour" were not recognized as the same entity:
1:@yongaryisback:*#IranianProtests THE DEMOCRATS AND* **LINDA SARSOUR** *HATE THESE PROTESTS*
2:@mattfwood:*@yongaryisback .. you do n't even look at her feed , you 'd see* **Linda Sarsour** *tweeting against ..*

We observed that 2% of errors in this category are of this type.

6. Missing or wrong mention matches with unclear reason:

This is a generic category to capture unclear cases of mention mismatches. We observe that 14% of errors in this category are of this type.

We also observed errors due to the Twitter phenomena we presented in Section 4. Since we don't have clear statistical information for these cases, we put these errors under this generic type. For instance, in the following example, both "he" and "his" refers to the same entity present in the attached media, but they were not put in the same chain by the resolver:

1:@MockingTheDraft: *Agree or disagree?* VISUAL_MEDIA_URL

3:@cmilner2: *@ChrisJBSnow @MockingTheDraft **He** 's 6' 3*

5:@bdbsport: *@ChrisJBSnow @cmilner2 @MockingTheDraft I 'm not saying anything until I hear **his** hand size.*

5.3.2 Missing chains

We are aware that the automated system that we tested against our data does not show singleton chains in the resulting files. But there are also non-singleton chains which do not appear in the automated results.

As indicated in Table 5, 12% of total errors are of this category.

5.3.3 Incorrect mention spans

1. Twitter names included in the span:
   Lists of usernames and hashtags in tweets can cause difficulties for the resolver. This holds in particular for the automatically-added usernames (mentioned in Section 3), which can erroneously be identified as antecedents. Removing these elements from the text could thus be an effective preprocessing step. But in general, usernames, display names and hashtags can also be used as linguistic constituents in the way that we mentioned in Section 4. Therefore, the preprocessing should be done with this consideration.

   7:@ToddXena: *@TippyStyle @nedryun there is a lot of " noise .. I would suggest is go back research the [Reagan]$_i$ years ..*

   8:@TippyStyle:*[@ToddXena @nedryun Todd Reagan]$_i$* actually had early onset Alzheimer 's during his presidency . Not giving me the warm an fuzzies here.*

   We observed that 36% of errors in this category are of this type.

2. Miscellaneous mention span errors:
   There are variety of errors with selecting the mention span, such as including emoticons[7] or unnecessary punctuations in the span.

   We observed that 64% of errors in this category are of this generic type.

[7]https://en.wikipedia.org/wiki/Smiley

6 Conclusions

Twitter conversations have so far not received much attention from the perspective of coreference or anaphora resolution. We argued that this genre shares certain features with other social media, multi-party chat, but also with spoken language. We explained how we constructed a corpus of 185 conversation threads, and what decisions we made in annotating pronominal anaphora on this somewhat unusual genre. A number of specific challenges surfaced in our annotation work, and we explained how we responded to them. Finally, we reported on our first experiments with an off-the-shelf resolution system (Stanford), showing the results as well as an error analysis. Our next steps are to experiment with different variants of preprocessing for measuring the effect on the resolver performance, and then conclude what fundamental problems remain for a resolver trained on "standard" text, when being confronted with this genre, and how they may be tackled.

Acknowledgements

We are grateful to Constanze Schmitt for her help in the annotation and qualitative error analysis. Our work was funded by the Deutsche Forschungsgemeinschaft (DFG), Collaborative Research Centre SFB 1287, Project A03.

References

Kevin Clark and Christopher D. Manning. 2015. Entity-centric coreference resolution with model stacking. In *Proceedings of the 53rd Annual Meeting of the Association for Computational Linguistics and the 7th International Joint Conference on Natural Language Processing (Volume 1: Long Papers)*, pages 1405–1415, Beijing, China. Association for Computational Linguistics.

Adèle Désoyer, Frédéric Landragin, Isabelle Tellier, Anas Lefeuvre, and Jean-Yves Antoine. 2016. Coreference resolution for french oral data: Machine learning experiments with ancor. In *7th International Conference on Intelligent Text Processing and Computational Linguistics (CICLing)*, Konya, Turkey.

Kevin Gimpel, Nathan Schneider, Brendan O'Connor, Dipanjan Das, Daniel Mills, Jacob Eisenstein, Michael Heilman, Dani Yogatama, Jeffrey Flanigan, and Noah A. Smith. 2011. Part-of-speech tagging for twitter: Annotation, features, and experiments. In *Proceedings of the 49th Annual Meeting of the*

Association for Computational Linguistics: Human Language Technologies: Short Papers - Volume 2, HLT '11, pages 42–47, Stroudsburg, PA, USA. Association for Computational Linguistics.

Yulia Grishina and Manfred Stede. 2015. Knowledge-lean projection of coreference chains across languages. In *In Proceedings of the 8th Workshop on Building and Using Comparable Corpora*, Beijing, China. Association for Computational Linguistics.

Iris Hendrickx and Vronique Hoste. 2009. Coreference resolution on blogs and commented news. In *Anaphora Processing and Applications*, Lecture Notes in Artificial Intelligence 5847, pages 43–53. Springer, Berlin/Heidlberg.

Prateek Jain, Manav Ratan Mital, Sumit Kumar, Amitabha Mukerjee, and Achla M. Raina. 2004. Anaphora resolution in multi-person dialogues. In *Proceedings of the 5th SIGdial Workshop on Discourse and Dialogue*, pages 47–50, Cambridge, Massachusetts, USA. Association for Computational Linguistics.

Xiaoqiang Luo, Radu Florian, and Todd Ward. 2009. Improving coreference resolution by using conversational metadata. In *Proceedings of Human Language Technologies: The 2009 Annual Conference of the North American Chapter of the Association for Computational Linguistics, Companion Volume: Short Papers*, pages 201–204, Boulder, Colorado. Association for Computational Linguistics.

Christopher D. Manning, Mihai Surdeanu, John Bauer, Jenny Finkel, Steven J. Bethard, and David Mc-Closky. 2014. The Stanford CoreNLP natural language processing toolkit. In *Association for Computational Linguistics (ACL) System Demonstrations*, pages 55–60.

Christoph Müller and Michael Strube. 2006. Multi-level annotation of linguistic data with MMAX2. In Sabine Braun, Kurt Kohn, and Joybrato Mukherjee, editors, *Corpus Technology and Language Pedagogy: New Resources, New Tools, New Methods*, pages 197–214. Peter Lang, Frankfurt a.M., Germany.

Nobal B. Niraula and Vasile Rus. 2014. A machine learning approach to pronominal anaphora resolution in dialogue based intelligent tutoring systems. In *Computational Linguistics and Intelligent Text Processing*, pages 307–318, Berlin, Heidelberg. Springer.

M. Poesio, A. Patel, and B. Di Eugenio. 2006. Discourse structure and anaphora in tutorial dialogues: An empirical analysis of two theories of the global focus. *Research on Language and Computation*, 4(2-3):229–257.

Sameer Pradhan, Xiaoqiang Luo, Marta Recasens, Eduard Hovy, Vincent Ng, and Michael Strube. 2014. Scoring coreference partitions of predicted mentions: A reference implementation. In *Proceedings of the 52nd Annual Meeting of the Association for Computational Linguistics (Volume 2: Short Papers)*, pages 30–35, Baltimore, Maryland. Association for Computational Linguistics.

Alan Ritter, Sam Clark, Mausam, and Oren Etzioni. 2011. Named entity recognition in tweets: An experimental study. In *Proceedings of the 2011 Conference on Empirical Methods in Natural Language Processing*, pages 1524–1534, Edinburgh, Scotland, UK. Association for Computational Linguistics.

Tatjana Scheffler. 2017. Conversations on twitter. In Darja Fier and Michael Beiwenger, editors, *Researching computer-mediated communication: Corpus-based approaches to language in the digital world*, pages 124–144. University Press, Ljubljana.

David Schlangen, Timo Baumann, and Michaela Atterer. 2009. Incremental reference resolution: The task, metrics for evaluation, and a Bayesian filtering model that is sensitive to disfluencies. In *Proceedings of the SIGDIAL 2009 Conference*, pages 30–37, London, UK. Association for Computational Linguistics.

Amanda Stent and Srinivas Bangalore. 2010. Interaction between dialog structure and coreference resolution. In *Proceedings of the IEEE Spoken Language Technology Workshop*, pages 342–347. IEEE.

Michael Strube and Christoph Müller. 2003. A machine learning approach to pronoun resolution in spoken dialogue. In *Proceedings of the 41st Annual Meeting of the Association for Computational Linguistics*, pages 168–175, Sapporo, Japan. Association for Computational Linguistics.

Joel Tetreault and James Allen. 2004. Semantics, dialogue, and pronoun resolution. In *Proceedings of the SemDial Conference (CATALOG)*, Barcelona, Spain.

Anaphora Resolution with the ARRAU Corpus

**Massimo Poesio,[1] Yulia Grishina,[2] Varada Kolhatkar,[3] Nafise Sadat Moosavi,[4]
Ina Roesiger,[5] Adam Roussel,[6] Fabian Simonjetz,[6] Alexandra Uma[1],
Olga Uryupina[7], Juntao Yu,[1] Heike Zinsmeister[8]**

[1]Queen Mary University of London, [2]University of Potsdam, [3]Simon Fraser University,
[4]HITS Heidelberg, [5]University of Stuttgart, [6]Ruhr University Bochum,
[7]University of Trento, [8]University of Hamburg

Abstract

The ARRAU corpus is an anaphorically annotated corpus of English providing rich linguistic information about anaphora resolution. The
most distinctive feature of the corpus is the
annotation of a wide range of anaphoric relations, including bridging references and discourse deixis in addition to identity (coreference). Other distinctive features include
treating all NPs as markables, including non-
referring NPs; and the annotation of a variety
of morphosyntactic and semantic mention and
entity attributes, including the genericity status of the entities referred to by markables.
The corpus however has not been extensively
used for anaphora resolution research so far.
In this paper, we discuss three datasets extracted from the ARRAU corpus to support the
three subtasks of the CRAC 2018 Shared Task–
identity anaphora resolution over ARRAU-style
markables, bridging references resolution, and
discourse deixis; the evaluation scripts assessing system performance on those datasets; and
preliminary results on these three tasks that
may serve as baseline for subsequent research
in these phenomena.

1 Introduction

The release of the ONTONOTES coreference corpus (Pradhan et al., 2007a) and the organization
of two CONLL shared tasks based on the dataset
(Pradhan et al., 2012) have resulted in a substantial increase in coreference research, both in terms
of quantity and in terms of quality. We expect
ONTONOTES to remain a key resource for the field
for many years.

However, ONTONOTES also has a number of
frequently mentioned limitations, including:

- Not all NPs of relevance to anaphora resolution are treated as markables. For instance,
  expletives are not annotated.

- And even among referring markables, singletons are not annotated, nor are references to
  abstract objects or many types of generic objects (Pradhan et al., 2012).

Furthermore, anaphora resolution involves a number of phenomena besides 'coreference', such as
bridging reference (Clark, 1975) and discourse
deixis (Webber, 1991). Only a simple form of
discourse deixis, event anaphora, is annotated in
ONTONOTES; bridging reference was not annotated, although a subset of the corpus has been
annotated with this information by Markert et al.
(2012).

A number of these limitations are overcome
in the ARRAU corpus (Uryupina et al., In press).
In ARRAU, all NPs are considered markables, including expletives and singletons. Both discourse
deixis and bridging reference have been annotated.

The corpus however, hasn't been widely used
for anaphora resolution research yet, with a few
exceptions (Rodriguez, 2010; Uryupina and Poesio, 2012; Marasović et al., 2017). There are a
number of reasons for this, ranging from the fact
that research in both bridging reference and discourse deixis is still limited, to the unusual markup
format. The objective of this paper is to introduce
the community to the three datasets extracted from
the ARRAU corpus to support this year's CRAC18
Shared task, the first evaluation campaign based
on ARRAU. Our hope is that making such datasets
available may, on the one hand, facilitate the use of
ARRAU; on the other, increase the community of
researchers working on these aspects of anaphora
resolution.

2 The ARRAU Corpus

2.1 Genres

The ARRAU corpus includes a substantial amount
of news text in the sub-corpus called RST, con-

Proceedings of the Workshop on Computational Models of Reference, Anaphora and Coreference, pages 11–22
New Orleans, Louisiana, June 6, 2018. ©2018 Association for Computational Linguistics

sisting of the entire subset of the Penn Treebank (Marcus et al., 1993) that was annotated in the RST treebank (Carlson et al., 2003). News data were annotated so that researchers could compare results on ARRAU with results on other news datasets; and these documents were chosen because they had already been annotated in a number of ways—not only syntactically (e.g., through the Penn Treebank (Marcus et al., 1993)) and for their argument structure (e.g., through Propbank (Palmer et al., 2005)) but also for rhetorical structure (Carlson et al., 2003). But one of the objectives of the ARRAU annotation was to cover genres other than news, so, in addition to RST, ARRAU includes three more sub-corpora. The TRAINS sub-corpus includes all the task-oriented dialogues in the TRAINS-93 corpus;[1] the PEAR sub-corpus consists of the complete collection of spoken narratives in the Pear Stories that provided some of the early evidence on salience and anaphoric reference (Chafe, 1980); and the GNOME sub-corpus covers documents from the medical and art history genres covered by the GNOME corpus (Poesio, 2000a, 2004b) used to study both local and global salience (Poesio et al., 2004, 2006). The same coding scheme was used for all sub-corpora, but separate guidelines were written for the textual and the spoken dialogue sub-corpora. Table 1 provides basic statistics about the four ARRAU sub-corpora. Note in particular the large number of non-referring markables. RST, TRAINS and PEAR were used for the CRAC 2018 shared task.

2.2 Markables

Markable definition Many, especially among the older, anaphorically annotated corpora impose syntactic, semantic or discourse-based restrictions on markables. For instance, in ONTONOTES neither expletives nor singletons are annotated (for a discussion of the state of the art in anaphoric annotation, see (Poesio et al., 2016)). By contrast, in ARRAU *all* NPs are considered as markables, also when they are non-referring because either expletives such as *it* or predicative NPs such as *a busy place* in (1), or when they do not corefer with any other markable and thus form a singleton coreference chain. Moreover, non-referring markables are manually sub-classified into expletives, predicative, and quantifiers. In addition, possessive

pronouns are marked as well, and all premodifiers are marked when the entity referred to is mentioned again, e.g., in the case of the proper name *US* in (2), and when the premodifier refers to a kind, like *exchange-rate* in (3).

(1)   [It] seems to be [a busy place]

(2)   ...The Treasury Department said that the $[US]_1$ trade deficit may worsen next year after two years of significant improvement...The statement was the $[US]_1$'s government first acknowledgment of what other groups, such as the International Monetary Fund, have been predicting for months.

(3)   The Treasury report, which is required annually by a provision of the 1988 trade act, again took South Korea to task for its $[exchange\text{-}rate]_1$ policies. "We believe there have continued to be indications of $[exchange\text{-}rate]_1$ manipulation ...

In ARRAU, the full NP is marked with all its modifiers; in addition, a MIN attribute is marked, as in the MUC corpora. For nominal markables, MIN is the head noun, whereas for (modified or not) named entities MIN is the entire proper name.

(4) $[^{min}$[Alan Spoon]^{min} , recently named Newsweek president] , said Newsweek's ad rates would increase 5% in January.

Markable properties All markables are manually annotated for a variety of properties according to the GNOME guidelines (Poesio, 2000b): these include morphosyntactic agreement (gender, number and person), grammatical function, and the semantic type of the entity. The guidelines and reliability studies leading to this scheme are discussed in (Poesio, 2000a, 2004a; Uryupina et al., In press). We will only mention one attribute here, the reference attribute, that specifies a combination of information about the logical form status of the NP (referring, expletive, quantificational, or predicative), and can be used to distinguish between referring and non-referring markables.

2.3 Types of anaphoric relations marked

The ARRAU guidelines support annotation of different types of anaphoric relations. All referring markables are marked as either discourse

---

	RST	GNOME	PEAR	TRAINS
documents	413	5	20	114
tokens	228901	21458	14059	83654
avg. doc length (tok)	554.2	4291.6	703.0	733.8
markables	72013	6562	4008	16999
avg. markables per doc	174.4	1312.4	200.4	149.1
non-referring markables	9552 (13.3%)	1047 (16.0%)	607 (15.1%)	2353 (13.8%)

Table 1: Corpus statistics for the four ARRAU sub-corpora.

`new` or `discourse old`. Discourse new mentions introduce new entities and thus are not marked as being coreferent with an entity already introduced (**antecedent**). For discourse-old mentions, an antecedent can be identified, either of type `phrase` (if the antecedent was introduced using a nominal markable) or `segment` (not introduced by a nominal markable, for **discourse deixis**). In addition, referring NPs can be marked as **related** to a previously mentioned discourse entity, to identify them as examples of associative (**bridging**) anaphora.

Bridging references The term **bridging reference** was introduced by Clark (1975) to refer to any reference that requires some sort of 'bridging' inference to be interpreted. Clark's very general definition covered both identity anaphora in which the description of the anaphor is different from the description of the antecedent, as in (5); and so-called **associative** anaphora (Hawkins, 1978), in which the anaphoric expression refers to an object that is associated with, but not identical to, the antecedent, as in (6). (These days, the term bridging reference is mostly used to refer to the associative cases.)

(5)   I saw a black Mercedes parked outside the restaurant. [The car] belonged to Bill.

(6)   I saw a black Mercedes parked outside the restaurant. [The engine] was still running.

Annotating—indeed, even identifying—bridging references in a reliable way is difficult (Vieira, 1998; Poesio and Vieira, 1998), which is one of the reasons why so few large-scale corpora for anaphora include this type of annotation (Poesio et al., 2016). The ARRAU guidelines for bridging anaphora are based on experiments that started with the work of Vieira and Poesio (Vieira, 1998; Poesio and Vieira, 1998) and continued in the GNOME project (Poesio, 2004a).

In GNOME, a subset of relations that could be annotated reliably was found (Poesio, 2004a), including three types of relations: `element-of`; `subset`; and a generalized possession relation `poss` covering both part-of relations and general possession relations. The ARRAU Release 1 guidelines followed the GNOME guidelines, but with an extension and a simplification. Annotators were asked to mark a markable as `related` to a particular antecedent if it stood to that antecedent in one of the relations identified in GNOME (indeed, the same examples were used), and in addition, if they stood in two additional relations (but without testing the reliability of this annotation):

- `other`, for *other* NPs, broadly following the guidelines in (Modjeska, 2003);

- an `undersp-rel` relation for 'obvious cases of bridging that didn't fit any other category'.

The simplification was that in ARRAU Release 1, coders were not asked to specify the relation—effectively, any associative bridging reference was considered a case of 'underspecified relation'. In ARRAU Release 2, the annotation of bridging references was revised for the RST domain only and coders were now asked to mark the relations only in that domain. Some statistics about bridging references in ARRAU Release 2 are shown in Table 2. A total of 5512 bridging references were marked, but a classification of the relations was only provided for the 3777 bridging references identified in the RST domain. In the table, we write P+S+E+O+U as category for the bridging references in the other domains, currently not classified.

Discourse deixis The term **discourse deixis** was introduced by Webber (1991) to indicate the reference to abstract entities which have not been introduced in the discourse through a nominal markable, as in the following example from the TRAINS corpus, where *that* in utterance 7.6 refers to the plan of shipping boxcars to oranges to Elmira.

	RST	TRAINS	GNOME	PEAR	TOTAL
all	3777	710	692	333	5512
poss	87				≥ 87
poss-inv	25				≥ 25
subset	1092				≥ 1092
subset-inv	368				≥ 368
element	1126				≥ 1126
element-inv	152				≥ 152
other	332				≥ 332
other-inv	7				≥ 7
undersp-rel	588				≥ 588
P+S+E+O+U	N/A	710	692	333	1735

Table 2: Distribution of bridging references in ARRAU.

(7)
7.3	:	so we ship one
7.4	:	boxcar
7.5	:	of oranges to Elmira
7.6	:	and <u>that</u> takes another 2 hours

Discourse deixis is a very complex form of reference, both to annotate (Artstein and Poesio, 2006) and to resolve. Very few anaphoric annotation projects have attempted annotating discourse deixis in its entirety (Artstein and Poesio, 2006; Dipper and Zinsmeister, 2012). More typical is a partial annotation, as in (Byron and Allen, 1998; Navarretta, 2000), who annotated pronominal reference to abstract objects; in ONTONOTES, where event anaphora was marked (Pradhan et al., 2007b); and in the work of Kolhatkar (2014), that focused on so-called shell nouns. In ARRAU,

1. A coder specifying that a referring expression is discourse old is asked whether its antecedent was introduced using a `phrase` (markable) or `segment` (discourse segment).

2. Coders choosing `segment` have to mark a sequence of *predefined* clauses.

Statistics about discourse deixis in ARRAU Release 2 are shown in Table 3. A total of 1633 cases of discourse deixis were marked.

2.4 Markup

ARRAU was annotated using the MMAX2 annotation tool (Müller and Strube, 2006). MMAX2 is based on **token standoff** technology: the annotated anaphoric information is stored in a `phrase` level whose markables point to a base layer in which each token is represented by a separate XML element.

2.5 Two releases

There have been two releases of the corpus. The first release, in 2008, is discussed in (Poesio and Artstein, 2008). This first release was relatively small (about 100K words in total), and focused primarily on identity anaphora and on the annotation of ambiguity, but its development involved extensive experiments with the annotation of discourse deixis and of ambiguity that led to the annotation guidelines used throughout the project (Poesio and Artstein, 2005b,a; Artstein and Poesio, 2006). The second release, via LDC in 2013, is substantially larger than the first (350K) and the annotation of bridging reference, discourse deixis and genericity is much more extensive. Another key annotation effort was the annotation of minimal spans of markables (MINs). Last but not least, extensive checks were run on the annotation of identity anaphora. This is the release used for the CRAC 2018 Shared Task.

3 Previous work on anaphora resolution with ARRAU

3.1 Identity anaphora

Rodriguez (2010) used BART (Versley et al., 2008) to compare the difficulty of ARRAU and the two more widely used corpora at the time, MUC-7 and ACE02, and the effect of using MIN information to ascribe partial credit (50%) whenever a system markable overlaps with the minimal span of a gold markable, and the boundaries of the system markable do not exceed those of the gold markable, as done in MUC. He found that assigning such partial credit substantially improves the scores.

Uryupina and Poesio (2012) explored the effect of domain adaptation in anaphora resolution, comparing the results obtained by training different versions of BART separately for each domain

RST	TRAINS	GNOME	PEAR	TOTAL
631	862	73	67	1633

Table 3: Distribution of discourse deixis in the subdomains of ARRAU.

	Soon et al 2001		Extended feature set	
	Domains	Union	Domains	Union
ARRAU				
GNOME	58.06	56.92	56.38	56.11
PEAR	66.74	67.36	66.29	65.24
RST	59.51	59.36	56.88	57.97
TRAINS-93	43.17	42.9	47.55	43.31
overall	56.66	56.04	54.84	55.29
ONTONOTES				
bc	55.04	55.62	60.71	59.52
mz	59.56	60.2	61.65	62.42
wb	51.07	53.05	53.91	53.36
whole	54.17	54.5	57.74	57.05

Table 4: (Uryupina and Poesio, 2012): Running BART on different ARRAU genres and on different ONTONOTES genres. MUC score.

or the entire dataset. They did that on both ARRAU 2 and ONTONOTES, thus providing what to our knowledge is the only comparison between the two corpora in terms of system performance. Table 4 summarizes the results.

3.2 Discourse Deixis

Marasović et al. (2017) developed an approach to abstract anaphora resolution based on bi-directional LSTMs to produce representations of the anaphor and the candidate sentence, and a mention ranking component adapted from the systems by Clark and Manning (2016) and Wiseman et al. (2015). The system was tested using both the dataset by Kolhatkar et al. (2013) (for shell nouns) and the discourse deixis cases in ARRAU.

4 The Three Tasks of CRAC 2018

The CRAC 2018 Shared Task was the evaluation campaign associated with this workshop. The task was articulated in three subtasks: a first task on identity anaphora resolution, a second one on bridging reference, and a third one on discourse deixis. Researchers could participate independently, and indeed no group participated in more than one task. In this Section we discuss how the datasets for the three tasks were created using ARRAU, and the evaluation scripts that were used.

4.1 Markable Settings

One characteristic in common to all three subtasks is that the official evaluation of systems was based on a **gold** setting, in that the markables were spec-ified in advance.[2] This was done because the organizers of Tasks 2 and 3 felt that the state of the art in bridging anaphora and discourse deixis resolution is such that the system markable setting would be too hard, so we would need to release data in a gold setting for those tasks–and then of course it would not make sense to release them in a system markables setting for Task 1. The evaluation scripts however supported both gold and predicted markables, and the evaluations reported below carried out both.

4.2 Task 1: Identity anaphora

In this task, systems have to decide

- whether a markable is referring or not;

- if referring, whether it introduces a new entity/coreference chain (discourse new) or refers to an entity already introduced (discourse old);

- in case it is classified as discourse old, the systems have to identify the antecedent (entity, or coreference chain).

Data format For this task, the documents were exported in the format used for EVALITA-2011 (Uryupina and Poesio, 2013), derived from the tabular CONLL-style format used in the SEMEVAL 2010 shared task on multilingual anaphora (Recasens et al., 2010). The format used involves three tab-separated columns, with one line per token:

```
TOKEN     MARKABLE       MIN
```

The first column specifies the token; the second column specifies whether the token belongs to a markable in BIO format (as said above, evaluation is on gold markables, although participants could also submit runs for systems-markables evaluation); and the third column specifies which token is the minimal span (MIN) of the markable, in the sense of MUC. So for example, the first line of the

---

[2]Given that non-referring NPs and NPs referring to singletons are annotated in ARRAU, however, the 'gold' setting in fact resembles more the 'gold markable boundaries' setting used in the CONLL 2012 shared task (Pradhan et al., 2012) than the gold setting for that task.

document `wsjarrau_2308.CONLL` consists of the following three columns:

```
Ripples B-markable_45     word_1
```

where `Ripples` is the token (in this case, the first token of the document, i.e., `word_1`); the second column says the token is the beginning of `markable_45`; and the third column says the `MIN` word of the markable is token 1, i.e., this very same token (note that token indices start from 1).

The task of a system is to decide whether a markable is referring, and if so, the coreference chain it belongs to (possibly a singleton). Participation in a coreference chain is represented using the `markable=set` notation from EVALITA, a slight variation of the standard CONLL notation which generalizes to representations for bridging reference and discourse deixis as well, as discussed below. In the case of the example line above, the gold version of the document contains the following line:

```
Ripples B-markable_45=set_37 word_1 new
```

which states that `markable_45` is referring; that the entity it refers to is discourse-new (fourth column); and that this entity is coreference chain `set_37`. (The EVALITA notation can easily be converted into the CONLL notation to use the standard CONLL scorer as well, as we did–see below.)

In case a token is part of distinct markables, the @ notation from EVALITA 2011 is used, derived from the | notation from SEMEVAL 2010. Consider for instance the first few lines of the same test set file, representing the NP

Ripples from the strike by 55,000 Machinists Union members against Boeing Co..

One plausible syntactic analysis of this NP can be represented using brackets as follows:

```
[Ripples from [the strike by [55,000
[Machinists Union] members] against
[Boeing Co.]]]
```

In EVALITA notation, the embedding of markables is represented as follows (to make the example more readable, coreference chain information has been omitted, and the annotation has been slightly formatted)

```
Ripples B-markable_45                       word_1
from    I-markable_45                       word_1
the     I-markable_45@B-markable_47         word_1@word_4
strike  I-markable_45@I-markable_47         word_1@word_4
by      I-markable_45@I-markable_47         word_1@word_4
55,000  I-markable_45@I-markable_47@B-markable_49
                                            word_1@word_4@word_6
Machinists  I-markable_45@I-markable_47@I-markable_49@
        B-markable_609                      word_1@word_4@word_6@word_8
union   I-markable_45@I-markable_47@I-markable_49
        @I-markable_609                     word_1@word_4@word_6@word_8
members I-markable_45@I-markable_47@I-markable_49
                                            word_1@word_4@word_6
against I-markable_45@I-markable_47         word_1@word_4
Boeing  I-markable_45@I-markable_47@B-markable_50
                                            word_1@word_4@word_11..word_12
Co.     I-markable_45@I-markable_47@I-markable_50
                                            word_1@word_4@word_11..word_12
```

This states that, for instance, the token `Machinists` is the Beginning of `markable_609`, which in turn is Inside `markable_49`, in turn `markable_47`, and then of `markable_45`. For each of these markables, the coreference chain to which it belongs is specified using the The third column specifies the `MINs` of each of these markables, again using the @ notation.

A system correctly interpreting these markables should output for every markable its coreference chain and information status (non referring, discourse new, or discourse old).

Evaluation script The coreference evaluation script developed by Moosavi and Strube was modified to produce the scorer for Task 1. We will refer to this script as 'the extended coreference scorer' below.[3] The extended scorer, when run excluding non-referring expressions and singletons and ignoring `MIN` information, evaluates a system's response using the same metrics (indeed, a reimplementation of the same code) as the standard CONLL evaluation script, v8 (Pradhan et al., 2014).[4] When required to use `MIN` information, the extended scorer follows the MUC convention, and considers a mention boundary correct if it contains the `MIN` and doesn't go beyond the annotated maximum boundary. When singletons are to be considered, singletons are also included in the scores (all metrics apart from MUC can deal with singletons). Finally, when run in all-markables mode, the script scores referring and non-referring expressions separately. Referring expressions are scored using the CONLL metrics; for non-referring expressions, the script evaluates P, R and F1 at non-referring expression identification. The extended coreference scorer is available from Moosavi's github at `https://github.com/ns-moosavi/coval`.

4.3 Task 2: Bridging Anaphora

Data format For the bridging task, the documents were exported in a similar format to that

---

[3]Discussions are under way to incorporate some of the aspects of this scorer in the official CONLL scorer.

[4]In addition to MELA and related metrics, the extended scorer also computes Moosavi and Strube's LEA metric (Moosavi and Strube, 2016).

of Task 1. Again, the test set already specifies the gold markables (in this case, only the bridging references). The test set provides four tab-separated columns, with one line for each token:

```
TOKEN MARKABLE MIN BRIDGE
```

The meaning of the first three columns is as in Task 1. The fourth column specifies whether the markable is a bridging reference. For example, the following lines

```
a           B-markable_311 word_695 B-markable_311
speedy      I-markable_311 word_695 I-markable_311
resolution  I-markable_311 word_695 I-markable_311
```

state that tokens `a`, `speedy`, and `resolution` are part of `markable_311`, with head token `word_695`, and that this markable is a bridging reference. The objective of participating systems is to identify which **anchor entity** and **anchor markable** referring to that entity the bridging reference refers to, using the notation

```
bridg_ref=bridg_rel=_anchor_mark=_anchor_ent
```

For example, in the case of `markable_311` above, the correct answer would be:

```
a       B-markable_311=set_148  word_695
        B-markable_311=undersp-rel=markable_308=set_3
speedy  I-markable_311=set_148  word_695
        I-markable_311=undersp-rel=markable_308=set_3
resolution      I-markable_311=set_148   word_695
        I-markable_311=undersp-rel=markable_308=set_3
```

stating that `markable_311` has been identified as belonging to entity `set_148` as well as being an associative reference to entity `set_3` through the `undersp-rel` relation.

Evaluation script The evaluation script for Task 2 is based on the evaluation method proposed in (Hou et al., 2013). The script separately measures precision and recall at anchor entity recognition (e.g., whether `set_3` is the right coreference chain) and at anchor markable detection (i.e., whether `markable_308` is the appropriate markable of `set_3`). Note that whereas the identification of the anchoring entity is considered correct whenever the right coreference chain is identified, irrespective of the particular anchor markable chosen, the identification of the anchor markable is strict, i.e., it is only considered correct if the same markable as annotated is found.

4.4 Task 3: Discourse deixis

Finally, in this task (discourse deixis) systems have to identify the **unit**–clausal text segment–that evokes the abstract entity the discourse deixis refers to.

For this task, the documents have been exported in a format again consisting of three columns, again with one line for each token:

```
TOKEN UNIT MARKABLE
```

The second column specifies which unit (= utterance in the case of dialogue data, clause in the case of textual data) the token belongs to. (All units have already been marked, so systems do not need to recognize them.) The third column specifies whether the token belongs to a discourse deixis - and if so, which unit (utterance) evoked the antecedent.

For example, consider the following fragment:

```
TOKEN       UNIT                        MARKABLE
But         B-markable_565
some        I-markable_565
investors   I-markable_565
might       I-markable_565
prefer      I-markable_565
a           I-markable_565
simpler     I-markable_565
strategy    I-markable_565
then        I-markable_565
hedging     I-markable_565@B-markable_106
their       I-markable_565@I-markable_106
individual  I-markable_565@I-markable_106
holdings    I-markable_565@I-markable_106
.           I-markable_565
They        B-markable_566
can         I-markable_566
do          I-markable_566
this        I-markable_566              B-markable_322
...
```

The first 14 lines contain tokens belonging to unit `markable_565`. The following 4 lines contain tokens belonging to unit `markable_566`. The last of these is marked as a discourse deixis:

```
this    I-markable_566  B-markable_322
```

This line states that token `this` belongs to unit `markable_566`[5], and it is the beginning of a discourse deixis, `B-markable_322`. The systems' task is to identify which unit the discourse deixis refers to. The gold interpretation, using the `=unit:<markable_ID>` format would be as follows:[6]

```
this    I-markable_566
        B-markable_322=unit:markable_565
```

Evaluation script The evaluation script for Task 3 computes the **Success@N** metric proposed by Kolhatkar (e.g., (Kolhatkar and Hirst, 2014)) and also used by Marasović et al. (2017). SUC-CESS@N is the proportion of instances where the gold answer–the unit label–occurs within a systems first n choices. (S@1 is standard precision.)

---

[5] All levels of annotation have markables named `markable_N` where N is an integer, but those names are independent: so unit `markable_566` is different from coreference `markable_566`.

[6] It is actually not entirely clear from the example whether demonstrative *this* refers to 'preferring a simpler strategy' or 'hedging their individual holdings' or, more likely, a more complex abstract object.

Configuration	P	R	F1
ONTONOTES			
CoreNLP CoNLL predicted	40.38	89.46	55.65
CoreNLP Rule-based	43.68	83.56	49.02
CoreNLP Hybrid	33.3	84.9	47.84
CoreNLP Dep	32.23	82.20	46.30
Our LSTM Best F1	73.53	74.01	73.77
Our LSTM High Recall	51.53	87.53	64.87
ARRAU RST			
CoreNLP Rule-based	70.95	62.74	66.59
CoreNLP Hybrid	71.55	67.28	69.35
CoreNLP Dep	70.27	66.08	68.11
Our LSTM	79.33	86.16	82.60

Table 5: Markable extraction in ARRAU and ONTONOTES.

5 Anaphoric Resolution with The Three New Datasets: Results

No system participated in Task 1 and Task 3 of the shared task. In this Section we discuss the results obtained with Task 2, as well as the baseline results for markable extraction and Task 1.

5.1 Markable extraction

One of the important differences between corpora for anaphora / coreference is the definition of mentions (or markables, in this case). In order to compare the difficulty of markable extraction in ARRAU with that of mention extraction ONTONOTES, we ran two markable extractors on both corpora: a few versions of a mention extractor based on the Stanford CORE pipeline, and our own implementation of an LSTM architecture for markable extraction. Our markable extractor is a modified version of the neural named entity recognition system proposed by Lample et al. (2016). Two versions of this markable extractor were run on the ONTONOTES dataset, one optimized for F1, one for recall. The results are shown in Table 5.

The results suggest that markable extraction in ARRAU is considerably easier than mention extraction in ONTONOTES. This might be due to the differences in markable definition, since singletons and non-referring NPs have to be excluded in ONTONOTES. But the accuracy gaps might also be a result of the domain differences between ONTONOTES and ARRAU. To test this we tested the Stanford pipeline on the WSJ portion of the ONTONOTES test set. The highest scores on the WSJ portion is obtained by the rule-based version of the pipeline, and is lower (43.1% F1) than that for the entire set. This suggests the difference in performance are due to the more releaxed notion of markable used in ARRAU.

Configuration	P	R	F1
Excluding singletons and non-referring			
MUC	72.32	58.88	64.91
B^3	67.85	48.45	56.53
CEAF$_e$	54.24	52.95	53.59
CONLL score			58.34
LEA	43.20	61.61	50.79
CoNLL official scorer			
MUC	72.12	59.02	64.92
B^3	67.56	48.55	56.50
CEAF$_e$	53.99	53.01	53.49
CONLL score	64.56	53.53	58.30
Including singletons but excluding non-referring			
MUC	72.08	58.88	64.81
B^3	77.46	77.12	77.29
CEAF$_e$	64.18	88.13	74.27
CONLL score			72.13
LEA	60.10	64.26	62.11
Results on non-referring			
Non-referring	0	0	0

Table 6: Baseline results on Task 1. Gold markables.

5.2 Task 1

The results from (Uryupina and Poesio, 2012) suggest that the resolution of identity anaphoric reference in ARRAU is no harder than in ONTONOTES, but to further test this the Stanford CORE deterministic coreference resolver (Lee et al., 2013) was run on the RST subset of the dataset for Task 1 as a baseline, using the division into training, development and test built-in the shared task for this subdomain. The system was run both on gold and on predicted mentions, and evaluated first using both the CONLL official scorer and the extended coreference scorer ignoring singletons and non-referring markables, then including those.

On gold markables The first 10 lines of Table 6 show the results obtained using the extended coreference scorer and the CONLL official scorer excluding both singletons (4161 markables) and non-referring markables (1391)–i.e., the same conditions as in the standard CONLL evaluations. In these conditions, the extended coreference scorer and the CONLL official scorer obtain the same scores modulo rounding. The following lines in Table 6 show the results when including in the assessment singletons; for this evaluation, the Stanford deterministic coreference resolver was made to output singletons instead of removing them prior to evaluation. When non-referring markables are included as well, the results for referring expressions remain identical, but in addition, the scorer outputs the results on those separately. (The Stanford deterministic coreference resolver does not attempt to identify non-referring markables, hence all values are 0.)

The first conclusion that can be obtained from this Table is that the results achieved by the Stan-

Configuration	P	R	F1
Exclude singletons and non-referring			
MUC	58.65	42.33	49.17
B^3	53.20	32.40	40.27
CEAF$_e$	42.77	37.88	40.18
CONLL score			43.21
LEA	27.61	46.17	34.55
CoNLL official scorer			
MUC	58.47	42.44	49.18
B^3	53.00	32.53	40.32
CEAF$_e$	42.64	37.98	40.18
CONLL score	51.37	37.65	43.23

Table 7: Baseline results on Task 1 with predicted mentions, without MIN information.

Configuration	P	R	F1
Exclude singleton and non-referring			
MUC	67.83	46.93	55.48
B^3	62.93	36.90	46.52
CEAF$_e$	47.48	42.05	44.60
CONLL score			48.87
LEA	56.71	32.27	41.13

Table 8: Baseline results on Task 1 with predicted mentions, using MIN information.

ford resolver on gold markables on this dataset are broadly comparable to the results the system achieved on gold markables at CONLL 2011, where it achieved a CONLL score of 60.7. The second observation is that the system appears quite good at identifying singletons, as its CONLL score in that case is over ten percentage points higher— in other words, the system is very much penalized when running on the CONLL dataset.

On Predicted Markables Table 7 shows the results obtained by the Stanford deterministic coreference resolver when evaluated on predicted markables instead of gold markables. These are the results that are more directly comparable with those obtained by this system in the CONLL 2011 shared task. We can see a substantial drop in CONLL score, from 58.3 on predicted markables in the CONLL 2011 shared task to 43.2 on predicted markables with the Task 1 dataset. Most likely, that indicates that some degree of optimization to the characteristics of CONLL dataset was carried out in the system even though the system is not trained.

Using the MIN information Finally, Table 8 shows the effect of using the MIN information. As can be seen from the Table, this results in five extra percentage points.

5.3 Task 2

One aspect of anaphoric interpretation for which there were no previous results with ARRAU is bridging reference. One group from the University of Stuttgart participated in this subtask (Roesiger, 2018). We summarize here the results; for further detail, see the paper.

Roesiger developed two systems, one rule-based, one ML-based. The results obtained by these systems on all three subdomains are summarized in Table 9 in the Appendix. The three columns present the result of the two systems at the tasks of (i) attempting to resolve all gold bridging references; (ii) only producing results when the system is reasonably convinced; and (iii) identifying and resolving bridging references. These results appear broadly comparable to those obtained by Hou et al. (2013) over the ISNotes corpus as far as the RST and TRAINS domain are concerned, but much lower for the PEAR domain– although given the small number of bridging references in this domain (354) not too much should be read into this. See Roesiger (2018) for some interesting hypotheses regarding the differences between the two corpora.

6 Conclusions

In this paper we discuss a dataset based on the ARRAU corpus that supports three fundamental anaphora resolution tasks: identity anaphora resolution, bridging reference resolution, and discourse deixis. We are not aware of any other dataset supporting all three tasks, which makes the resource fairly unique. In this paper we have discussed preliminary experiments with the data that can give other groups an idea of how to use them and what results have been achieved so far.

Acknowledgments

The original work on the ARRAU corpus was supported by EPSRC project ARRAU, GR/S76434/01.[7] This research was supported in part by the ERC project DALI.[8] We wish to thank LDC for their support with the organization and the running of the shared task.

---

[7]https://arrauproject.wordpress.com/
[8]http://www.dali-ambiguity.org

References

R. Artstein and M. Poesio. 2006. Identifying reference to abstract objects in dialogue. In *Proc. of BRANDIAL*, Potsdam.

D. Byron and J. Allen. 1998. Resolving demonstrative anaphora in the trains-93 corpus. In *Proceedings of the Second Colloquium on Discourse, Anaphora and Reference Resolution*. University of Lancaster.

L. Carlson, D. Marcu, and M. E. Okurowski. 2003. Building a discourse-tagged corpus in the framework of rhetorical structure theory. In J. Kuppevelt and R. Smith, editors, *Current Directions in Discourse and Dialogue*, pages 85–112. Kluwer.

W. L. Chafe. 1980. *The Pear Stories: Cognitive, Cultural and Linguistic Aspects of Narrative Production*. Ablex, Norwood, NJ.

H. H. Clark. 1975. Bridging. In *Proceedings of TINLAP*.

K. Clark and C. D. Manning. 2016. Improving coreference resolution by learning entity- level distributed representations. In *Proc. of ACL*, Berlin.

S. Dipper and H. Zinsmeister. 2012. Annotating abstract anaphora. *Language Resources and Evaluation*, 46(1):37–52.

J. A. Hawkins. 1978. *Definiteness and Indefiniteness*. Croom Helm, London.

Y. Hou, K. Markert, and M. Strube. 2013. Global inference for bridging anaphora resolution. In *Proc. of the NAACL*, pages 907–917, Atlanta, Georgia.

V. Kolhatkar. 2014. *Resolving Shell Nouns*. Ph.D. thesis, University of Toronto.

V. Kolhatkar and G. Hirst. 2014. Resolving shell nouns. In *Proc. of EMNLP*, pages 499–510, Doha, Qatar.

V. Kolhatkar, H. Zinsmeister, and G. Hirst. 2013. Interpreting anaphoric shell nouns using antecedents of cataphoric shell nouns as training data. In *Proc. of EMNLP*, Seattle.

G. Lample, M. Ballesteros, S. Subramanian, K. Kawakami, and C. Dyer. 2016. Neural architectures for named entity recognition. In *Proceedings of NAACL*, pages 260–270. Association for Computational Linguistics.

H. Lee, A. Chang, Y. Peirsman, N. Chambers, M. Surdeanu, and D. Jurafsky. 2013. Deterministic coreference resolution based on entity-centric, precision-ranked rules. *Computational Linguistics*, 39(4):885–916.

A. Marasović, L. Born, J. Opitz, and A. Frank. 2017. A mention-ranking model for abstract anaphora resolution. In *Proc. of EMNLP*, pages 221–232, Copenhagen.

M. P. Marcus, B. Santorini, and M. A. Marcinkiewicz. 1993. Building a large annotated corpus of english: the Penn Treebank. *Computational Linguistics*, 19(2):313–330.

K. Markert, Y. Hou, and M. Strube. 2012. Collective classification for fine-grained information status. In *Proc. of the ACL*, Jeju island, Korea.

N. N. Modjeska. 2003. *Resolving other anaphors*. Ph.D. thesis, University of Edinburgh.

N. S. Moosavi and M. Strube. 2016. A proposal for a link-based entity aware metric. In *Proc. of ACL*, pages 632–642, Berlin.

C. Müller and M. Strube. 2006. Multi-level annotation of linguistic data with MMAX2. In S. Braun, K. Kohn, and J. Mukherjee, editors, *Corpus Technology and Language Pedagogy. New Resources, New Tools, New Methods*, volume 3 of *English Corpus Linguistics*, pages 197–214. Peter Lang.

C. Navarretta. 2000. Abstract anaphora resolution in Danish. In *Proc. of the 1st SIGdial Workshop on Discourse and Dialogue*, pages 56–65. ACL.

M. Palmer, D. Gildea, and Kingsbury. 2005. The proposition bank: A corpus annotated with semantic roles. *Computational Linguistics*, 31(1):71–106.

M. Poesio. 2000a. Annotating a corpus to develop and evaluate discourse entity realization algorithms: issues and preliminary results. In *Proc. of LREC*, pages 211–218, Athens.

M. Poesio. 2000b. *The GNOME Annotation Scheme Manual*, fourth version edition. University of Edinburgh, HCRC and Informatics, Scotland. Available from `http://cswww.essex.ac.uk/Research/nle/corpora/GNOME/anno_manual_4.htm`.

M. Poesio. 2004a. Discourse annotation and semantic annotation in the GNOME corpus. In *Proceedings of the ACL Workshop on Discourse Annotation*, pages 72–79, Barcelona.

M. Poesio. 2004b. The MATE/GNOME scheme for anaphoric annotation, revisited. In *Proceedings of SIGDIAL*, Boston.

M. Poesio and R. Artstein. 2005a. Annotating (anaphoric) ambiguity. In *Proceedings of the Corpus Linguistics Conference*, Birmingham.

M. Poesio and R. Artstein. 2005b. The reliability of anaphoric annotation, reconsidered: Taking ambiguity into account. In *Proceedings of ACL Workshop on Frontiers in Corpus Annotation*, pages 76–83.

M. Poesio and R. Artstein. 2008. Anaphoric annotation in the ARRAU corpus. In *Proc. of LREC*, Marrakesh.

M. Poesio, A. Patel, and B. Di Eugenio. 2006. Discourse structure and anaphora in tutorial dialogues: an empirical analysis of two theories of the global focus. *Research in Language and Computation*, 4:229–257. Special Issue on Generation and Dialogue.

M. Poesio, S. Pradhan, M. Recasens, K. Rodriguez, and Y. Versley. 2016. Annotated corpora and annotation tools. In M. Poesio, R. Stuckardt, and Y. Versley, editors, *Anaphora Resolution: Algorithms, Resources and Applications*, chapter 4. Springer.

M. Poesio, R. Stevenson, B. Di Eugenio, and J. M. Hitzeman. 2004. Centering: A parametric theory and its instantiations. *Computational Linguistics*, 30(3):309–363.

M. Poesio and R. Vieira. 1998. A corpus-based investigation of definite description use. *Computational Linguistics*, 24(2):183–216.

S. Pradhan, X. Luo, M. Recasens, E. Hovy, V. Ng, and M. Strube. 2014. Scoring coreference partitions of predicted mentions: A reference implementation. In *Proc. of the ACL*, pages 30–35, Baltimore.

S. S. Pradhan, E. Hovy, M. Marcus, M. Palmer, L. Ramshaw, and R. Weischedel. 2007a. Ontonotes: A unified relational semantic representation. *International Journal on Semantic Computing*, 1(4):405–419.

Sameer Pradhan, Alessandro Moschitti, Nianwen Xue, Olga Uryupina, and Yuchen Zhang. 2012. Conll-2012 shared task: Modeling multilingual unrestricted coreference in ontonotes. In *Joint Conference on EMNLP and CoNLL - Shared Task*, pages 1–40, Jeju Island, Korea. Association for Computational Linguistics.

Sameer Pradhan, Lance Ramshaw, Ralph Weischedel, Jessica MacBride, and Linnea Micciulla. 2007b. Unrestricted Coreference: Indentifying Entities and Events in OntoNotes. In *in Proceedings of the IEEE International Conference on Semantic Computing (ICSC)*.

M. Recasens, L. Màrquez, E. Sapena, M. A. Martí, M. Taulé, V. Hoste, M. Poesio, and Y. Versley. 2010. Semeval-2010 task 1: Coreference resolution in multiple languages. In *Proc. SEMEVAL 2010*, Uppsala.

K. Rodriguez. 2010. *Resources for linguistically motivated multilingual anaphora resolution*. Ph.D. thesis, Universitá di Trento.

I. Roesiger. 2018. Rule- and learning-based methods for bridging resolution in the ARRAU corpus. In *Proc. of CRAC*.

W. M. Soon, D. C. Y. Lim, and H. T. Ng. 2001. A machine learning approach to coreference resolution of noun phrases. *Computational Linguistics*, 27(4).

O. Uryupina, R. Artstein, A. Bristot, F. Cavicchio, F. Delogu, K. Rodriguez, and M. Poesio. In press. Annotating a broad range of anaphoric phenomena, in a variety of genres: the arrau corpus. *Journal of Natural Language Engineering*.

O. Uryupina and M. Poesio. 2012. Domain-specific vs. uniform modeling for coreference resolution. In *Proc. of LREC*, pages 187–191, Istanbul. ELRA.

O. Uryupina and M. Poesio. 2013. Evalita 2011: Anaphora resolution task. In *Evaluation of Natural Language and Speech Tools for Italian*, number 7689 in Lecture Notes in Computer Science, pages 146–155. Springer.

Y. Versley, S. Ponzetto, M. Poesio, V. Eidelman, A. Jern, J. Smith, X. Yang, and A. Moschitti. 2008. Bart: A modular toolkit for coreference resolution. In *Proc. of ACL, demo session*, Columbus, OH.

R. Vieira. 1998. *Definite Description Resolution in Unrestricted Texts*. Ph.D. thesis, University of Edinburgh, Centre for Cognitive Science.

B. L. Webber. 1991. Structure and ostension in the interpretation of discourse deixis. *Language and Cognitive Processes*, 6(2):107–135.

S. J. Wiseman, A. M. Rush, S. M. Shieber, and J. Weston. 2015. Learning anaphoricity and antecedent ranking features for coreference resolution. In *Proc. of the ACL*, Bejing.

A   Appendix

	Gold bridges-all			Gold bridges-partial			Full bridging resolution		
	P	R	F1	P	R	F1	P	R	F1
RST									
Rule (IR, entity)	39.8	39.8	39.8	63.6	22.0	32.7	18.5	20.6	19.5
Rule (official, phrase)	32.2	32.9	32.5	54.0	19.1	28.2	16.2	12.7	14.2
Rule (official, entity)	36.5	35.7	36.1	58.4	20.6	30.5	16.8	13.2	14.8
ML (IR, entity)	-	-	-	47.0	22.8	30.7	17.7	20.3	18.6
ML (official, phrase)	-	-	-	41.4	13.0	19.8	10.8	12.0	11.4
ML (official, entity)	-	-	-	51.7	16.2	24.7	12.6	15.0	13.7
PEAR									
Rule (IR, entity)	28.2	28.2	28.2	69.2	13.7	22.9	57.1	12.2	20.1
Rule (official, phrase)	22.0	23.8	22.9	40.6	7.3	12.4	43.8	4.0	7.3
Rule (official, entity)	30.5	28.2	29.3	62.5	11.3	19.1	53.1	4.8	8.8
ML (IR, entity)	-	-	-	26.6	5.7	9.4	5.47	12.5	7.61
ML (official, phrase)	-	-	-	15.0	1.7	3.1	15.5	4.8	7.3
ML (official, entity)	-	-	-	37.5	4.2	7.6	23.6	7.3	11.2
TRAINS									
Rule (IR, entity)	48.9	48.9	48.9	66.7	36.0	46.8	27.1	21.8	24.2
Rule (official, phrase)	41.7	47.8	41.7	58.0	32.4	41.6	28.4	11.3	16.2
Rule (official, entity)	47.5	47.3	47.4	64.4	36.0	46.2	28.4	11.3	16.2
ML (IR, entity)	-	-	-	56.6	23.6	33.3	10.3	14.6	12.1
ML (official, phrase)	-	-	-	58.8	11.9	19.8	17.4	10.1	12.8
ML (official, entity)	-	-	-	63.2	12.8	21.3	19.0	11.0	13.9

Table 9: Roesiger's results on Task 2 for all domains.

Rule- and Learning-based Methods
for Bridging Resolution in the ARRAU Corpus

Ina Rösiger
Institute for Natural Language Processing
University of Stuttgart, Germany
roesigia@ims.uni-stuttgart.de

Abstract

We present two systems for bridging resolution, which we submitted to the CRAC shared task on bridging anaphora resolution in the ARRAU corpus (track 2): a rule-based approach following Hou et al. (2014) and a learning-based approach. The re-implementation of Hou et al. (2014) achieves very poor performance when being applied to ARRAU. We found that the reason for this lies in the different bridging annotations: whereas the rule-based system suggests many referential bridging pairs, ARRAU contains mostly lexical bridging. We describe the differences between these two types of bridging and adapt the rule-based approach to be able to handle lexical bridging. The modified rule-based approach achieves reasonable performance on all (sub-)tasks and outperforms a simple learning-based approach.

1   Introduction

Bridging (Clark, 1975) is an anaphoric phenomenon where the interpretation of a bridging anaphor, sometimes also called associative anaphor (Hawkins, 1978), is based on the non-identical associated antecedent.

The related NLP task of bridging resolution is about linking these anaphoric noun phrases and their antecedents, where both do not refer to the same referent, but are related in a way that is not explicitly stated. Bridging anaphors are thus discourse-new, but dependent on previous context.

(1)   The 2018 Winter Olympics was a major multi-sport event held in February 2018 in Pyeongchang County, South Korea. **Ticket prices** were announced in April 2016 ...

Full bridging resolution combines two subtasks: (i) detecting bridging anaphors (anaphor recogni-

tion) and (ii) finding an antecedent for given bridging anaphors (anaphor resolution).

Recently, there has only been few work on these tasks (Hou et al., 2014, 2013b,a; Markert et al., 2012; Rahman and Ng, 2012), which is partly due to the lack of annotated data, which makes the application of statistical methods difficult. Most recent work has focused on the corpus ISNotes (Markert et al., 2012), on which Hou et al. (2014)'s rule-based system currently achieves state-of-the-art results.

The first shared task on bridging resolution, co-located with the workshop on computational models of reference, anaphora and coreference (CRAC), deals with the task of bridging anaphora resolution in the RST domain of the ARRAU corpus (Poesio and Artstein, 2008). The dataset used in the shared task is part of the second release of the ARRAU corpus (Uryupina et al., to appear).

This paper presents a rule-based and a learning-based system, as submitted to the shared task. We start with a re-implementation of Hou et al. (2014)'s rule-based approach, which we then apply to the ARRAU corpus. Although the approach was designed for the same domain (news), we find that the performance is very poor. Our analysis shows that this is due to two different phenomena being defined as bridging, namely referential and lexical bridging. We present the differences between lexical and referential bridging and adapt the rule-based model so that it can also handle lexical bridging. We also compare the rule-based approach with a learning-based model which has access to the same information than the rule-based system. We report the results achieved for bridging anaphora detection, bridging anaphora resolution as well as full bridging resolution on all three domains of the ARRAU corpus: the RST domain (news), TRAINS (dialogue) and PEAR (narratives). For the shared task's main focus, bridg-

Proceedings of the Workshop on Computational Models of Reference, Anaphora and Coreference, pages 23–33
New Orleans, Louisiana, June 6, 2018. ©2018 Association for Computational Linguistics

ing anaphora resolution in the RST domain of AR-RAU, i.e. finding an antecedent for a given bridging anaphor, we achieve an accuracy of 39.8%. Surprisingly, although the rules were designed for the RST domain of ARRAU, they perform even better on the two other domains. The rule-based system outperformed the learning-based one in every setting.

2   The ARRAU corpus

The second release of the ARRAU corpus, first published in Poesio and Artstein (2008), was used as the data basis for the shared task. It is a multi-domain corpus that aims at "providing much needed data for the next generation of coreference/anaphora resolution systems" (Uryupina et al., to appear). The current version of the dataset contains 350K tokens and 5512 bridging anaphors. The shared task data comprises text from three domains: RST (newspaper), TRAINS (dialogues) and the PEAR stories (narrative text). Following earlier attempts on the reliable annotation of bridging (Poesio, 2004), where it became evident that better annotation quality could be achieved by limiting the annotation to the three relations `subset`, `element` and `poss`, most of the bridging relations in ARRAU are of these types, as shown in Table 2. Additionally, comparative anaphora are included and marked as `other`, and bridging cases which do not fit the pre-defined relations, but are obvious cases of bridging, are marked with the relation `undersp-rel`.

Domain	Number of bridging anaphors
RST	3777
TRAINS	710
PEAR stories	333
Total	5512

Table 1: Number of bridging anaphors in the single domains of the ARRAU corpus

Relation	Number of bridging relations
Poss	87
Poss-inverse	25
Subset	1092
Subset-inv	368
Element	1126
Element-inverse	152
Other	332
Other-inverse	7
Underspecified	588

Table 2: Bridging relations in ARRAU

3   Bridging definition

Bridging has been studied in many theoretical studies (Clark, 1975; Hawkins, 1978; Hobbs et al., 1993; Asher and Lascarides, 1998) as well as in corpus and computational studies (Fraurud, 1990; Poesio et al., 1997; Vieira and Teufel, 1997; Poesio and Vieira, 1998; Poesio et al., 2004; Nissim et al., 2004; Nedoluzhko et al., 2009; Lassalle and Denis, 2011; Baumann and Riester, 2012; Cahill and Riester, 2012; Markert et al., 2012; Hou et al., 2013b,a; Hou, 2016; Zikánová et al., 2015; Grishina, 2016; Roitberg and Nedoluzhko, 2016; Riester and Baumann, 2017). Unlike in work on coreference resolution, these studies do not follow an agreed upon definition of bridging. Many issues have been controversial for a long time, for example whether definiteness should be a requirement for bridging anaphors, or the restriction to certain pre-defined relations. In this paper, we do not want to go deeper into the definition of bridging, but we would like to discuss one additional aspect that will be relevant in our discussion of the experiments with the ARRAU corpus: the distinction between referential and lexical bridging, inspired by, though different from, the two-level *RefLex* scheme by Baumann and Riester (2012).

Referential vs. lexical bridging We propose the terms *referential* and *lexical bridging* to distinguish two different phenomena which are currently both defined – and annotated – as bridging. **Referential bridging** describes bridging on the level of referring expressions, i.e. we are considering bridging anaphors that are truly anaphoric, in the sense that they need an antecedent in order to be interpretable, as in (2). As such, (referential) bridging anaphors are context-dependent expressions.

(2)   The city is planning <u>a new townhall</u> and **the construction** will start next week.

Referential bridging is often a subclass of (referential) information status annotation. The corpus ISNotes (Markert et al., 2012) is one example of a corpus which solely includes referential bridging.

Lexical bridging (called *lexical accessibility* in Baumann and Riester (2012)), on the other hand, describes lexical semantic relations, such as meronymy, at the word/concept level (*house – door*), rather than at the level of referring expressions (*a house – the door*). It is important to realise that lexical relations are defined as part of the intrinsic meaning of a pair of concepts, thus, abstracting away from specific discourse referents: it is the word *door* which is a meronym of *house*, not some actual physical object or its mental image. The proper nouns *Europe* and *Spain* are in a meronymic relation and can thus be considered a case of lexical bridging. However, *Spain*, is not anaphoric, as its interpretation does not depend on the antecedent *Europe*. Lexical bridging is often annotated when certain pre-defined relations are defined as bridging.

It should be noted that lexical and referential bridging are two different phenomena with completely different properties, although they often co-occur in one and the same expression, such as in (3), where we have a relation of meronymy between the content word *house* and *door*, but also an anaphoric referring expression *the door* on the referential level.

(3)   <u>a house</u> ... **the door**.

The second release of the ARRAU corpus contains instances of both referential and lexical bridging, with the majority of the bridging links being purely lexical bridging pairs, i.e. most expressions labeled as bridging are actually not context-dependent. This is probably because the focus of the annotation was set on the pre-defined relations.

Another relation often brought up in connection with bridging is the *subset* or *element-of* relation, which is the most common relation in ARRAU. In principle, an expression referring to an element or a subset of a previously introduced group can be of the referential type of bridging, e.g. in (4).

(4)   I saw <u>some dogs</u> yesterday. **The small pug** was the cutest.

It should be noted, however, that at the lexical level, subset/element-of pairs have more in common with coreference pairs, e.g. (5), since the lexical relation between their head nouns tends to be hypernymy, synonymy or plain word repetition, i.e. relations which are summarised as *lexical givenness* in Baumann and Riester (2012).

(5)   I saw <u>a dog</u> yesterday. **The small pug** was very cute.

Finally, the subset relations identified as bridging in ARRAU often comprise cases such as in

(6), where *supercomputers priced between [...]* is a subset of *supercomputers*. Even if this is justifiable at the lexical level (the concept *supercomputer* is lexically given), we should note that there is, once more, no referential bridging involved here, since the expression denoting the subset can be interpreted independently of the context.

(6)   Cray Computer also will face intense competition, not only from Cray Research, which has about 60 % of the world-wide <u>supercomputer</u> market and which is expected to roll out the C-90 machine, a direct competitor of the Cray-3, in 1991. The new company said it believes there are fewer than 100 potential customers for **supercomputers priced between 15 million and 30 million [...]**.

Distinguishing referential and lexical cases in AR-RAU automatically is non-trivial, although our assumption is that many referential cases of bridging are probably included in `undersp-rel`.

4   Data preparation

The ARRAU corpus was published in the MMAX format, an XML-based format of different annotation layers. We converted the data into our own, CoNLL-12-style format and used the following annotation layers to extract information:
the word level, to obtain the words, document names and word number, the sentence level, to obtain sentence numbers, the part-of-speech level to extract POS tags and the phrase level to extract bridging anaphors, their antecedent, the bridging relation, coreference information, as well as the following attributes of the markables: gender, number, person, category, genericity, grammatical function and head word.

A couple of non-trivial issues came up during the preparation of the data: anaphors with multiple antecedents, antecedents spanning more than one sentence, empty antecedents and discontinuous markables, such as in

(7)   **those in** Asia or **Europe seeking foreign stock-exchange**.

After filtering out these cases, the corpus statistics have changed, which are given in Table 3.

Domain	Number of bridging anaphors		
	Train/dev	Test	Total
RST	2715	588	3303
TRAINS	419	139	558
PEAR	175	128	303

Table 3: Number of bridging anaphors in the shared task after filtering out problematic cases.

5 Evaluation scenarios and metrics

We report the performance of our systems for four different tasks.

5.1 Tasks/evaluation scenarios

Full bridging resolution This tasks is about finding bridging anaphors and linking them to an antecedent. Gold bridging anaphors are not given. We use gold markables.

Bridging anaphora resolution (all) This subtask is about finding antecedents for given bridging anaphors. In this setting, we predict an antecedent for every anaphor. This is the official task of the shared task.

Bridging anaphora resolution (partial) This subtask is about finding antecedents for given bridging anaphors, but in this case, we only predict an antecedent if we are relatively sure that this is a bridging pair. This means that we miss a number of bridging pairs, but the precision for the predicted pairs is much higher.

Bridging anaphora detection This subtask is about recognising bridging anaphors (without linking them to an antecedent), again using gold markables.

5.2 Evaluation metrics

We report our results in the form of the widely known metrics of precision, recall and F1 measure.

Internal scorer We take coreference chains into account during the evaluation, i.e. the predicted antecedent does not have to be the exact gold antecedent to be considered correct, as long as they are in the same coreference chain.

For bridging anaphora resolution (all), i.e. when anaphors are given and one antecedent has to be determined for all anaphors, precision and recall are the same, so in this case we report accuracy.

Official scorer Recently, the official scorer for the evaluation of the shared task has become available, which differs from our internal evaluation in the handling of some of the special cases (cf. Section 4 and Table 3). As we ignored these special cases, the official scores will most likely be lower than our own scores, in most of the cases.

In Section 9, we will report the performance using our own and the official scorer script (in the entity setting, which also takes coreference into account).

5.3 Data splits

We design rules and optimise parameters on the training/dev sets of the RST domain, and report performance on the test sets.

6 Applying Hou et al. (2014)'s rule-based system to ARRAU

As a starting point, we adopt the approach by Hou et al. (2014) and re-implement a rule-based system for full bridging resolution[1]. The system contains eight rules. The input to the rules are the gold markables. Before applying the rules, we filter out coreferent anaphors, as this increases precision, even with predicted coreference. Each rule then proposes bridging pairs, independently of the other rules. For a more detailed description, please refer to the original paper.

Our re-implementation achieves comparable results to the original version on ISNotes (Markert et al., 2012), the corpus on which the rules were designed, with an F1 score of 17.8 for full bridging resolution (Hou et al. (2014) report an F1 score of 18.4, but on a different, unknown test-development split).

When applying the re-implementation to the complete RST dataset, the performance drops to an F1 score of 0.3 for the task of full bridging resolution, although both datasets are of the same domain (WSJ articles). We investigated the reasons for this huge difference and analysed the rules and their predicted bridging pairs. Table 4 shows the rules and their performance on the RST dataset.

We soon realised that the annotations differ quite a lot with respect to the understanding of the category bridging, as described in the section about referential and lexical bridging. We noticed that besides predicting wrong pairs, the original system would suggest bridging pairs which are fine from a referential point of view on bridging, but are not annotated in the corpus, such as in

---

[1]The system will be made available: `https://github.com/InaRoesiger/BridgingSystem`

(8) As competition heats up in <u>Spain's</u> crowded bank market, [...]. **The government** directly owns 51.4% and ...

(9) <u>I</u> heard from **friends** yesterday that ...

Additionally, it would miss a lot of lexical bridging pairs, as these often involve mentions with matching heads, which are filtered out in the pre-processing step of the system because they tend to signal coreferent anaphors, such as in

(10) Her husband and <u>older son</u> [...] run a software company. Certainly life for her has changed considerably since the days in Kiev, when she lived with her parents, her husband and **her two sons** in a 2 1/2-room apartment. (*relation: element-inverse*).

This is why the performance is so poor: a lot of referential bridging pairs which are not annotated were predicted, while the system missed almost all cases of lexical bridging.

In the remainder of this section, we give examples of some of the correct and incorrect pairs (according to the gold standard in ARRAU), as proposed by the respective rules. Note that some of the incorrect cases (according to the gold standard) might actually be good bridging pairs.

Rule 1: Building parts

(11) Once inside, she spends nearly four hours measuring and diagramming each room in <u>the 80 year-old house</u> [...] She snaps photos of **the buckled floors** ... (correct)

(12) And now Kellogg is indefinitely suspending work on what was to be <u>a 1 billion cereal plant</u>. The company said it was delaying **construction** ... (wrong)

Rule 2: Relatives

(13) <u>I</u> heard from **friends** that state farms are subsidized, ... (wrong)

Rule 3: GPE jobs

(14) The fact that <u>New England</u> proposed lower rate increases [...] complicated negations with **state officials** (wrong)

It is probably controversial whether *state officials*

should be annotated as bridging, as it can also be a generic reference to the class. However, in this case, it is neither annotated as generic nor as bridging.

Rule 4: Professional roles

(15) Meanwhile <u>the National Association of Purchasing Management</u> said its latest survey indicated ...[]. **The purchasing managers**, however, also said that orders turned up in October ... (correct)

(16) A series of explosions tore through the huge <u>Phillips Petroleum Co.</u>pred plastics plant near here_{gold}, injuring more than a hundred and [...]. There were no immediate reports of deaths, but **officials** said a number of workers ... (different antecedent)

Rule 5: Percentage expressions

(17) Only 19% of <u>the purchasing managers</u> reported better export orders [...]. And **8%** said export orders were down ... (correct)

Rule 6: Set members

(18) Back in 1964, the <u>FBI had five black agents</u>. **Three** were chauffeurs for ... (correct)

(19) ... <u>a substantial number of people</u> will be involved. **Some** will likely be offered severance package ... (wrong)

Rule 7: Argument-taking I

(20) In ending <u>Hungary's</u> part of the project, **Parliament** authorized ... (wrong)

(21) <u>Sales of information-processing products</u>pred increased and accounted for 46% of total sales_{gold}. In audio equipment, **sales** rose 13 % to ... (different antecedent)

Rule 8: Argument-taking II

(22) As aftershocks shook <u>the San Francisco Bay Area</u>, rescuers searched through rubble for survivors of Tuesday's temblor, and **residents** picked their way through ... (correct)

	Anaphor recognition		Bridging resolution	
Rule	Correct pairs	Wrong pairs	Correct pairs	Wrong pairs
Rule 1: Building parts	2	28	1	29
Rule 2: Relatives	1	26	0	27
Rule 3: GPE jobs	0	30	0	30
Rule 4: Professional roles	10	251	1	260
Rule 5: Percentage NPs	6	3	5	4
Rule 6: Set members	8	4	4	8
Rule 7: Arg-taking I	3	38	0	41
Rule 8: Arg-taking II	14	163	4	173

Table 4: Applying Hou et al. (2014) on the RST part of the ARRAU corpus

(23) Lonnie Thompson, a research scientist at <u>Ohio State</u>$_{pred}$ gold who dug for and analyzed the ice samples. To compare temperatures over the past 10,000 years, **researchers** analyzed ...
(different antecedent)

7 Rules for lexical and referential bridging in ARRAU

As the rule-based system is very modular, it is easy to design new rules that can also handle lexical bridging. We add a number of rather specific rules, which are meant to increase precision, but also include more general rules to increase recall. We also leave in three rules of the original rule-based system: building parts (Rule 1), percentage expressions (Rule 5) as well as set members (Rule 6).

Comparative anaphora While comparative anaphors are a different information status class in ISNotes, the ARRAU corpus contains comparative anaphors as a subclass of bridging anaphors, which are labeled as `other`. For a markable to be considered a comparative anaphor, it must contain a comparative marker[2], e.g. *two additional rules, the other country*, etc.

We then search for the closest markable which is of the same category than the anaphor and whose head matches its head in the last seven sentences. If this search is not successful, we search for an antecedent of the same category than the anaphor in the same and previous sentence. If this fails too, we search for a markable with the same head or a WordNet synonym appearing before the anaphor.

(24) <u>the issue</u> ... **other issues in memory**

We exclude a couple of very general terms, such as *things, matters* as potential anaphors, as they are typically used non-anaphorically, such as in *Another thing is that ...*[3].

Subset/Element-of bridging This is a rather general rule to capture mostly lexical bridging cases of the relations `subset/element`.

As the anaphor is typically more specific than the antecedent (except for cases of the relation `subset-inverse/element-inverse`), it must be modified by either an adjective, a noun or a relative clause. We then search for the closest antecedent of the same category with matching heads in the last three sentences.

(25) <u>computers</u> ... **personal computers**

If this fails, we check whether the head of the anaphor is a country. If so, we look for the closest antecedent with *country* or *nation* as its head in the same sentences or the previous five sentences. This is rather specific, but helps to find many pairs in the news domain.

(26) <u>countries</u>... **Malaysia**

If this also fails, we take the closest WordNet synonym of the same category within the last three sentences as the antecedent. Again, we use our small list of general terms to exclude rather frequent general expressions, which are typically not of the category bridging.

Time subset For this rule, we list a number of time expressions, such as *1920s, 80s, etc.*. The anaphor must have time annotated as its category and must be one of the above mentioned time expressions. We then search for the closest antecedent of the same category in the last seven sentences for which the decade numbers match.

---

[2]other, another, similar, such, related, different, same, extra, further, comparable, additional

[3]The full list is: *thing, matter, year, week, month.*

(27)   1920s ... **1929**.

(28)   the 1950s ... **the early 1950s**

One anaphora   We search for expressions where *one* is followed by a common noun. We then remember the common noun part of the expression, and search for the closest plural entity of the same category whose common noun part matches the common noun part of the anaphor. Taking into account all words with a common noun tag turned out to work better than just comparing the heads of the phrases.

(29)   board members ... **one board member**

If this rule does not apply, we look for anaphor candidates of the pattern *one of the N* and again search for the closest plural entity for which the common noun parts of the expressions match.

(30)   the letters ... **one of the letters**

As in a few of the other rules, we exclude a couple of very general terms as they typically do not refer back to something that has been introduced before.

Locations   In the RST data, a lot of cities or areas are linked to their state/country. We can find these bridging pairs with the WordNet relation partHolonym. To be considered an anaphor, the markable must be of the category space or organization whose size is three words or less (as to exclude modification). We then search for the closest antecedent of the same category that is in a WordNet partHolonym relation with the anaphor.

(31)   California ... **Los Angeles**

(32)   Lebanon ... **Beirut**

Same heads   This rule is very similar to the subset/element-of rule, but is designed to find more cases that have not yet been proposed by the subset/element-of rule. For a markable to be considered an anaphor, it must be a singular, short NP (containing four words or less). We then search for the closest plural expression of the same category whose head matches the head of the anaphor or that is in a WordNet synonym relation with the anaphor's head, in the last five sentences.

(33)   Democrats ... **a democrat**

If this fails, we look for singular markables with a maximum size of three words which contain an adjective as anaphor candidates, and then search for a plural antecedent of the same category whose head matches the head of the anaphor or that is in a WordNet synonymy relation with the anaphor's head, in the last seven sentences.

(34)   the elderly ... **the young elderly**

(35)   market conditions ...   **current market conditions**

If this also fails, we look for inverse relations, i.e. a plural anaphor and a singular antecedent of the same category and matching heads/WN synonym in the last seven sentences.

(36)   an automatic call processor that ...   **Automatic call processors**

Persons   In this rather specific rule, we search for expressions containing an apposition which refer to a person, e.g. *David Baker, vice president*. For this, the anaphor candidate must match such a pattern and be of the category person. As the antecedent, we choose the closest plural person NP whose head matches the head of the apposition.

(37)   Specialists ... **John Williams, a specialist**

The rest   This rule is also very specific and aims to resolve occurrences of *the rest*, which, in many cases, is annotated as a bridging anaphor. We thus search for occurrences of *the rest* and propose as an antecedent a number expression within the last three sentences.

(38)   90 % of the funds ... **The rest**

Proposing antecedents for all remaining anaphors   For the task of bridging anaphora resolution, i.e. choosing an antecedent for a given anaphor, we need to force the system to propose an antecedent for every bridging anaphor.

This is why we include a couple of rules, which are applied in the order presented here and which propose an antecedent for every anaphor which has not yet been proposed as an anaphor by the other rules.

1. Pronoun anaphors
    The anaphor must be a pronoun of the category person. As the antecedent, we choose the closest plural person NP in the last two sentences.

(39)   At a recent meeting of manufacturing executives, everybody I talked with was very positive, he says. Most say **they** plan to ...

This is in a way a strange annotation, as pronouns should in theory alway be coreferent anaphors, not bridging anaphors. An alternative annotation would be to link *they* back to *most*, and *most* as a bridging anaphor to *manufacturing executives*.

2. WordNet synonyms in the last three sentences

(40)   The purchasing managers ...
250 purchasing executives

3. Cosine similarity greater than 0.5 in the last seven sentences
This is meant to find more general related cases of bridging. For the cosine similarity, we take the word2vec pre-trained vectors (Mikolov et al., 2013).

(41)   "Wa" is Japanese for team spirit and Japanese ballplayers have miles and miles of it. **A player's commitment** to practice ...

4. The anaphor is a person and the antecedent is the closest organisation in the last two sentences.

5. First word head match
We choose the closest antecedent within the last two sentences, where the anaphor and the antecedent both start with a proper noun.

6. Same category in the last three sentences, choose closest

(42)   ... that have funneled money into his campaign. After **his decisive primary victory over Mayor Edward I. Koch**

7. Global headmatch/WordNet synonyms: global in this case means that we search for an antecedent in the whole document, without a distance restriction.

8. Global same category

9. Choose closest NP as a fallback plan.

8 A learning-based method

To compare the performance of the rule-based system with a learning-based method, we set up an SVM classifier[4], which we provide with the same information than the rule-based system.

The classifier follows a pair-based approach similar to Soon et al. (2001), where the instances to be classified are pairs of markables. For training, we pair every gold bridging anaphor with its gold antecedent as a positive instance. As a negative instance, we pair every gold bridging anaphor with a markable that occurs in between the gold anaphor and gold antecedent[5]. During testing, we pair every markable except the first one in the document with all preceding markables. As the classifier can classify more than one antecedent-anaphor-pair as bridging for one anaphor, we choose the closest antecedent (closest-first decoding).

As the architecture of the machine learning is not designed to predict at least one antecedent for every given bridging anaphor, we cannot report results for bridging anaphora resolution (all). However, we report results for partial bridging anaphora resolution, where, during training, we pair the gold bridging anaphors with all preceding markables, instead of pairing all markables with all preceding markables.

We define the following features[6]:

Markable features   words in the markable, gold head form, predicted head form, noun type (proper, pronoun, nominal), category, determiner (def, indef, demonstr, bare), number, gender, person, nested markable?, grammatical role, genericity, partial previous mention?, full previous mention?, modified by a comparative marker?, modified by an adjective?, modified by one?, modified by a number?, lengths in words.

Pair features   distance in sentences, distance in words, head match?, modifier match?, WordNet synonym?, WordNet hyponym?, wordNet

---

[4]Using Weka's SMO classifier with a string to vector filter

[5]This is a common technique in coreference resolution, to reduce the number of negative instances and help the imbalance issue.

[6]Features marked with a ? are boolean features.

	anaphor recognition			anaphora-res.-all			anaphora-res.-partial			full bridging resolution		
	P	R	F1	P	R	F1	P	R	F1			
RST												
Rule (internal)	29.2	32.5	30.7	39.8	39.8	39.8	63.6	22.0	32.7	18.5	20.6	19.5
Rule (official)	-	-	-	36.5	35.7	36.1	58.4	20.6	30.5	16.8	13.2	14.8
ML (internal)	-	-	-	-	-	-	47.0	22.8	30.7	17.7	20.3	18.6
ML (official)	-	-	-	-	-	-	51.7	16.2	24.7	12.6	15.0	13.7
PEAR												
Rule (internal)	75.0	16.0	26.4	28.2	28.2	28.2	69.2	13.7	22.9	57.1	12.2	20.1
Rule (official)	-	-	-	30.5	28.2	29.3	62.5	11.3	19.1	53.1	4.8	8.8
ML (internal)	-	-	-	-	-	-	26.6	5.7	9.4	5.47	12.5	7.61
ML (official)	-	-	-	-	-	-	37.5	4.2	7.6	23.6	7.3	11.2
TRAINS												
Rule (internal)	39.3	21.8	24.2	48.9	48.9	48.9	66.7	36.0	46.8	27.1	21.8	24.2
Rule (official)	-	-	-	47.5	47.3	47.4	64.4	36.0	46.2	28.4	11.3	16.2
ML (internal)	-	-	-	-	-	-	56.6	23.6	33.3	10.3	14.6	12.1
ML (official)	-	-	-	-	-	-	63.2	12.8	21.3	19.0	11.0	13.9

Table 5: Performance of the different systems on the tests sets of ARRAU, using gold markables (and gold bridging anaphors in the anaphora resolution settings). We report performance using the official and our own internal scorer.

	Anaphor recognition			Full bridging resolution		
Rule	Correct pairs	Wrong pairs	Precision	Correct pairs	Wrong pairs	Precision
1: Building parts	0	0	-	0	0	-
2: Percentage	1	0	1.0	1	0	1.0
3: Set members	1	1	0.50	0	2	0.0
4: Comp anaphora	44	16	0.73	26	34	0.43
5: Subset/element	57	247	0.19	34	270	0.11
6: Time subset	3	6	0.33	3	6	0.33
7: One anaphora	0	0	-	0	0	-
8: Locations	25	11	0.69	22	14	0.61
9: Head matching	72	236	0.23	42	266	0.14
10: The rest	1	1	0.50	0	2	0.0
11: Person	10	1	0.91	8	3	0.73

Table 6: Performance of the single rules for full bridging resolution on the test set of RST, using gold markables

meronym?, WordNet partHolonym?, semantic connectivity score, highest semantic connectivity score in document?, cosine similarity.

9 Final performance

Table 5 shows the results of the modified rule-based approach and the learning-based approach for all tasks. It can be seen that the rule-based approach outperforms the learning-based one in every setting[7]. Surprisingly, in spite of the fact that the rules were designed on the training/dev sets of the RST domain, the performance for the PEAR and TRAINS domain is even better in most settings. However, these datasets are small, which is why this result should be taken with a grain of salt. Table 6 shows the rules and their performance in the final system for full bridging resolution. Some rules are included which do not predict any pairs because they predicted pairs in the training/dev setting (on which the system was designed).

10 Conclusion

We have presented two systems for full bridging resolution and bridging anaphora resolution. We started with a re-implementation of the state-of-the-art rule-based method by Hou et al. (2014), which did not achieve satisfactory performance when being applied to the ARRAU corpus. We found that the reasons for this lie in the different bridging annotations. Whereas the rule-based system suggests many referential bridging pairs, ARRAU contains mostly lexical bridging. The adapted rule-based approach achieves reasonable performance on all (sub-)tasks and outperforms a simple learning-based method.

Acknowledgments

I would like to thank Arndt Riester for his valuable comments as well as the anonymous reviewers for their insightful remarks. This work was funded by the Collaborative Research Center SFB 732, Project A6.

---

[7]We compute significance using the Wilcoxon signed rank test (Siegel and Castellan, 1988) at the 0.01 level.

References

Nicholas Asher and Alex Lascarides. 1998. Bridging. *Journal of Semantics*, 15(1):83–113.

Stefan Baumann and Arndt Riester. 2012. Referential and Lexical Givenness: semantic, prosodic and cognitive aspects. In Gorka Elordieta and Pilar Prieto, editors, *Prosody and Meaning*, number 25 in Interface Explorations. Mouton de Gruyter, Berlin.

Aoife Cahill and Arndt Riester. 2012. Automatically acquiring fine-grained information status distinctions in German. In *Proceedings of the 13th Annual Meeting of the Special Interest Group on Discourse and Dialogue*, pages 232–236. Association for Computational Linguistics.

Herbert H. Clark. 1975. Bridging. In *Proceedings of the 1975 workshop on Theoretical issues in natural language processing*, pages 169–174. Association for Computational Linguistics.

Kari Fraurud. 1990. Definiteness and the processing of noun phrases in natural discourse. *Journal of Semantics*, 7(4):395–433.

Yulia Grishina. 2016. Experiments on bridging across languages and genres. In *Proceedings of the first Workshop on Coreference Resolution Beyond OntoNotes (NAACL-HLT)*, pages 7–15, San Diego, USA.

John A Hawkins. 1978. Definiteness and indefiniteness: A study in reference and grammaticality prediction. atlantic highlands.

Jerry R Hobbs, Mark E Stickel, Douglas E Appelt, and Paul Martin. 1993. Interpretation as abduction. *Artificial Intelligence*, 63:69–142.

Yufang Hou. 2016. *Unrestricted Bridging Resolution*. Ph.D. thesis.

Yufang Hou, Katja Markert, and Michael Strube. 2013a. Cascading collective classification for bridging anaphora recognition using a rich linguistic feature set. In *Proceedings of the Conference on Empirical Methods in Natural Language Processing*, pages 814–820, Seattle, USA.

Yufang Hou, Katja Markert, and Michael Strube. 2013b. Global inference for bridging anaphora resolution. In *Proceedings of the 2013 Conference of the North American Chapter of the Association for Computational Linguistics: Human Language Technologies*, pages 907–917, Atlanta, USA.

Yufang Hou, Katja Markert, and Michael Strube. 2014. A rule-based system for unrestricted bridging resolution: Recognizing bridging anaphora and finding links to antecedents. In *Proceedings of the Conference on Empirical Methods in Natural Language Processing*, pages 2082–2093, Seattle, USA.

Emmanuel Lassalle and Pascal Denis. 2011. Leveraging different meronym discovery methods for bridging resolution in french. *Anaphora Processing and Applications*, pages 35–46.

Katja Markert, Yufang Hou, and Michael Strube. 2012. Collective classification for fine-grained information status. In *Proceedings of the 50th Annual Meeting of the Association for Computational Linguistics: Long Papers-Volume 1*, pages 795–804, Jeju Island, Korea. Association for Computational Linguistics.

Tomas Mikolov, Kai Chen, Greg Corrado, and Jeffrey Dean. 2013. Efficient estimation of word representations in vector space. *CoRR*, abs/1301.3781.

Anna Nedoluzhko, Jiří Mírovský, Radek Ocelák, and Jiří Pergler. 2009. Extended coreferential relations and bridging anaphora in the prague dependency treebank. In *Proceedings of the 7th Discourse Anaphora and Anaphor Resolution Colloquium (DAARC 2009), Goa, India*, pages 1–16.

Malvina Nissim, Shipra Dingare, Jean Carletta, and Mark Steedman. 2004. An annotation scheme for information status in dialogue. *Proceedings of The fourth international conference on Language Resources and Evaluation*.

Massimo Poesio. 2004. Discourse annotation and semantic annotation in the gnome corpus. In *Proceedings of the 2004 ACL Workshop on Discourse Annotation*, DiscAnnotation '04, pages 72–79, Stroudsburg, PA, USA. Association for Computational Linguistics.

Massimo Poesio and Ron Artstein. 2008. Anaphoric Annotation in the ARRAU Corpus. In *International Conference on Language Resources and Evaluation (LREC)*, Marrakech, Morocco.

Massimo Poesio, Rahul Mehta, Axel Maroudas, and Janet Hitzeman. 2004. Learning to resolve bridging references. In *Proceedings of the 42nd Annual Meeting on Association for Computational Linguistics*, page 143. Association for Computational Linguistics.

Massimo Poesio and Renata Vieira. 1998. A corpus-based investigation of definite description use. *Computational Linguistics*, 24(2):183–216.

Massimo Poesio, Renata Vieira, and Simone Teufel. 1997. Resolving bridging references in unrestricted text. In *Proceedings of a Workshop on Operational Factors in Practical, Robust Anaphora Resolution for Unrestricted Texts*, pages 1–6. Association for Computational Linguistics.

Altaf Rahman and Vincent Ng. 2012. Learning the fine-grained information status of discourse entities. In *Proceedings of the 13th Conference of the European Chapter of the Association for Computational Linguistics*, EACL '12, pages 798–807, Stroudsburg, PA, USA. Association for Computational Linguistics.

Arndt Riester and Stefan Baumann. 2017. The RefLex Scheme – Annotation guidelines. SinSpeC. Working papers of the SFB 732 Vol. 14, University of Stuttgart.

Anna Roitberg and Anna Nedoluzhko. 2016. Bridging corpus for russian in comparison with czech. In *CORBON@ HLT-NAACL*, pages 59–66.

Sidney Siegel and N. John Jr. Castellan. 1988. *Nonparametric Statistics for the Behavioral Sciences*, 2nd edition. McGraw-Hill, Berkeley, CA.

Wee Meng Soon, Hwee Tou Ng, and Daniel Chung Yong Lim. 2001. A machine learning approach to coreference resolution of noun phrases. *Computational linguistics*, 27(4):521–544.

Olga Uryupina, Ron Artstein, Antonella Bristot, Frederica Cavicchio, Francesca Delogu, Kepa Rodriguez, and Massimo Poesio. to appear. Annotating a broad range of anaphoric phenomena, in a variety of genres: the arrau corpus. *Journal of Natural Language Engineering*.

Renata Vieira and Simone Teufel. 1997. Towards resolution of bridging descriptions. In *Proceedings of the eighth conference on European chapter of the Association for Computational Linguistics*, pages 522–524. Association for Computational Linguistics.

Šárka Zikánová, Eva Hajicová, Barbora Hladká, Pavlína Jínová, Jirí Mírovskỳ, Anja Nedoluzhko, Lucie Poláková, Katerina Rysová, Magdaléna Rysová, and Jan Václ. 2015. Discourse and coherence. *From the Sentence Structure to Relations in Text. Institute of Formal and Applied Linguistics*.

A Predictive Model for Notional Anaphora in English

Amir Zeldes

Department of Linguistics
Georgetown University
Washington, DC, USA
`amir.zeldes@georgetown.edu`

Abstract

Notional anaphors are pronouns which disagree with their antecedents' grammatical categories for notional reasons, such as plural to singular agreement in: "the government ... they". Since such cases are rare and conflict with evidence from strictly agreeing cases ("the government ... it"), they present a substantial challenge to both coreference resolution and referring expression generation. Using the OntoNotes corpus, this paper takes an ensemble approach to predicting English notional anaphora in context on the basis of the largest empirical data to date. In addition to state of the art prediction accuracy, the results suggest that theoretical approaches positing a plural construal at the antecedent's utterance are insufficient, and that circumstances at the anaphor's utterance location, as well as global factors such as genre, have a strong effect on the choice of referring expression.

1 Introduction

In notional agreement, nouns which ostensibly belong to one agreement category are referred back to using a different category, as in (1) (Quirk et al., 1985), with singular/plural verb and pronoun.

(1)   [The government] has/have voted and [it] has/[they] have announced the decision

Although examples such as (1) are often taken to represent a single phenomenon, subject-verb (SV) agreement and pronoun number represent distinct agreement phenomena and can disagree in some cases, as shown in (2) and (3), taken from the OntoNotes corpus (Hovy et al., 2006).

(2)   [CNN] **is** my wire service; [they]**'re** on top of everything.

(3)   [One hospital] in Ramallah **tells** us [they] **have** treated seven people

While previous studies have focused on SV agreement (den Dikken 2001, Depraetere 2003, Martinez-Insua and Palacios-Martinez 2003), there have been few corpus studies of notional pronouns, due at least in part to the lack of sizable corpora reliably annotated for coreference, and the low accuracy of automatic systems on difficult cases. In this paper we take advantage of the OntoNotes corpus, the largest corpus manually annotated for coreference in English (about 1.59 million tokens with coreference annotations), to build a predictive model of the phenomenon, which can be used for both coreference resolution and referring expression generation (see Krahmer and van Deemter 2012 for an overview).

2 Previous work

Theoretical linguistic discussions have focused on SV agreement, especially in expletive constructions (ECs, Sobin 1997; i.e. 'there is' vs. 'there are'). Reid (1991) discusses SV agreement and notional pronouns, and posits reference to persons as facilitating plural pronouns, as in (4) and (5), where a relative 'who' forces a +PERSON reading.

(4)   And this fall [the couple] expects [its] first child.

(5)   A Florida court ruled against [a Pennsylvania couple] **who** contend May's 10-year-old daughter is actually [their] child.

This suggests that inferred entity type may be a relevant predictor of notional anaphora. Other theoretical papers suggest a formal analysis with empty pronoun heads bearing a plural feature, e.g. the analysis in (6) from den Dikken (2001) (see also Sauerland 2003 for a similar analysis).

(6) $[_{DP1}$ pro$_{[+pl]}$ $[_{DP2}$ the committee$_{[-pl]}]]$ are ...

34

Proceedings of the Workshop on Computational Models of Reference, Anaphora and Coreference, pages 34–43
New Orleans, Louisiana, June 6, 2018. ©2018 Association for Computational Linguistics

This suggests that speakers decide on the notional agreement category already at the point of uttering the antecedent. However psycholinguistic studies have shown effects localized to the point of uttering the anaphor, due to processing constrains (see Eberhard et al. 2005, Wagers et al. 2009, Staub 2009). We hypothesize that processing constraints may make it difficult for speakers to remember the exact expression used for the antecedent after a long distance from the first point of utterance, and therefore consider some length and distance-based metrics as features below (see Section 3.3).

Corpus-based studies have shown that notional anaphora likelihood varies by modality (more often in speech), variety of English (more often in UK English) and genre (see Quirk et al. 1985: 758, Leech and Svartvik 2002: 201, Levin 2001). Depraetere (2003) explored the idea that verb semantics influence agreement choice, especially whether verbs imply decomposition or categorization of the unit (e.g. *consist of, be gathered, scatter*), or signify differentiation within a set (e.g. *disagree, quarrel*). Annala (2008) provides a detailed corpus study of nine nouns in the written part of the British National Corpus (`http://www.natcorp.ox.ac.uk/`) and the Corpus of Late Modern English Texts (CLMETEV, `http://www.helsinki.fi/varieng/CoRD/corpora/CLMETEV/`). The study found tense to be relevant for the nine nouns, with past tense of 'be' being particularly susceptible to triggering plural agreement, while for nouns which generally prefer plural, singular agreement appeared more often in the present. Taken together, these studies suggest that tense and verb classes may be relevant features, as well as indicating the importance of some conventional usage effects. The latter are also backed by psycholinguistic evidence that speakers process notional anaphora more quickly than strict agreement in contexts that are biased towards the non-agreeing plural (Gernsbacher, 1986).

3 Experimental setup

3.1 Types of cases included

In this paper we focus exclusively on plural pronouns referring back to singular headed phrases, but the exact nature of cases included requires some decisions. Since the number for second person pronouns (*you, your*, etc.) is ambiguous, we omit all second person cases. First person cases

are rare but possible, especially in reference to organizations, as in (7), taken from OntoNotes.

(7)   Bear Stearns stepped out of line in the view of [the SEC]$_i$ ... [we]$_i$'re deadly serious about bringing reform into the marketplace

Some of the same lexical heads can appear with both singular and plural first person reference, either for metonymical reasons ("when a country says 'I/we'...") or by coincidental homonymy.[1] These cases are therefore all included whenever a relevant NP is annotated as coreferent in OntoNotes.

Three main types of plural reference to singular antecedents can be distinguished in our data (see Section 3.2 for some statistics): the most common, which will be referred to as Type I, is reference to complex/distributive entities (so called 'committee' nouns) seen e.g. in (2). These are distinct from Type II, which has bleached quantity noun heads, (e.g. 'a number of X' or 'a majority of X') which may sometimes be referenced as a plurality, as in (8), and sometimes as a unit, as in (9).

(8)   [the vast silent **majority** of these Moslems] are not part of the terror and the incitement , but [they] also do not stand up political leaders

(9)   [the vaunted Republican **majority**] is just not now nor has [it] ever been ready for prime time governing

A third type (Type III) occurs in cases such as (10), denoting unspecified gender (these are sometimes called generic or epicene pronouns; see also Huddleston and Pullum 2002:493-494, Curzan 2003). This construction has been gaining popularity (Paterson, 2011), and has recently been approved by the 2017 Associated Press Stylebook as standard (`https://www.apstylebook.com/`).

(10)   I'll go and talk to [the person here] cause [they] get cheap tickets

Although this type of agreement is semantically and pragmatically very different from the other two types above, it must be addressed in this paper for several reasons. Firstly, if we want to be

---

[1] For example one speaker in a forum discussion in the corpus has the user name 'A Very Ordinary Native Country', leading to coreference with the pronoun 'I'.

able to predict pronoun form for computational applications such as coreference resolution or natural language generation, then such cases should be covered in some way. Secondly, there are cases in which either a computer, or in some cases even a human would find it difficult or impossible to be sure of the class that a case falls under, as shown in (11) and (12), both real examples from OntoNotes.

(11)   [The enemy] attacked several times, and each time [they] were repelled

(12)   [a publisher] is interested in my personal ad book ... I looked [them] up

While in (11) it may seem unlikely that use of 'they' is meant to obscure gender, this reading cannot be ruled out, especially by automatic analysis. In (12), it is possible to get either reading: either the 'publisher' is a company, and therefore plural (Type I; but notice singular 'is' as a verb), or the speaker spoke with the director of a publishing house, disregarding that person's gender (Type III). Note that in singular agreement, these would result in saying 'she' or 'he' versus 'it', as in (13) (also from OntoNotes).

(13)   [the Des Moines-based publisher] said [it] created a new Custom Marketing

Additionally, there are Type III cases in which plural pronoun agreement for singular-like reference is not motivated by gender constraints, e.g. (14).

(14)   [Nobody] is going to like Bolton a year from now, are [they]?

Due to these complications, we include all cases of plural anaphora annotated as coreferent with singular NPs, though we will re-examine these types in the data in analyzing the results.

3.2 Data

The data for the present study comes from the OntoNotes corpus (Hovy et al., 2006), Version 5, the largest existing corpus with coreference annotations. OntoNotes contains gold POS tags and syntactic constituent parses, as well as coreference resolution for pronominal anaphora and definite or proper noun NPs (but not for indefinites, see below), and named entity annotations for proper nouns. The coreference annotated portion of the corpus contains 1.59 million tokens from multiple genres, presented in Table 1.

Table 1: Coarse text types in OntoNotes

Spoken		Written	
bc.conv	137,223	news	68,6455
bc.news	244,425	bible	243,040
phone	110,132	trans.	98,143
		web	71467
total	491,780	**total**	1,099,105
	total 1,590,885		

Written data constitutes the large bulk of material, primarily from newswire (Wall Street Journal data), as well as some data from the Web and the New Testament, and some translations of news and online discussions in Arabic and Chinese. The translated data has been placed in its own category: it behaves more conservatively in preferring strict agreement than non-translated language (see Section 4.2), perhaps due to translators' editorial practices. The spoken data comes primarily from television broadcasts, including dialogue data from MSNBC, Phoenix and other broadcast sources (bc.conv), or news, from CNN, ABC and others (bc.news), as well as phone conversations.

The relevant cases from the corpus for the present study were extracted by finding all lexical NPs headed by singulars (tagged NNP or NN) whose phrases are referred back to by an immediate antecedent (the next mention) which is a first or third person pronoun, then filtering to keep only those singular NPs headed by a token which is attested as taking plural agreement somewhere in the corpus, but also including its attestation with singular pronouns. In other words, this study makes no *a priori* interpretation of anaphora as notional in isolation: all and only items actually attested in both forms are considered.

These selection criteria, followed by manual filtering for errors, led to the extraction of 3,488 anaphor-antecedent pairs, of which 1,209 exhibited notional agreement (34.6%), including a subset of 207 cases (5.9% of the data) which were unambiguously identifiable as Type III, gender neutral plural pronouns.

OntoNotes contains 17,263 direct anaphoric links to a singular NP, meaning we can estimate the frequency of all agreement types addressed here at a not insubstantial 7% of pronominal reference to a singular lexical NP antecedent, with gender neutral type III at about 1.2% and Types I-II covering 5.8% of the total corpus.

As a test data set, we reserve a random 10% of the data, amounting to 349 cases, stratified to include approximately the same proportions of genres, as well as notional vs. strict agreement cases. This stratification is important in order to test the classifier in Section 4.1 using realistically distributed data.

3.3 Feature extraction

To predict the occurrence of notional anaphora we will use a range of categorical features indicated to be relevant in previous studies (see Section 2): POS tags and dependency functions for the anaphor, antecedent and their governing token, entity types, genre/modality, and definiteness/previous mention of the antecedent. These features indirectly give us access to tense, grammatical constructions and some measures of salience (especially subjecthood and repeated mention). Additionally, we will consider a number of numerical features which may be relevant from a processing perspective, such as the distance in tokens between the anaphor and antecedent, length in characters and tokens for the antecedent NP, document token count, and the positions of the expressions in the document, expressed as a percentage of document length (e.g. an antecedent may begin at the 75th percentile of document token count). Most of these features can be extracted from the data automatically.

A limitation of using OntoNotes is that many antecedents of pronominal anaphora are not named entities (unnamed 'committees', etc.), meaning we do not have gold entity types for all NPs. In order to overcome this problem and expand the range of features available in this study, the entire corpus was annotated automatically for non-named entities using xrenner, a non-named entity recognizer (Zeldes and Zhang, 2016).

A second problem is that the coreference annotation guidelines for OntoNotes preclude antecedents for indefinite NPs, meaning cases such as (15) are marked as multiple entities (BBN Technologies 2007:4).

(15)   [Parents]$_x$ should be involved with their children's education at home, not in school. [They]$_x$ should see to it ... [Parents]$_y$ are too likely to blame schools for the educational limitations of [their]$_y$ children.

The second instance of 'parents' is regarded as a separate, 'discourse new' entity. This will be relevant for using previous mention of the antecedent as a feature: we can only detect previous mention of the antecedent if it is annotated, and this will never be the case for indefinites.

In order to assess the influence of grammantical function and semantic classes of verbs governing either the anaphor or the antecedent, the syntax trees in the corpus were converted to a dependency representation using Stanford CoreNLP (Manning et al., 2014), allowing for a simpler use of dependency functions as a predictor. This also allows us to identify the governing verb (or noun etc.) for each mention. Governing verbs were then tagged automatically using VerbNet classes (Kipper et al. 2006), which give rough classes based on semantics and alternation behaviors in English, such as ALLOW for verbs like {*allow, permit, ...*} or HELP: {*aid, assist, ...*}, etc.

Because some verb classes are small or rare, potentially leading to very sparsely attested feature values, classes attested fewer than 60 times were collapsed into a class OTHER (for example Verb-Net class 22.2, AMALGAMATE). Verbs attested in multiple classes were always given the majority class, for example the verb *say* appears both in VerbNet class 37.7 SAY and class 78, INDICATE, but was always classified as the more common SAY. Finally, some similar classes were collapsed in order to avoid replacement by OTHER, such as LONG + WANT + WISH, which were fused into a class DESIRE. Nominal governors (e.g. for possessive NPs, whose governor is the possessor NP) were classified by their NER entity class or non-named class predicted by the entity recognizer.

4 Results

4.1 Predictive ensemble model

In this section we construct a model to predict, given properties of a singular antecedent NP from a lexeme known to exhibit notional agreement, and properties of the position of the anaphor referring back to it, whether or not the pronoun will in fact be plural. Considering the highly contextual nature of notional anaphora, we would ideally want to use the entire sequence of text before and after each of the entity mentions to predict the choice of pronoun, for example using a Recurrent Neural Network. However, despite being the largest available dataset for English, the amount of gold standard examples we have (less than 4,000) makes a Deep Learning approach problematic. We therefore train an ensemble of decision trees on the features presented in Section 3, more specifically using the Extra Trees algorithm (Geurts et al., 2006), which outperforms the standard Random Forest algorithm and linear models on our data.

Using a grid search with 5 fold cross validation on the training data, the optimal hyper-parameters for the classifier were found, leading to the use of 300 trees with unlimited depth, limited to the default number of features in the scikit-learn implementation, which is the square root of the number of features rounded up. The best performance was achieved using the 20 features outlined in Figure 1, meaning that each tree receives 5 features to work with, thereby reducing the chance of overfitting training data. The classifier achieves a classification accuracy of 86.81% in predicting the correct form in the test set, an improvement of over 20% above the majority baseline of always guessing 'strict agreement' (65.6% accuracy).

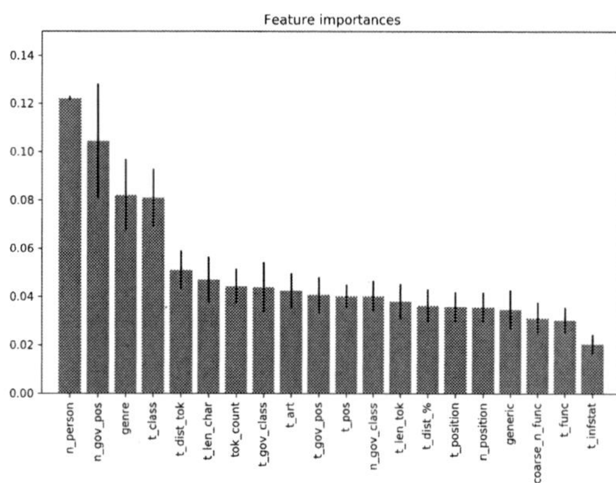

Figure 1: Variable importances for the classifier. Features beginning with n_ apply to the anaphor, and features with t_ to the antecedent.

To evaluate the importance of features in Figure 1 we use the Gini index of purity achieved at splits using each respective feature across all trees. Error bars indicate the standard deviation from the average importance across all trees in the ensemble. A Gini index of 0 means complete homogeneity (for our task, a 50-50 split on both sides), whereas 1 would mean perfect separation based on that feature. In addition to features discussed above, a feature 'generic' was introduced for phrases such as 'anyone', 'someone', 'somebody', etc. which behave differently from other PERSON entities, as

well as a feature 't_art' coding the antecedent's article as definite, indefinite, demonstrative, or none.

The most important feature is 1st vs. 3rd person anaphor ('n_person'), as these are rather different situations: 1st person cases occur mainly with individuals speaking for aforementioned organizations, introduced as proper nouns (e.g. 'the SEC ... we' in (7)). Next is the POS tag of the anaphor's governor, which includes information about tense and can work in conjunction with verbs' semantic classes and grammatical functions (cf. Depraetere 2003, Annala 2008). Genre is surprisingly important in third place (cf. Levin 2001), indicating that settings licensing notional anaphora are genre specific. Replacing genre with a more coarse grained spoken/written variable degrades accuracy. Genre is closely followed by the semantic class of the antecedent, i.e. the entity in question, which is clearly relevant (+/-PERSON and more, see Section 4.2 for details).

Subsequent variables are less important, including distance, length and position in the document. Though both are helpful, using the article form ('t_art') is more important than the information status or previous mention ('t_infstat') based on antecedents to the antecedent (keeping in mind limitations of the coreference annotations, cf. Section 3.2). Grammatical functions are helpful, but less so than other features.

Looking at the actual classifications obtained by the classifier produces the confusion matrix in Table 2. The matrix makes it clear that the classifier is very good at avoiding errors against the majority class: it almost never guesses 'notional' when it shouldn't. Conversely, about 1/3 of actual notional cases are misclassified, predicted to be 'strict'. Among the erroneous cases, only 6 belong to Type III (about 15% of errors) , showing that the classifier largely handles this type quite well next to the other types, since Type III covers about 20% of plural-to-singular agreement cases.

Table 2: Confusion matrix for test data classification

		Predicted		
		Sg	Pl	Total
Actual	Sg	222	39	261
	Pl	7	81	88
	Total	229	120	349

4.2 Analysis of predictors

To understand why the features used in the previous section are helpful we analyze the distribution of notional anaphors for several non-obvious predictors individually. Beginning with processing factors, we can consider the effect of distance between anaphor and antecedent and position in the document, shown in Figures 2 and 3.

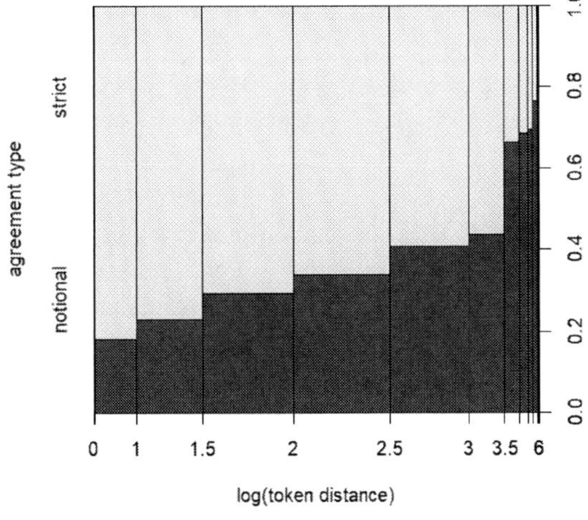

Figure 2: Log token distance between anaphor and antecedent.

In Figure 2, token distance is shown in log-scale, as greater distances are attested sparsely, and the breadth of each column in the spine plot corresponds to the amount of data it is based on. It is easy to see the perfectly monotonic rise in the proportion of notional agreement, beginning with under 20% at a log-distance of ~1, all the way to over 50% at log-distances of ~3.5 or higher (approximately 33 tokens and above).

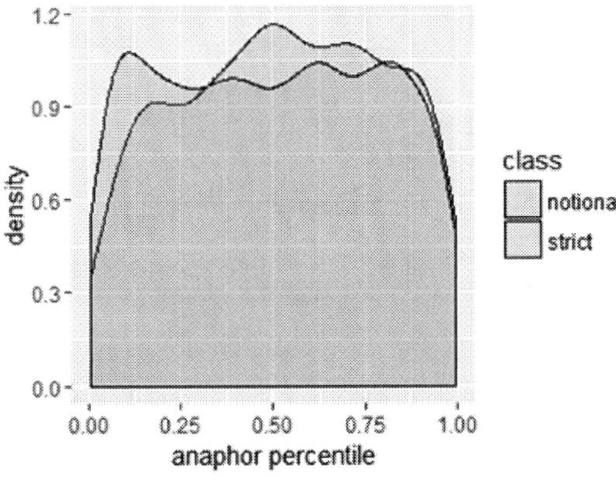

Figure 3: Position of anaphor as percentile of document length in tokens.

Figure 3 shows why position in the document matters: there is a slightly higher frequency of notional agreement after the halfway point of documents. This can be related to a speaker fatigue effect (speakers/writers become less constrained and exhibit less strict agreement as the document goes on), or due to editorial fatigue in written data (editors correct notional agreement, but notice it less frequently further in the document). However while we would only expect an editorial motivation to affect written data, the effect is found in both spoken and written documents, meaning a possible speaker fatigue effect cannot be discounted.

Next we can consider the effect of genre, and expectations that speech promotes notional agreement. This is confirmed in Table 3. However we note that individual genres do behave differently: data from the Web is closer to spoken language. The most restrictive genre in avoiding notional agreement is translations. Both of these facts may reflect a combination of modality, genre and editorial practice effects. However the strong differences suggest that genre is likely crucial to any model attempting to predict this phenomenon.

Table 3: Agreement patterns across genres

genre written	notional	strict	% notional
bible	169	487	25.76
newswire	344	843	28.98
translations	55	210	20.75
web	48	71	40.33
total written	616	1611	27.66
spoken	*notional*	*strict*	*% notional*
bc.conv	237	201	54.11
bc.news	296	378	43.91
phone	60	89	40.26
total spoken	593	668	47.02

Moving on to grammatical and semantic factors, we consider the entity type of the referring expression in Figure 4. The plot shows the chi square residuals for the association of each entity type with the two agreement types. Lines sloping top-right to bottom-left correspond to entity types preferring strict agreement (OBJECT, PLACE, PERSON), while top-left to bottom-right slopes correspond to types preferring notional agreement (QUANTITY, TIME, ORGANIZATION).

The result that PERSON somewhat prefers

strict agreement is surprising given the expectation that agentive, human-associated predicates have an effect promoting notional agreement (Depraetere, 2003). This is because many of those predicates were most often associated in our data with an ORGANIZATION telling, having or wanting to do something, and then being construed as a group of humans. This leads to the notional preference of the ORGANIZATION class. NPs actually classified as PERSON often included heads such as the very common *family* (mostly singular agreement), or potential Type III nouns which often take explicit gender (e.g. gender-specific *'baby ... her/his'*). Less surprising is the association of QUANTITY and TIME with notional agreement, covering cases such as *'a third of ... they'*, and counted time units in Type II phrases such as *'a couple of (minutes/hours)'*.

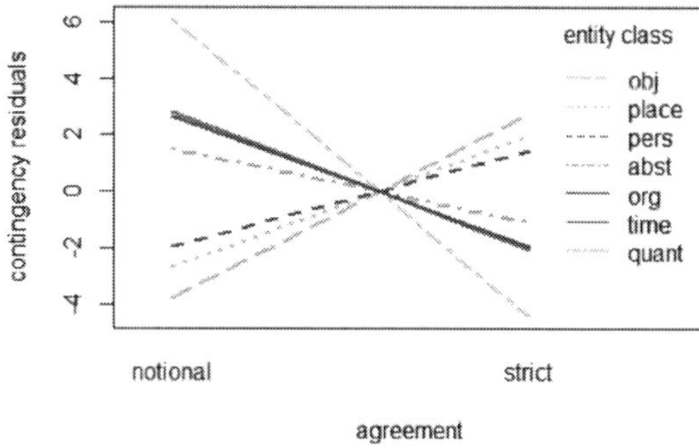

Figure 4: Chi square residuals for notional agreement by entity type. The legend is ordered by strictness.

Looking at the distribution of grammatical forms and functions, Table 4 shows imbalances based on the POS tag of the token governing the anaphor, and Figure 5 shows an association plot between dependency functions[2] and agreement patterns (rare POS and dependency labels have been omitted for clarity).

The table confirms the observations by Annala (2008) that present tense favors plural agreement more than past tense (VBD/VBN), but also reveals that nominal governors (NNP and more so NN, primarily possessed nouns of the entity in question), also promote singular agreement. This is

Table 4: Agreement by anaphor governor POS

	notional	strict	% notional
VBG	112	94	54.36
VBpres[3]	218	255	46.08
VB	244	291	45.61
JJ	48	82	36.92
VBD	183	313	36.89
IN	65	117	35.71
VBN	81	163	33.19
NNP	8	18	30.76
NN	141	645	17.93

echoed in the association plot in Figure 5. Possessive anaphors ('poss') prefer strict agreement and anaphoric subjects promote plural agreement, while the opposite is true for antecedents: if the antecedent is a subject, it is more likely to be realized later as a singular, and the opposite if it is a possessive.

It is possible that the increased salience of subjects adds to speakers' tendency to refer back to them in keeping with the morphological number of the previous mention, while a late mention as a subject allows the salient anaphor position to select a disagreeing form more easily, without depending on previous mentions. Investigating this hypothesis further may require psycholinguistic data.

5   Conclusion

One of the fundamental challenges of notional agreement is the apparent unpredictability shown often in previous studies: the same nouns can appear under seemingly similar conditions with both types of agreement. The ensemble classifier presented here shows that despite this unpredictability, comparatively good predictions can be made on unseen data, with an accuracy of 86.81%, substantially improving on a baseline of 65.6%.[4]

---

[2]Two versions of the function labels were tested: coarse labels as used in Figure 5 (e.g. 'subj', 'clausal') and all available labels in the Stanford CoreNLP basic label set (distinguishing active 'nsubj' and passive 'nsubjpass', different types of clauses, etc.). The classifier works best with coarse labels for the anaphor's function but fine grained ones for the antecedent.

[3]The tags VBP and VBZ have been collapsed into VBpres, since they trivially imply whether the anaphor was singular or plural.

[4]An anonymous reviewer has asked to what extent state of the art coreference resolution systems also err on notional cases in general and the cases targeted here in particular: this is an interesting question which probably depends on the system, but it certainly seems possible that some architectures could benefit from notional agreement probability estimation, similarly to preprocessors predicting singleton status (Recasens et al., 2013) or other special constructions (e.g. anaphoric 'one' in English, Recasens et al. 2016).

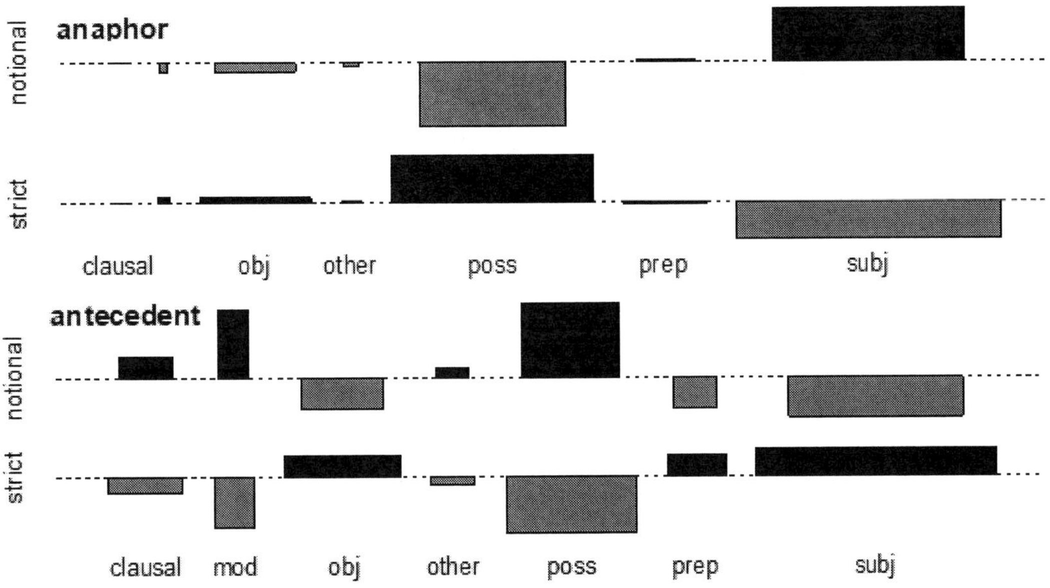

Figure 5: Association of pronoun choice and dependency functions of the anaphor and antecedent (top: anaphor; bottom: antecedent). The category 'clausal' collapses the labels 'csubj', 'ccomp' and 'advcl'.

The classifier showed a good ability to recognize the majority class, but also learned to be 'cautious', guessing 'strict' in 1/3 of notional cases. A possible interpretation of this result is that for ambiguous cases, in which either form could be acceptable, the classifier chooses the safer majority class. In many such misclassified cases it seems likely that speakers would accept either variant, as in (16), which the classifier gets wrong:

(16)   [Comsat Video, which distributes pay-per-view programs to hotel rooms], plans to add Nuggets games to [their] offerings

In this example, multiple signals suggest strict agreement, including an aforementioned, subject antecedent, and short distance to the 3rd person possessive anaphor. Based on features from the training data, it is a fair example of the environment of a 'strict' case; at the same time, it seems likely that speakers would accept a version with 'its', and it is not difficult to find similar examples, with similar distances, syntax and governing items, as in (17).[5]

(17)   Ultimately, Lewis said, [her school] added African-American history to [its] offerings

---

[5]An anonymous reviewer has suggested that checking human acceptability of such deviating cases would be an interesting follow up study, and we certainly agree.

Another aspect worth considering is the feature space used here, and some possible alternatives. Among the features tested but ultimately rejected in this study, we examined the presence of relative clause markers as suggested by Reid (1991), as well as some alternative semantic representations for governing verb semantics. For relative clauses, the importance of cases with 'who' as in example (4) turned out not to be useful in practice, despite the presence of well over 200 relative clauses in the data and over 150 with 'who(m)'. It can be suspected that relative pronouns modifying the antecedent at the point it is mentioned have less interactions with anaphors, which can appear much later in the text, than with immediate subject-verb agreement cases which motivated the observation in Reid (1991).

For encoding verb semantics, the choice of VerbNet categories and the lack of disambiguation for ambiguous cases are both far from optimal. VerbNet classes do not necessarily map well onto verb groups' preferences for notional agreement. It seems likely that other thematic, cluster-based or vector space-based methods of classifying verb semantics could be helpful for the present task. To this end we tested using semantic classes as assigned by the UCREL Semantic Analysis System (USAS, Rayson et al. 2004), which performed worse than VerbNet. Some VerbNet classes are mirrored in the USAS classes (e.g. communication verbs, the USAS coarse domain Q, or sub-classes in domain Q2); however in many cases it is possible that, by being much more specific (classes such as 'science and technology' in USAS), content domain classes encourage the classifier to memorize specific training instances, which do not generalize well. Ideally, a flexible semantic representation such as trainable embeddings would likely be helpful, but would require training on an external dataset beyond the notional agreement pairs, which only amount to a few thousand examples.

For future work, we can point out that while the classifier achieved overall good accuracy above chance, there is substantial room for improvement, and more features could be considered. These include phonological features (e.g. phonotactics around anaphors, metrical factors), morphological features (affixes, types of compounding), semantic features (more directly targeting predicates with distributive readings) and further context cues such as modifiers (adjectives, adverbs) and other words in the context not directly governing or governed by the noun in question. For NLP and NLG applications, it would be most useful to consider those variables for which we can build automatic taggers or generated contexts in real-time. At the same time, it will probably remain impossible to achieve perfect accuracy: it is expected that, as with many high level alternations, some element of inter- and even intra-speaker variation, as well as speakers' communicative intentions, will always create a certain degree of unpredictability in settings which are otherwise comparable.

References

Henri Annala. 2008. *Changes in Subject-Verb Agreement with Collective Nouns in British English from the 18th Century to the Present Day*. Pro gradu thesis, University of Tampere.

BBN Technologies. 2007. Co-reference guidelines for English OntoNotes. version 6.0. Technical report.

Anne Curzan. 2003. *Gender Shifts in the History of English*. Studies in English Language. Cambridge University Press, Cambridge.

Marcel den Dikken. 2001. "Pluringulars", pronouns and quirky agreement. *The Linguistic Review* 18:19–41.

Ilse Depraetere. 2003. On verbal concord with collective nouns in British English. *English Language and Linguistics* 7(1):85–127.

Kathleen Eberhard, J. Cooper Cutting, and Kathryn Bock. 2005. Making sense of syntax: Number agreement in sentence production. *Psychological Review* 112:531–559.

Morton Ann Gernsbacher. 1986. Comprehension of conceptual anaphora in discourse processing. In *Proceedings of the Eigth Annual Conference of the Cognitive Science Society*. Amherst, MA, pages 110–125.

Pierre Geurts, Damien Ernst, and Louis Wehenkel. 2006. Extremely randomized trees. *Machine Learning* 63(1):3–42.

Eduard Hovy, Mitchell Marcus, Martha Palmer, Lance Ramshaw, and Ralph Weischedel. 2006. OntoNotes: The 90% solution. In *Proceedings of the Human Language Technology Conference of the NAACL, Companion Volume: Short Papers*. New York, pages 57–60.

Rodney Huddleston and Geoffrey K. Pullum. 2002. *The Cambridge Grammar of the English Language*. Cambridge University Press, Cambridge.

Emiel Krahmer and Kees van Deemter. 2012. Computational generation of referring expressions: A survey. *Computational Linguistics* 38(1):173–218.

Geoffrey Leech and Jan Svartvik. 2002. *A Communicative Grammar of English*. Longman, London.

Magnus Levin. 2001. *Agreement with Collective Nouns in English*. Lund Studies in English 103. Lund University, Lund.

Christopher D. Manning, Mihai Surdeanu, John Bauer, Jenny Finkel, Steven J. Bethard, and Davide McClosky. 2014. The Stanford CoreNLP natural language processing toolkit. In *Proceedings of ACL 2014: System Demonstrations*. Baltimore, MD, pages 55–60.

Ana E. Martinez-Insua and Ignacio M. Palacios-Martinez. 2003. A corpus-based approach to non-concord in present day English existential there-constructions. *English Studies* 84(3):262–283.

Laura L. Paterson. 2011. *The Use and Prescription of Epicene Pronouns: A Corpus-based Approach to Generic he and Singular they in British English*. Ph.D. thesis, Loughborough University.

Randolph Quirk, Sydney Greenbaum, Geoffrey Leech, and Jan Svartvik. 1985. *A Comprehensive Grammar of the English Language*. Longman, London.

Paul Rayson, Dawn Archer, Scott Piao, and Tony McEnery. 2004. The UCREL semantic analysis system. In *Proceedings of the Workshop Beyond Named Entity Recognition: Semantic Labelling for NLP Tasks*. Lisbon, Portugal, pages 7–12.

Marta Recasens, Marie-Catherine de Marneffe, and Christopher Potts. 2013. The life and death of discourse entities: Identifying singleton mentions. In *Proceedings of NAACL 2013*. Atlanta, GA, pages 627–633.

Marta Recasens, Zhichao Hu, and Olivia Rhinehart. 2016. Sense anaphoric pronouns: Am I one? In *Proceedings of the Workshop on Coreference Resolution Beyond OntoNotes (CORBON 2016), co-located with NAACL 2016*. San Diego, CA, pages 1–6.

Wallis Reid. 1991. *Verb and Noun Number in English: A Functional Explanation*. Longman, London.

Uli Sauerland. 2003. A new semantics for number. In *Proceedings of SALT 13*. CLC Publications, Ithaca, NY.

Nicholas Sobin. 1997. Agreement, default rules, and grammatical viruses. *Linguistic Inquiry* 28(2):318–343.

Adrian Staub. 2009. On the interpretation of the number attraction effect: Response time evidence. *Journal of Memory and Language* 60(2):1–39.

Matthew W. Wagers, Ellen F. Lau, and Colin Phillips. 2009. Agreement attraction in comprehension: Representations and processes. *Journal of Memory and Language* 61:206–237.

Amir Zeldes and Shuo Zhang. 2016. When annotation schemes change rules help: A configurable approach to coreference resolution beyond OntoNotes. In *Proceedings of the NAACL2016 Workshop on Coreference Resolution Beyond OntoNotes (CORBON)*. San Diego, CA, pages 92–101.

Integrating Predictions from Neural-Network Relation Classifiers into Coreference and Bridging Resolution

Ina Rösiger, Maximilian Köper, Kim Anh Nguyen and **Sabine Schulte im Walde**
Institut für Maschinelle Sprachverarbeitung
Universität Stuttgart, Germany
`{roesigia,koepermn,nguyenkh,schulte}@ims.uni-stuttgart.de`

Abstract

Cases of coreference and bridging resolution often require knowledge about semantic relations between anaphors and antecedents. We suggest state-of-the-art neural-network classifiers trained on relation benchmarks to predict and integrate likelihoods for relations. Two experiments with representations differing in noise and complexity improve our bridging but not our coreference resolver.

1 Introduction

Noun phrase (NP) coreference resolution is the task of determining which noun phrases in a text or dialogue refer to the same discourse entities (Ng, 2010). The most difficult cases in NP coreference are those which require semantic knowledge to infer the relation between the anaphor and the antecedent, as in Example (1) where we need to know that *Malaria* is a *disease*.

(1)   <u>Malaria</u> is a mosquito-borne infection. **The disease** is transmitted via a bite ...

Related, but even more complicated is the task of bridging resolution: it requires linking anaphoric noun phrases and their antecedents which however do not refer to the same referent, but are related in a way that is not explicitly stated (Poesio and Artstein, 2005; Poesio and Vieira, 1998). Bridging anaphors are discourse-new but still depend on the preceding context. For example, for resolving *the windows* in (2) to *the room*, we need to know that a room typically has windows.

(2)   I went into <u>the room</u>. **The windows** were broken.

The semantic relation information necessary for anaphora resolution is typically integrated into a system through a knowledge base, by relying on WordNet, Wikipedia or similar resources (cf. Vieira and Poesio (2000), Ponzetto and Strube (2007), a.o.). Up to date, few approaches have tried to integrate automatically induced information about semantic relations (e.g. Poesio et al. (2002); Feuerbach et al. (2015)). In the current study, we suggest state-of-the-art neural-network classifiers to predict semantic relations between noun pairs, and integrate the relation predictions into existing systems for coreference and bridging resolution.

2 Relation Hypotheses

Coreference signals a relation of identity, so we assume that coreference resolution should benefit from relations that link identical or highly similar entities. Obviously, synonymy is a member of this set of relations, as exemplified in Example (3):

(3)   I live on <u>Shortland Street</u>. **The road** will be closed for repair work next week.

Hypernymy can also be used to refer to a previously introduced entity, as in Example (4):

(4)   <u>My neighbour's dog</u> has been getting on my nerves lately. **The stupid animal** kept barking all night.

Note that the direction of this relation is important, as we can introduce a hyponym and then later refer to it via a hypernym, but not vice versa[1].

The relations between a bridging anaphor and its antecedent are assumed to be more diverse. The prototypical bridging relation is represented by meronymy:

---

[1] Although, in news text, you might find a certain writing style which allows for hypernyms to later be referred to via a hyponym, e.g. in "Today we are celebrating <u>a great athlete</u>. **The olympic swimmer** has always been one of our personal favorites."

44

Proceedings of the Workshop on Computational Models of Reference, Anaphora and Coreference, pages 44–49
New Orleans, Louisiana, June 6, 2018. ©2018 Association for Computational Linguistics

(5)   My car broke down yesterday. It turned out to be a problem with **the engine**.

However, other relations come into play, too, such as attribute-of and part-of-event (Hou, 2016).

3   Experimental Setup

Data   We based our experiments on the benchmark dataset for coreference resolution, the OntoNotes corpus (Weischedel et al., 2011). For bridging, we used the ISNotes corpus, a small subset of OntoNotes annotated with information status (Markert et al., 2012). In order to obtain candidate pairs for semantic relation prediction, we considered all heads of noun phrases in the OntoNotes corpus (Weischedel et al., 2011) and combined them with preceding heads of noun phrases in the same document. Due to the different corpus sizes, the generally higher frequency of coreferent anaphors and the transitivity of the coreference relation, we obtained many more coreference pairs (65,113 unique pairs) than bridging pairs (633 in total, including 608 unique pairs).

Bridging resolver   As there is no publicly available bridging resolver, we re-implemented the rule-based approach by Hou et al. (2014). It contains eight rules which all propose anaphor-antecedent pairs, independently of the other rules. The rules are applied in order of their precision. Apart from information on the connectivity of two nouns, which is derived from counting how often two nouns appear in a $noun_1$ preposition $noun_2$ pattern in a large corpus, the tool does not contain information about general relations.

Coreference resolver   We used the IMS Hot-Coref resolver (Björkelund and Kuhn, 2014) as a coreference resolver, because it allows an easy integration of new features. While its performance is slightly worse than the state-of-the-art neural coreference resolver (Clark and Manning, 2016), the neural resolver relies on very few basic features and word embeddings, which already implicitly contain semantic relations.

Evaluation metrics   For coreference resolution, we report the performance as CoNLL score, version 8.01 (Pradhan et al., 2014). For bridging resolution, we report performance in precision, recall and F1. For bridging evaluation, we take coreference chains into account during the evaluation, i.e. the predicted antecedent is considered correct if it is in the same coreference chain as the gold antecedent. We applied train-development-test splits, used the training and development set for optimisation, and report performance on the test set.

4   First Experiment

4.1   Semantic Relation Classification

We used the publicly available relation resource BLESS (Baroni and Lenci, 2011), containing 26,546 word pairs across the six relations co-hyponymy/coordination, attribute, meronymy, hypernymy, and random. As classification method, we relied on the findings from Shwartz and Dagan (2016), and used a plain distributional model combined with a non-linear classifier (neural network) with only word representations. As many of our target word pairs rarely or never occurred together in a shared sentence, we could not integrate intervening words or paths as additional features.

We took the publicly available 300-dimensional vectors from ConceptNet (Speer et al., 2017), combined the word representations with the semantic relation resources, and trained a feed-forward neural network for classification. The input of the network is simply the concatenation of the two words, and the output is the desired semantic relation. At test time we present two words and output the class membership probability for each relation. In addition we provide information about the semantic similarity by computing the cosine.

We relied on the training, test and validation split from Shwartz and Dagan (2016). The hyper-parameter were tuned on the validation set and obtained the best performance by relying on two hidden layers with 200 and 150 neurons respectively. As activation function we applied rectified linear units (ReLU). Despite, we set batch size to 100 and used a dropout rate of 20%.

Intrinsic Evaluation   To validate that the semantic relation classification works to a sufficient degree, we performed an intrinsic evaluation. On the test set from Shwartz and Dagan (2016), our model achieved an accuracy of 87.8%*, which is significantly[2] better than the majority class baseline (i.e. the random class with 45%). Shwartz and Dagan report a weighted average F-score of

____
[2]We used the χ^2 test * with $p < 0.001$.

89, which is only marginally better than our reimplementation (88).

While this performance seems very good and confirms the quality of our reimplementation, the work by Levy et al. (2015) pointed out that such supervised distributional models often just memorise whether a word is a prototypical example for a certain relation. Indeed, we found many of these cases in our dataset. For example the term 'gas' appeared $\frac{9}{10}$ times in a meronym relation in training and $\frac{4}{4}$ times as a meronym in the test set. To encounter this effect we conducted a second evaluation where we made sure that training and test set contained different terms.

With an accuracy of 58.6%* and a weighted mean F-score of .52, the performance of this second evaluation was still significantly better than the majority class baseline but considerably worse than the reported results on the BLESS train/test split with lexical overlap. Still, we assume that this evaluation provides a more realistic view on the relation classification. Results per relation are given in Table 1. It can be seen that the model is skewed towards the majority class (random), whereas in particular the hypernym relation seems to be difficult. Here we observed many false decision between coord/hyper.

Rel.	P	R	F1
Random	63.7	93.8	75.9
Coord	46.6	41.2	43.7
Attri	68.9	18.7	29.4
Mero	31.1	22.4	26.0
Hyper	25.0	0.4	0.7

Table 1: Results of the intrinsic evaluation on BLESS (without lexical overlap).

4.2 Relation Analysis

Before using the predicted relations for coreference and bridging resolution, we analysed the distribution of relations across the bridging and coreference pairs, as well as across all other, non-related pairs. Table 2 shows the average cosine similarities (COS) of these pairs. As expected, the average cosine similarity is highest for coreference pairs and a little lower for bridging pairs, but still much higher in comparison to all other pairs. In the rows below cosine similarity, we give the averages of the output probabilities of the classifier for each relation. Random represents the class for non-related pairs without a relation. Such non-related pairs have indeed a high

score for not being in a relation, whereas coreference and bridging pairs have lower scores in this category. Non-related random pairs have a high score for not being in a relation, whereas coreference and bridging pairs have lower scores in this category. Both coreference and bridging pairs have high meronym values, which is surprising for the coreference pairs. Bridging pairs also have a higher coordination value (i.e. co-hyponymy), and a slightly higher value for hypernymy.

	Coref pairs	Bridging pairs	Other pairs
COS	0.26	0.19	0.05
Random	0.39	0.49	0.78
Coord	0.22	0.13	0.03
Attri	0.07	0.07	0.06
Mero	0.22	0.23	0.10
Hyper	0.09	0.07	0.02

Table 2: Average cosine similarities and relation classifier probabilities for coreferent and bridging pairs in comparison to other pairs of nouns, experiment 1.

4.3 Relations for Bridging Resolution

As short, unmodified NPs are generally considered useful bridging anaphor candidates, because they often lack an antecedent in the form of an implicit modifier, we add the following new rule to our bridging resolver: "search for an unmodified NP, in the form of *the N*", e.g. in *the advantages*. As bridging antecedents typically appear in a rather close window (cf. Hou (2016)), we search for an antecedent within the last three sentences. As bridging pairs have a higher cosine value than non-related pairs, we experiment with an additional cosine similarity constraint: if the pair is in a certain relation and the cosine similarity is greater than 0.2, it is proposed.

Table 3 shows the results for the different relations as well as the versions with and without a cosine similarity threshold, which are explored further in Table 4. Note that both tables do not give absolute numbers of correct and wrong bridging pairs, but only the bridging pairs which were proposed by the newly added semantic rule.

Meronymy seems to be the best predictor for bridging, with a significant gain of 2.38% in F1 score[3], followed by the not-random version. The precision slightly decreased, but since the rule was designed to increase recall, this is acceptable. In the best setting (meronymy, cosine threshold of

---

[3]We compute significance using the Wilcoxon signed rank test (Siegel and Castellan, 1988) at the 0.05 level.

Baseline	-	-	-	-	-	-	-	59.82	10.58	18.0
Relation	*without cosine threshold*					*with cosine threshold of 0.2*				
	Correct	Wrong	Precision	Recall	F1	Correct	Wrong	Precision	Recall	F1
Coord	5	41	45.57	11.37	18.20	5	32	48.3	11.37	18.41
Attri	3	46	43.48	11.06	17.63	2	8	56.56	10.9	18.28
Mero	14	101	35.69	12.80	18.84	14	36	50.00	12.80	**20.38**
Hyper	2	7	57.02	10.90	18.3	2	4	58.47	10.9	18.38
Not random	17	105	35.90	13.27	19.37	15	54	45.3	12.95	**20.15**

Table 3: Correct and wrong bridging pairs which are found by the additional semantic rule, with and without additional cosine threshold constraint (> 0.2).

Threshold	Correct	Wrong	P	R	F1
0.15	16	56	44.20	12.64	19.66
0.20	14	36	50.00	12.80	**20.38**
0.25	10	26	52.03	12.16	19.72
0.30	2	22	50.74	10.90	17.95

Table 4: Effect of the cosine threshold constraint, for the relation meronymy.

0.2) we now find 14 additional correct pairs, for example:

(6)   IBM said it expects industrywide efforts to become prevalent because <u>semiconductor manufacturing</u> has become so expensive. A state-of-the-art plant cost 40 million in the mid-1970s but costs 500 million today because **the technology** is so complex.

We also find 36 more wrong pairs, for example:

(7)   In the 1980s, the Justice Department and lower federal courts that enforce the Voting Rights Act have required state legislatures and <u>municipal governments</u> to create the maximum number of "safe" minority election districts – districts where minorities form between 65% and 80% of **the voting population** .

4.4   Relations for Coreference Resolution

We used the following features in the resolver:

- *Random as the highest class*: a boolean feature which returns true if the random class got assigned the highest value of all the relations.
- *Cosine binned into low, middle, high*: this is a binned version of cosine similarity. We experimented with two different bins, the first one {0-0.3,0.3-0.49,>0.49}, the second one {0-0.3,0.3-0.6,>0.6}
- *Relation with the highest value*: a multi-value feature with 6 potential values: none, mero, coord, attri, hyper and random. The class with the highest value is returned.

We added one feature at a time and analysed the change in CoNLL score. The results are not shown in detail, as the score decreased in every version. For coreference resolution, where the baseline performance is already quite high, the additional semantic information thus does not seem to improve results. This is in line with Björkelund and Kuhn (2014), where integrating a WordNet synonym/hypernym lookup did not improve the performance, as well as Durrett and Klein (2013), where increased semantic information was not beneficial either.

5   Second Experiment

The first experiment had a few major shortcomings. First, we did not have lemmatised vectors, and as a result, singular and plural forms of the same lemma had different values. Sometimes, this led to the wrong analysis, cf. Example (8), where the singular and plural versions of *novel* make different predictions, and where a lemmatised version would have preferred the correct antecedent:

W1	W2	COS	coord	attri	mero
characters	novel	0.35	**0.69**	0.02	0.27
characters	novels	0.43	0.28	0.05	**0.38**

(8)   In   <u>novels of an earlier vintage</u>$_{predicted}$, David would have represented excitement and danger; Malcom, placid, middle-class security. The irony in <u>this novel</u>$_{gold}$ is that ... **The characters** confront a world ...

Second, many proper nouns were assigned zero values, as they were not covered by our vector representations. These pairs thus could not be used in the new rule. Third, the relations in the benchmark dataset BLESS do not completely match our hypotheses. We thus designed a second experiment to overcome these shortcomings.

5.1 Semantic Relation Classification

To address the problem with out-of-vocabulary words we relied on fasttext (Bojanowski et al., 2016), which uses subword information to create representations for unseen words. We created 100-dimensional representations by applying a window of 5 to a lemmatised and lower-cased version of DECOW14 (Schäfer, 2015). The semantic relations were induced from WordNet (Fellbaum, 1998), by collecting all noun pairs from the relations: synonymy, antonymy, meronymy, hyponymy, hypernymy. To obtain a balanced setup, we sampled 2,010 random pairs from each relation, and in addition we created random pairs without relations across files. Hyper-parameters of the neural network were identical to the ones used in the first experiment.

Intrinsic Evaluation   We obtained a similar performance as before, an accuracy of 55.8%* (exp1: 58.6) and a mean weighted f-score of 55 (exp1: 52). Results per relation are shown in Table 5. Interestingly, the performances with respect to the individual relations differ strongly from the first experiment. In this second experiment, with balanced relations, meronym and antonym are well-detected whereas random performs inferior.

Rel.	P	R	F1
Random	56.7	39.0	46.2
Ant	70.0	83.4	76.3
Syn	46.3	46.5	46.4
Mero	62.1	69.5	65.6
Hyper	48.9	49.1	49.0
Hypo	47.5	47.6	47.6

Table 5: Results of the intrinsic evaluation on WordNet.

5.2 Relation Analysis

Table 6 shows that –unexpectedly– the coreference and bridging pairs in comparison to other pairs differ much less than in the first experiment.

	Coref pairs	Bridging pairs	Other pairs
COS	0.38	0.31	0.22
Random	0.13	0.15	0.21
Mero	0.18	0.15	0.17
Hyper	0.25	0.23	0.23
Hypo	0.20	0.27	0.19
Syn	0.16	0.15	0.15
Ant	0.08	0.06	0.05

Table 6: Average relation classifier probabilities and cosine similarities for coreferent and bridging pairs in comparison to other pairs of nouns, experiment 2.

5.3 Relations for Anaphora Resolution

The two setups for integrating the relation classification into bridging and coreference resolution were exactly the same as in the first experiment. The outcome is however a little disappointing. The baseline system for bridging resolution was only improved in one condition, for the relation meronymy and with a cosine threshold of 0.3, reaching F1=18.92 (in comparison to F1=20.38 in the first experiment). Regarding coreference resolution we did not obtain any improvements over the baseline, as in the first experiment.

These results correspond to the less clear differences in the relation analysis (cf. Table 6) but are unexpected because in our opinion the setup for experiment 2 in comparison to the setup for experiment 1 was clearly improved regarding the task requirements.

6 Discussion and Conclusion

As the data for which we predicted the relations does not contain labeled relations that match the categories in our hypotheses, it is difficult to assess how well the classifiers work on this data. Despite the fact that we applied state-of-the-art methods, annotating at least a small part of the data would be necessary to assess the quality of the predictions. Our analysis shows that while some of our hypotheses have been confirmed, e.g. that meronymy is the most important relation for bridging, which can be used to improve the performance of a bridging resolver, the distribution of the relations in actual corpus data seems to be more complex than our hypotheses suggested, as we find for example also cases of meronymy in the coreference pairs.

For some of the relations, the missing direction can be problematic, as the system sometimes proposes pairs where the anaphor is a superordinate to the antecedent (e.g. <u>residents</u> ... **city**), although as mentioned in the introduction, it typically only works vice versa (<u>city</u> ... **residents**).

As the performance for coreference resolution is already quite high, the predicted relations did not improve the performance. For bridging resolution, however, the performance is typically low, and further work on finding general cases of bridging seems promising.

Acknowledgments

This work was funded by the Collaborative Research Center SFB 732, projects A6 and D12.

References

Marco Baroni and Alessandro Lenci. 2011. How we blessed distributional semantic evaluation. In *Proceedings of the GEMS 2011 Workshop on GEometrical Models of Natural Language Semantics*, GEMS '11, pages 1–10, Stroudsburg, PA, USA.

Anders Björkelund and Jonas Kuhn. 2014. Learning structured perceptrons for coreference resolution with latent antecedents and non-local features. In *Proceedings of the 52nd Annual Meeting of the Association for Computational Linguistics (Volume 1: Long Papers)*, pages 47–57, Baltimore, Maryland. Association for Computational Linguistics.

Piotr Bojanowski, Edouard Grave, Armand Joulin, and Tomas Mikolov. 2016. Enriching word vectors with subword information. *arXiv preprint arXiv:1607.04606.*

Kevin Clark and Christopher D. Manning. 2016. Deep reinforcement learning for mention-ranking coreference models. In *Proceedings of the 2016 Conference on Empirical Methods on Natural Language Processing*, Austin, USA.

Greg Durrett and Dan Klein. 2013. Easy victories and uphill battles in coreference resolution. In *Proceedings of the 2013 Conference on Empirical Methods in Natural Language Processing*, pages 1971–1982, Seattle, USA.

Christiane Fellbaum. 1998. *WordNet: An Electronic Lexical Database.* Bradford Books.

Tim Feuerbach, Martin Riedl, and Chris Biemann. 2015. Distributional semantics for resolving bridging mentions. In *Proceedings of the International Conference Recent Advances in Natural Language Processing*, pages 192–199, Hissar, Bulgaria.

Yufang Hou. 2016. *Unrestricted Bridging Resolution.* Ph.D. thesis.

Yufang Hou, Katja Markert, and Michael Strube. 2014. A rule-based system for unrestricted bridging resolution: Recognizing bridging anaphora and finding links to antecedents. In *Proceedings of the Conference on Empirical Methods in Natural Language Processing*, pages 2082–2093, Seattle, USA.

Omer Levy, Steffen Remus, Chris Biemann, and Ido Dagan. 2015. Do supervised distributional methods really learn lexical inference relations? In *Proceedings of the 2015 Conference of the North American Chapter of the Association for Computational Linguistics: Human Language Technologies*, pages 970–976, Denver, USA.

Katja Markert, Yufang Hou, and Michael Strube. 2012. Collective classification for fine-grained information status. In *Proceedings of the 50th Annual Meeting of the Association for Computational Linguistics: Long Papers-Volume 1*, pages 795–804, Jeju Island, Korea. Association for Computational Linguistics.

Vincent Ng. 2010. Supervised noun phrase coreference research: The first fifteen years. In *Proceedings of the 48th Annual Meeting of the Association for Computational Linguistics*, pages 1396–1411, Uppsala, Sweden. Association for Computational Linguistics.

Massimo Poesio and Ron Artstein. 2005. The reliability of anaphoric annotation, reconsidered: Taking ambiguity into account. In *Proceedings of the workshop on frontiers in corpus annotations ii: Pie in the sky*, pages 76–83. Association for Computational Linguistics.

Massimo Poesio, Tomonori Ishikawa, Sabine Schulte Im Walde, and Renata Vieira. 2002. Acquiring lexical knowledge for anaphora resolution. In *Proceedings of the third international conference on language resources and evaluation (LREC)*, Las Palmas, Spain.

Massimo Poesio and Renata Vieira. 1998. A corpus-based investigation of definite description use. *Computational Linguistics*, 24(2):183–216.

Simone Paolo Ponzetto and Michael Strube. 2007. Knowledge derived from wikipedia for computing semantic relatedness. *J. Artif. Intell. Res.(JAIR)*, 30:181–212.

Sameer Pradhan, Xiaoqiang Luo, Marta Recasens, Eduard Hovy, Vincent Ng, and Michael Strube. 2014. Scoring coreference partitions of predicted mentions: A reference implementation. In *Proceedings of the 52nd Annual Meeting of the Association for Computational Linguistics (Volume 2: Short Papers)*, pages 30–35, Baltimore, Maryland. Association for Computational Linguistics.

Roland Schäfer. 2015. Processing and Querying Large Web Corpora with the COW14 Architecture. In *Proceedings of the 3rd Workshop on Challenges in the Management of Large Corpora*, pages 28 – 34.

Vered Shwartz and Ido Dagan. 2016. Path-based vs. distributional information in recognizing lexical semantic relations. In *Proceedings of the 5th Workshop on Cognitive Aspects of the Lexicon (CogALex-V), in COLING*, Osaka, Japan.

Sidney Siegel and N. John Jr. Castellan. 1988. *Nonparametric Statistics for the Behavioral Sciences*, 2nd edition. McGraw-Hill, Berkeley, CA.

Robert Speer, Joshua Chin, and Catherine Havasi. 2017. Conceptnet 5.5: An open multilingual graph of general knowledge. In *AAAI*.

Renata Vieira and Massimo Poesio. 2000. An empirically based system for processing definite descriptions. *Computational Linguistics*, 26(4):539–593.

Ralph Weischedel, Sameer Pradhan, Lance Ramshaw, Martha Palmer, Nianwen Xue, Mitchell Marcus, Ann Taylor, Craig Greenberg, Eduard Hovy, Robert Belvin, et al. 2011. Ontonotes release 4.0. *LDC2011T03, Philadelphia, Penn.: Linguistic Data Consortium.*

Towards Bridging Resolution in German:
Data Analysis and Rule-based Experiments

Janis Pagel and Ina Rösiger
Institute for Natural Language Processing
University of Stuttgart, Germany
`{pageljs,roesigia}@ims.uni-stuttgart.de`

Abstract

Bridging resolution is the task of recognising bridging anaphors and linking them to their antecedents. While there is some work on bridging resolution for English, there is only little work for German. We present two datasets which contain bridging annotations, namely DIRNDL and GRAIN, and compare the performance of a rule-based system with a simple baseline approach on these two corpora. The performance for full bridging resolution ranges between an F1 score of 13.6% for DIRNDL and 11.8% for GRAIN. An analysis using oracle lists suggests that the system could, to a certain extent, benefit from ranking and re-ranking antecedent candidates. Furthermore, we investigate the importance of single features and show that the features used in our work seem promising for future bridging resolution approaches.

1 Introduction

Bridging (Clark, 1975) or *associative anaphora* (Hawkins, 1978) is an anaphoric phenomenon, where a discourse-new entity stands in a prototypical or inferable relationship to a previously introduced entity. Crucially, these two entities are not coreferent.

(1) Und man muss jetzt aufpassen, dass man sich nicht zum Sprachrohr von Leuten macht, die eben <u>den Mindestlohn</u> umgehen wollen. Einer **der Hauptstreitpunkte** ist ja **die Dokumentationspflicht**[1].

(And now you have to be careful that you do not become the voice for the people who just want to avoid <u>the minimum wage</u>. One of **the main points of contention** is **the documentation requirement**...)

Bridging anaphors can be considered expressions with an implicit argument, e.g. *die Dokumentationspflicht beim Mindestlohn (the documentation requirement relevant to the minimum wage)*.

The related NLP task of bridging resolution is to identify bridging anaphors and link them to their antecedents. Most of the work on bridging resolution, with its subtasks of anaphor detection and antecedent selection, has focused on English (e.g. Hou et al., 2014; Markert et al., 2012; Rahman and Ng, 2012). For German, Grishina (2016) has presented a corpus of 432 bridging pairs as well as an in-depth analysis on some properties of bridging, e.g. on the distance between anaphors and their antecedents and on the distribution of bridging relations. Apart from Cahill and Riester (2012)'s work on bridging anaphor detection as a subclass in information status classification and Hahn et al. (1996)'s early work on bridging resolution, there have been no automatic approaches to bridging resolution in German.

This paper gives an overview on German corpora containing bridging annotations and presents experiments on bridging anaphor detection and full bridging resolution on two available corpora, DIRNDL and GRAIN. The performance for full bridging resolution ranges between an F1 score of 13.6% for DIRNDL and 11.8% for GRAIN. We investigate this difference in performance by using oracle lists, which evaluate the antecedent search techniques of the rules.

2 Related work

2.1 Available corpora

This section briefly presents the three German corpora that contain bridging annotations.

GRAIN Recently, the GRAIN release of the SFB732 Silver Standard Collection (Schweitzer et al., 2018) has been announced. It contains

---

[1] Anaphors are marked in bold face, their antecedents are underlined.

Proceedings of the Workshop on Computational Models of Reference, Anaphora and Coreference, pages 50–60
New Orleans, Louisiana, June 6, 2018. ©2018 Association for Computational Linguistics

23 German radio interviews of about 10 minutes each, whose transcripts were annotated with referential information status (Baumann and Riester, 2012), following the annotation guidelines in Riester and Baumann (2017). This means that all referring expressions in the interviews were categorised as to whether they are given/coreferential, bridging anaphors, deictic, discourse-new, idiomatic, etc. The interviews also contain coreference chains and bridging links. 274 bridging pairs were annotated in total[2]. While the referential information status was hand-annotated, the other annotation layers consist of predicted annotations. GRAIN contains spontaneous speech about rather diverse topics.

DIRNDL The DIRNDL corpus (Eckart et al., 2012; Björkelund et al., 2014), a corpus of radio news, also contains bridging annotations as part of its information status annotation (again, on transcripts of the news), following older guidelines of the RefLex scheme (Baumann and Riester, 2012). Overall, 655 bridging pairs have been annotated. Apart from the manual information status annotation, other linguistic annotation layers (POS-tagging, parsing, morphological information) have been created automatically.

Corefpro corpus The corefpro corpus (Grishina, 2016) contains news and narrative text as well as medicine instruction leaflets, and comprises 432 annotated bridging pairs. There are three different types of anaphors: coreferent, bridging or near-identity, following Recasens and Hovy (2010). Only definite anaphors were annotated. The corpus was not available when we performed our experiments, but has recently been made publicly available[3].

2.2 Computational approaches

As mentioned in the introduction, there has only been little work on bridging for German so far. Cahill and Riester (2012) presented a CRF-based automatic classification of information status, which included bridging as a subclass. However, they did not state the accuracy per class, which is why we cannot derive any performance estimation for the task of bridging anaphor detection. They stated that bridging cases "are difficult to capture by automatic techniques", which

confirms findings from information status classification for English, where bridging is typically a category with rather low accuracy (Markert et al., 2012; Rahman and Ng, 2012; Hou, 2016a). Hahn et al. (1996) and Markert et al. (1996) have presented a resolver for bridging anaphors, back then called textual ellipsis or functional anaphora, in which they resolved bridging anaphors in German technical texts using centering theory and a knowledge base. The corpus and the knowledge base as well as the overall system are, however, not available, which makes a comparison with our system difficult. As far as we know, the rule-based system from Hou et al. (2014) is the only system proposed for full bridging resolution so far, following earlier work on bridging anaphor detection (Hou et al., 2013a) and antecedent selection (Hou et al., 2013b).

3 Bridging definition in RefLex

As both available corpora, DIRNDL and GRAIN, were annotated according to the RefLex scheme (Baumann and Riester, 2012; Riester and Baumann, 2017), we present the main idea of this scheme, as well as its implications for bridging anaphors.

RefLex (Riester and Baumann, 2017) distinguishes information status at two different dimensions, namely a referential and a lexical dimension. The referential level analyses the information status of referring expressions (i.e. noun phrases) according to a fine-grained version of the given/new-distinction, whereas the lexical level analyses the information status at the word level, where content words are analysed as to whether the lemma or a related word has occurred before.

Bridging anaphors are a subclass of referential information status and are labeled as `r-bridging`. On the referential level, indefinite expressions are considered to be discourse-new and are thus treated as expressions of the information status category `r-new`. Therefore, the bridging anaphors in our data are always definite.

In RefLex, `r-briding-contained` is a separate information status class, where the anaphor is modified by the antecedent in either a prepositional modification or a possessive pre-modification, e.g. in *the approach's **accuracy*** or ***the accuracy** of the approach*. In this paper, we do not cover these cases.

---

[2]In a preliminary version of the data, in which one interview is missing as it is currently being validated.

[3]https://github.com/yuliagrishina/corefpro

4 Analysis: Bridging in GRAIN

Before resolving bridging references in an automatic approach, we analysed the newest of the available corpora, the GRAIN corpus, with respect to the bridging annotations, in order to get a better feeling for the annotations. As GRAIN contains natural discourse in the form of radio interviews, we believe that it is well-suited for this type of analysis.

We categorise the occurrences of bridging in GRAIN into three main categories: *prototypical*, *world-knowledge-dependent* and *unspecified*. These types reflect our intuition about the bridging phenomena in GRAIN[4]. Prototypical bridging means that the anaphor stands in a prototypical relationship to its antecedent, see Example (2). Here, *caretakers* and *patients* are prototypical members of a retirement home.

(2) Aber jetzt zum Beispiel am Bürokratiewahnsinn in <u>den Heimen,</u> der **den Pflegekräften** die Zeit für **die Patienten** nimmt, ändert sich ja dadurch erst einmal nichts.
(But for now, it changes nothing about the bureaucracy madness in <u>the retirement homes</u>, which takes all the time that **the caretakers** could spend on **the patients**.)

Prototypical relations can also be sub-categorised, leading to sub-types that others have also observed, e.g. *building-part* or *professional-role* (cf. Hou et al. (2014)). Additionally, due to GRAIN's domain, many prototypical bridging pairs are related to countries and properties of countries (see Rule 9 in Section 7.2.1).

Example (3) presents a case of bridging where world-knowledge is necessary in order to infer that *athletes* are the athletes of the sports events in Sochi for the Winter Olympics in 2014.

(3) [...], dass ich nicht nach <u>Sotschi</u> fahren konnte, obwohl ich als Sportlerin da wirklich sehr, sehr gerne jetzt auch in der neuen Rolle hingefahren wäre, um **die Sportler** zu unterstützen.
([...], that I couldn't go to <u>Sochi</u>, even though I really, really would have liked to go as an athlete and also in my new role, in order to support **the athletes**.)

Finally, many bridging anaphors do not fall in any of the other two categories, see Example (4). *Beginning* is not prototypically related to *reform* and there is no world-knowledge involved in knowing that a reform can have a beginning (it is probably more of an inference that a reform is a process, which typically has an end and a beginning).

(4) Das ist <u>das größte Reformwerk seit Jahrzehnten in Deutschland</u>. Und kein Wunder, dass es da **am Anfang** ruckelt.
(This is <u>the biggest reform in Germany for decades</u>. No wonder that it is unstable **in the beginning**.)

We manually counted the types of bridging in GRAIN and observe counts for our three main types and for the types proposed in Hou et al. (2014), as shown in Table 1. We also find instances of comparative anaphora (see Markert et al., 2012).

Type	Sub-type	Count
	Building-part	3
Prototypical	Professional role	1
	Country-related	19
	Other prototypical	69
World-Knowledge		23
Unspecified		101
Comparative		8

Table 1: Types of bridging in GRAIN and their counts.

5 Experimental setup

5.1 Data

GRAIN GRAIN (Schweitzer et al., 2018) will be released soon[5]. As the annotation project is associated with our project, we have received an early version of the data, in which one of the 23 interviews is missing[6]. As no train-test-development split has yet been specified, we split the data ourselves[7].

---

[4]As the categorisation was performed by only one person (the first author), it has to be taken with a grain of salt. Still, we believe it is helpful to get a better feeling for the data.

[5]The release, as well as a detailed documentation is published in the framework of CLARIN 8 and available via a persistent identifier: `http://hdl.handle.net/11022/1007-0000-0007-C632-1`.

[6]The missing interview is: 20140524 Laumann

[7]The five development interviews are: 20140614 Maas, 20140802 Dressler, 20150124 Wendt, 20150404 Wagenknecht and 20151024 Peter. The five test interviews are: 20140517 Giegold, 20140927 Lemke, 20141011 Özoguz, 20150110 Bentele and 20150620 Münch. The rest of the documents make up the training data.

DIRNDL The DIRNDL anaphora corpus with updated bridging annotations was downloaded from the webpage[8]. We adopt the official train-development-test split.

5.2 Evaluation metrics

The evaluation of bridging resolution is computed using the widely known precision and recall measures (and the harmonic mean between them, F1). Additionally, we consider an antecedent correct if the predicted antecedent is one of the mentions in the coreference chain of the gold antecedent. For this, we take into account gold coreference chains. For optimisation, we use the development sets[9], and we report performance on the test set, if not indicated otherwise.

6 Baseline

In order to better judge how well the rule-based system performs, we create a baseline for anaphor and antecedent prediction. We first filter out all coreferent markables as annotated in the gold-standard. The baseline predicts a markable to be a bridging anaphor if it contains a definite article and is not modified by a prepositional phrase (PP), an adjective or does not contain a demonstrative pronoun (pre-processing is exactly the same as for the rule-based system, which we will describe later). The antecedent is then the subject of the previous sentence.

The baseline reflects the common ground that bridging anaphors are usually short, unmodified NPs and their antecedents usually appear in the previous sentence (cf. Hou, 2016b). The results of the baseline for DIRNDL and GRAIN are reported in Table 2 and 3.

The baseline achieves good performance for anaphor detection, suggesting that many bridging anaphors are indeed unmodified NPs, more so for GRAIN than for DIRNDL. The high recall is expected since the baseline suggests many candidates to be an anaphor, independent of other properties of the candidate. As a consequence, the precision is very low. The poor performance on the full prediction task is not surprising: Even though the antecedent often occurs in close proximity of

	Precision	Recall	F1
Anaphor Rec.	12.6%	65.1%	21.1%
Bridging Res.	0.5%	2.3%	0.8%

Table 2: Baseline results for anaphor detection and full bridging resolution on the test set of DIRNDL.

	Precision	Recall	F1
Anaphor Rec.	15.8%	69.8%	25.9%
Bridging Res.	0.4%	1.6%	0.6%

Table 3: Baseline results for anaphor detection and full bridging resolution on the test set of GRAIN.

its anaphor and subjects are the most preferred grammatical role, it is not necessarily the subject in the previous sentence.

7 A rule-based approach

In this section, we describe our rule-based approach to bridging resolution. For this, we adapted the approach by Hou et al. (2014) to German. The system consists of three parts: (i) pre-processing, (ii) rule application and (iii) post-processing. For a more detailed explanation of the adaptation process, please refer to the supplementary material[10].

7.1 Pre-processing

We extract all gold markables of the information status annotation as our set of gold markables.

As potential bridging anaphor candidates, we filter out a number of noun types, as they are not considered bridging anaphors: all pronouns, indefinite expressions, proper names as well as markables which have embedded NPs and NPs whose head has appeared before in the document (as an approximation for coreferent anaphors). We also investigate the role of coreference information, as described in Section 7.3.1.

7.2 Rules

We implemented and adapted to German all eight rules as proposed by Hou et al. (2014). The input to the rules are the extracted markables. Each rule then proposes bridging pairs, independently of the other rules. The rules are summarised in Table 4. Some of the rules use the concept of semantic connectivity and argument-taking ratio, which we also adapted. The main idea behind the concept of semantic connectivity between two words can be ap-

---

[8]www.ims.uni-stuttgart.de/forschung/ressourcen/korpora/dirndl.en.html

[9]From now on, we use the term *development set* for the combination of the development set and the training set of the respective corpus. By combining the two sets, we ensure a higher variety of bridging phenomena for tuning our system.

[10]www.ims.uni-stuttgart.de/institut/mitarbeiter/roesigia/bridging-resolution-german-supplementary.pdf

Rule	Example	Anaphor	Antecedent search	Window
1	A white woman's house ← The basement	building part	semantic connectivity	2
2	She ← Husband David Miller	relative	closest person NP	2
3	The UK ← The prime minister	GPE job title	most frequent GEO entity	–
4	IBM ← Chairman Baker	professional role	most frequent ORG NP	4
5	The firms ← Seventeen percent	percentage expression	modifying expression	2
6	Several problems ← One	number/indefinite pronoun	closest plural, subject/object NP	2
7	Damaged buildings ← Residents	head of modification	modifying expression	–
8	A conference ← Participants	arg-taking noun, subj pos.	semantic connectivity	2

Table 4: Overview of rules in Hou et al. (2014). For details, please refer to the supplementary material of this paper or the original paper.

proximated by the number of times two words occur in a N PREP N pattern. We computed the semantic connectivity scores using the SdeWaC corpus (Faaß and Eckart, 2013), a web corpus of 880 M tokens. The argument-taking ratio is a measure that describes the likelihood of a noun to take an argument. We derive the number of times in which a noun takes an argument automatically, by defining a number of patterns of modification (e.g. PP-postmodification, possessive modification), again using the SdeWac corpus. For a more detailed description, please refer to the original paper or the supplementary material of this paper.

7.2.1 New rules

In addition to adapting the rules from the English system to German, we also added a couple of new rules, which are tailored to our domain of news and interviews.

Rule 9: Country-related It is common in our data that a country is introduced into the discourse and then a country-related entity is picked up as a bridging anaphor. Note that by country we mean both geographical locations as well as political entities.

(5)   **Die Regierung** → Australien
        (the government → Australia)

(6)   **Die Westküste** → Japan
        (the west coast → Japan)

We therefore introduce a new rule: If the anaphor is a non-demonstrative definite expression without adjectival or nominal pre-modification and without PP post-modification that occurs on our list of country parts, we search for the most salient country. Salience is determined by frequency in the document, with the exception of the subject in the very first sentence, which overrides frequency in terms of salience. The list of country parts consists of terms like *Regierung (government), Einwohner (residents)*, etc.

Rule 10: High semantic connectivity Rule 10 is similar to Rule 8 in Hou et al. (2014), but without the constraint that the anaphor has to be in subject position. However, it must be a non-modified NP or PP. If the semantic connectivity score to a previously introduced mention is higher than a certain threshold (15.0 in our experiments), it is proposed as the antecedent. The antecedent should appear in the last four sentences. The feature is designed to capture more general cases of bridging by looking for a high semantic connectivity between the anaphor and the antecedent.

Rule 11: Political topics This is a domain specific rule, based on the observation that many bridging anaphors in DIRNDL and GRAIN are related to political issues.

(7)   **Parteivorsitzende** → die Grünen
        (party leaders → the Green Party)

We obtain a list of nouns of the political domain from GermaNet (Hamp and Feldweg, 1997; Henrich and Hinrichs, 2010). A markable is considered as an anaphor, if its head occurs in this list. Additionally, markables modified by adjectives or PPs are excluded. The antecedent is chosen by taking the markable with the highest semantic connectivity in the previous four sentences.

Rule 12: Exclusion of `r-unused-known`
The evaluation of the baseline in Section 6 has shown that bridging anaphors are generally short and not modified by adjectives or PPs. Since we remove coreferent and indefinite expressions as possible anaphor candidates, the only other information status categories that frequently contain such expressions are `r-bridging` and `r-unused-known`. In Riester and Baumann (2017), the label `r-unused-known` is used for definite expressions which are generally known to the annotator. Rule 12 is identical to Rule 10, but aims to exclude such markables by only considering markables which only occur once in a document. The intuition is that known expressions are more salient and potentially occur multiple times in a discourse, while bridging anaphors are unique with respect to their context.

(8)   im Internet ... im Internet ... im Internet
        (on the Internet ... on the Internet ...
        on the Internet)

(9)   **Den Haken** $\rightarrow$ Das Kästchen
        (the tick mark $\rightarrow$ the check box)

In the above examples, taken from one exemplary document, *Internet* appears three times in the whole document, while *Haken* only appears once. *Internet* is labeled as `r-unused-known`, since it is a generally known entity, while *Haken* is a bridging anaphor. Thus, in this case, Rule 12 will exclude all occurrences of *im Internet* as a potential bridging anaphor.

Post-processing In order to avoid conflicts of rules predicting different antecedents for the same anaphor, rule precision is evaluated on the development set. The rules are then ordered by precision and applied to the test set in descending order. Thus, a rule with a higher precision gets precedence over a rule with lower precision. The maximal sentence distance of the respective rules is also trained on the development set.

7.3 Results on DIRNDL

Table 5 shows the performance for both anaphor detection and full bridging resolution. As mentioned above, the performance was optimised on the development set and tested on the test set. Obviously, the scores for anaphor detection are higher, as the task of full bridging resolution predicts antecedents for the previously determined bridging anaphors. If all predicted antecedents are correct, the performance of full bridging resolution and anaphor detection are the same, which is of course not the case in our experiments.

	Precision	Recall	F1
Test set			
Anaphor Rec.	26.0%	18.9%	21.9%
Bridging Res.	16.3%	11.6%	13.6%
Dev set			
Anaphor Rec.	47.6%	19.0%	27.2%
Bridging Res.	26.7%	10.5%	15.1%
Whole set			
Anaphor Rec.	39.1%	19.1%	25.6%
Bridging Res.	22.2%	10.7%	14.4%

Table 5: Performance of the rule-based system on DIRNDL.

	Precision	Recall	F1
Test set			
Anaphor Rec.	45.5%	15.9%	23.5%
Bridging Res.	22.7%	7.9%	11.8%
Dev set			
Anaphor Rec.	29.4%	15.2%	20.0%
Bridging Res.	17.4%	9.0%	11.9%
Whole set			
Anaphor Rec.	32.1%	15.3%	20.7%
Bridging Res.	18.3%	8.8%	11.9%

Table 6: Performance of the rule-based system on GRAIN.

On the test set, the system achieves an F1 score of 21.9% for anaphor detection and 13.6% for bridging resolution. The precision is always higher than the recall, which is due to the focus on high precision rules. We also tested how the system performs on the development set, also displayed in Table 5. Overall, the performance is higher, which was to be expected, since the system was optimised on this subset. However, the differences are not very large, suggesting that the system is not overfitting to the development set and the rule ordering and maximum sentence distances that it learned also work well on unseen data. Table 5 also presents the performance for the whole data set, for both anaphor detection and full bridging resolution[11].

Most of the rules transferred from the English bridging resolver do not predict any bridging pairs in our data. For some cases, this can be explained by the different bridging definitions (e.g. no indefinite bridging anaphors in our data). Rule 6, for example, which is designed to resolve anaphors containing a number expression or indefinite pro-

---

[11]These values are later used as references when we investigate possible sources of error for our system.

nouns, cannot propose any correct pairs due to guideline differences.

Of course, ISNotes (Markert et al., 2012), the corpus on which the experiments in the English bridging resolver were based on, and DIRNDL are also of slightly different domains (news text in IS-Notes vs. radio news in DIRNDL), which might explain some of the differences.

Table 7 shows the performance of the single rules when being applied to DIRNDL. From the original English system, only Rule 4 (GPE job titles) and the very general Rule 8 (which is based on semantic connectivity) fire. Our new rules also predict pairs: While Rule 9 (country-related) is rather specific and has a high precision, Rule 10 proposes a lot of pairs, thus increasing the recall. Rule 12 is highly similar to Rule 10, and, for DIRNDL, does not seem to help more than Rule 10, indicating that filtering out `r-unused-known` entities was not successful for DIRNDL. Rule 11 (political topics) is very specific and similarly to Rule 9, it is also based on lexical lists of potential bridging anaphors, but cannot achieve a similarly high precision.

7.3.1 Bridging resolution with gold coreference

To test the effect of coreference information, we also run the system without filtering out coreferent anaphors. In Table 9, we show that, as expected, the precision and, as a result, the F1 score are significantly higher in the setting with coreference[12].

7.4 Results on GRAIN

In order to test the generalisability of the findings, we also report results on GRAIN. The results of the system's performance on GRAIN are shown in Table 6. For anaphor detection, the system performs better on GRAIN than on DIRNDL with an F1 score of 23.5%, compared to 21.9% for DIRNDL. However, this effect was only observed on the test data, not on the development set. Overall, the performance on GRAIN for full bridging resolution is notably and consistently lower than on DIRNDL (11.8% vs. 13.6%). The data sets for GRAIN also seem to be fairly distributed in terms of bridging anaphors, since all F1 values are rather close together.

While 97.9% of all nouns appearing in DIRNDL have an argument-taking ratio score and 45.9% of the noun-noun combinations have a semantic connectivity score, we find that in GRAIN, 98.3% of all nouns have an argument-taking ratio score, but only 24.0% of the noun-noun combinations have a semantic connectivity score. We believe that this is one of the reasons for the overall lower score on full bridging resolution. Another reason could be that while the radio news in DIRNDL are scripted and have prototypical topics such as politics, the weather, etc., GRAIN contains spontaneous speech of very diverse topics.

Results on the precision of the single rules are displayed in Table 8. Overall, the rules perform worse than for DIRNDL. In addition to that, Rule 11 does not seem to work for GRAIN very well.

8 Oracle lists

For GRAIN, finding the correct antecedent for a bridging anaphor is noticeably more difficult than for DIRNDL. In order to investigate why this is the case, we do some experiments using oracle lists to find antecedents in both GRAIN and DIRNDL. An oracle list represents a ranked suggestion of antecedents for an anaphor, with the most likely antecedent on top. Despite the fact that the rules in our system only predict one antecedent, we can change them so that they predict several antecedents. For this, we use the antecedent search technique of the respective rule and extend it to predict several candidates, instead of just one antecedent. For example, some of the rules are based on distance (often combined with a restriction, e.g. the closest organisation). Instead of predicting only the closest organisation, we can now come up with a list of organisations, ranked by distance. Other rules are based on the semantic connectivity scores, where we can then use the scores to create the list of potential antecedents. Note that we do not change the rules, nor do we involve any sort of re-ranking: we simply use the rule's search technique to create a list of antecedents, rather than a single antecedent[13]. This way, we can evaluate

---

[12]We compute significance using the Wilcoxon signed rank test (Siegel and Castellan, 1988) at the 0.05 level.

[13]To avoid ties, we perform simple modifications in order to influence the ranking. For example, Rule 3 also ranks according to document frequency of candidates, but we take into account the sentence and word distance, to penalise candidates which are further away from the anaphor. In case a rule already predicted a candidate to be a potential antecedent for a previous anaphor, we push these candidates higher on the ranking by adding a fixed value. This is meant to take into account the fact that antecedents are often the antecedent of multiple anaphors (cf. Hou (2016b)'s findings on sibling anaphors).

Rule	Anaphor detection			Full bridging resolution		
	Correct	Wrong	Precision	Correct	Wrong	Precision
Rule 4:	4	0	100.00%	0	4	0.0%
Rule 8:	23	24	48.9%	8	39	17.0%
Rule 9:	27	7	79.4%	22	12	64.7%
Rule 10:	50	63	44.2%	20	93	17.7%
Rule 11:	10	10	50.0%	4	16	20.0%
Rule 12:	50	63	44.2%	20	93	17.7%

Table 7: Rule precision on the development set of DIRNDL.

Rule	Anaphor detection			Full bridging resolution		
	Correct	Wrong	Precision	Correct	Wrong	Precision
Rule 1:	1	5	16.6%	1	5	16.6%
Rule 4:	0	2	0.0%	0	2	0.0%
Rule 8:	10	16	38.5%	3	23	11.5%
Rule 9:	15	17	46.9%	13	19	40.6%
Rule 10:	7	30	18.9%	3	34	8.1%
Rule 11:	1	13	7.1%	0	14	0.0%
Rule 12:	6	28	17.6%	3	31	8.8%

Table 8: Rule precision on the development set of GRAIN.

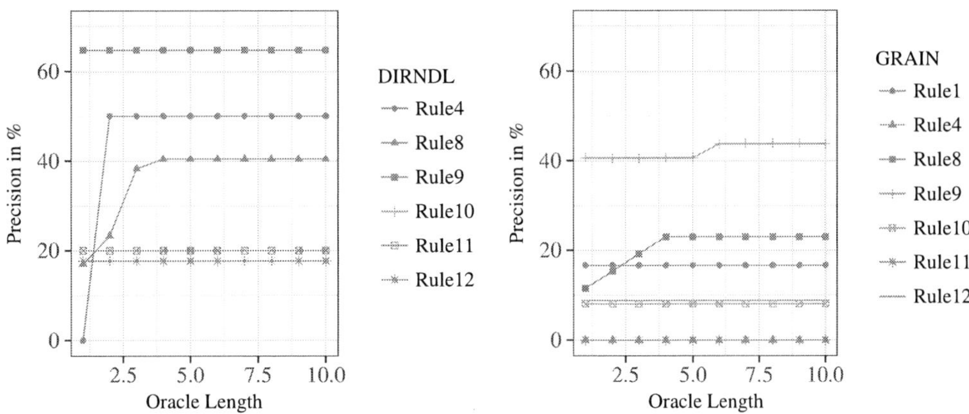

Figure 1: Performance of rules on the development set for DIRNDL and GRAIN, using different lengths of oracle lists.

Setting	Precision	Recall	F1
No coref	10.7%	11.6%	11.1%
Gold coref	14.9%	11.6%	14.4%

Table 9: Bridging resolution with different types of coreference information in DIRNDL (Gold markables).

the antecedent search strategies of the respective rules.

Figure 1 shows the precision for each rule based on the length of the oracle list, evaluated on the development set. We can see that the rules benefit from the oracle lists to a different extent. Rule 9 in DIRNDL is not changing its precision, suggesting that its performance is already quite good and all correct antecedents are already ranked on top of the oracle. Other rules like Rule 4 or 8 benefit a lot, indicating that the correct antecedents are generally in the scope of the rule, but simply not ranked high enough. Rule 4 and 11 in GRAIN stay at 0% precision. This means that these rules are not able to capture the correct antecedents at all.

In Figure 2, the overall performance of the system on the whole dataset is shown, dependent on the oracle length. Both datasets benefit from the oracle lists, but especially GRAIN could benefit from re-ranking the oracle lists in order to push the correct antecedent higher. Overall improvement through re-ranking is however limited, since many rules are restricted in their search for an antecedent by the maximum sentence distance. The fact that some of the rules cannot show their full

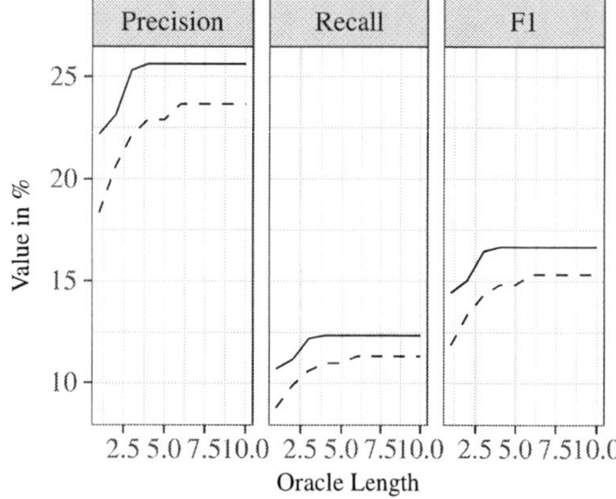

Figure 2: Performance of the rule-based system on the whole data set for DIRNDL and GRAIN, using different lengths of oracle lists.

potential even for a higher oracle list length suggests that these rules have no access to the correct antecedent at all and need to be revised.

9 Variable Importance

We investigated different machine learning techniques, but due to the small amount of data, the results were lower than for the rule-based approach and thus not shown here. However, we use machine learning in order to evaluate the importance of different features that were also used in the rule-based system. Doing so, we get a better understanding of what features are actually beneficial for the rule-based system.

We look closer at the prediction power of a few selected features. These are the length and number of words of the anaphor, the POS of the head of the anaphor, the anaphor's argument taking ratio, the sentence distance from the anaphor, the POS and named entity (NE) category of the head of the antecedent, its length and word count and the semantic connectivity.

We report variable importance values using the random forest technique (Ho, 1995) with 10-fold cross validation on GRAIN. Variable importance is estimated by leaving out a single feature for prediction and evaluating the decrease in performance for the random forest classifier. Table 10 shows the results for anaphor detection and bridging resolu-

tion.

It becomes clear that semantic connectivity, the argument-taking ratio of the anaphor and the length in characters of the anaphor/antecedent are overall good predictors. This substantiates the use of these features, since the rule-based system makes extensive use of them. However, coverage and computation of semantic connectivity should be improved in order to obtain better results of antecedent detection for GRAIN.

Feature	Variable Importance
SemanticConnectivity	32.2
AnaCharLength	31.6
AnteCharLength	30.5
AnaArgTakingRatio	29.3
AnteWordCount	25.9
AnaWordCount	22.5
SentDist	14.9
AnteHeadPOS	5.9
AnteHeadNE	5.8
AnaHeadPOS	3.3

Table 10: Variable importance estimated with a random forest classifier on GRAIN.

10 Conclusion

We have presented an analysis of bridging in two available corpora for German, DIRNDL and GRAIN. We have implemented a baseline for bridging resolution, which achieved good results for anaphor detection, indicating that short, unmodified NPs are good bridging anaphor candidates, but resulting in poor performance for bridging resolution. We have also presented a rule-based system following Hou et al. (2014), which has achieved reasonable results on both corpora. Oracle lists have shown the potential of the single rules if they were better at finding the correct antecedent, which could be exploited in a re-ranking approach. The features and information used by the rule-based system seem to be promising, but could still be improved and extended.

Acknowledgments

We would like to thank Arndt Riester for his valuable comments as well as the anonymous reviewers for their insightful remarks. This work was funded by the Collaborative Research Center SFB 732, Project A6.

References

Stefan Baumann and Arndt Riester. 2012. Referential and Lexical Givenness: semantic, prosodic and cognitive aspects. In Gorka Elordieta and Pilar Prieto, editors, *Prosody and Meaning*, number 25 in Interface Explorations. Mouton de Gruyter, Berlin.

Anders Björkelund, Kerstin Eckart, Arndt Riester, Nadja Schauffler, and Katrin Schweitzer. 2014. The extended DIRNDL corpus as a resource for automatic coreference and bridging resolution. In *Proceedings of the 9th International Conference on Language Resources and Evaluation*, LREC 2014, pages 3222–3228.

Aoife Cahill and Arndt Riester. 2012. Automatically acquiring fine-grained information status distinctions in German. In *Proceedings of the 13th Annual Meeting of the Special Interest Group on Discourse and Dialogue (SIGdial)*, pages 232–236, Seoul.

Herbert H. Clark. 1975. Bridging. In *Proceedings of the 1975 workshop on Theoretical issues in natural language processing*, pages 169–174. Association for Computational Linguistics.

Kerstin Eckart, Arndt Riester, and Katrin Schweitzer. 2012. A discourse information radio news database for linguistic analysis. In *Linked Data in Linguistics*, pages 65–76. Springer.

Gertrud Faaß and Kerstin Eckart. 2013. SdeWaC - A corpus of parsable sentences from the web. In *Language Processing and Knowledge in the Web - 25th International Conference, GSCL 2013, Darmstadt, Germany, September 25-27, 2013. Proceedings*, pages 61–68.

Yulia Grishina. 2016. Experiments on bridging across languages and genres. In *Proceedings of the first Workshop on Coreference Resolution Beyond OntoNotes (NAACL-HLT)*, pages 7–15, San Diego, USA.

Udo Hahn, Michael Strube, and Katja Markert. 1996. Bridging textual ellipses. In *Proceedings of the 16th Conference on Computational Linguistics - Volume 1*, COLING '96, pages 496–501, Stroudsburg, PA, USA. Association for Computational Linguistics.

Birgit Hamp and Helmut Feldweg. 1997. GermaNet - a lexical-semantic net for German. In *Proceedings of the ACL workshop Automatic Information Extraction and Building of Lexical Semantic Resources for NLP Applications*, Madrid.

John A Hawkins. 1978. *Definiteness and indefiniteness: A study in reference and grammaticality prediction*. Crook Helm.

Verena Henrich and Erhard Hinrichs. 2010. GernEdiT – The GermaNet editing tool. In *Proceedings of the Seventh Conference on International Language Resources and Evaluation*, LREC 2010, pages 2228–2235.

Tin Kam Ho. 1995. Random decision forests. In *Proceedings of the 3rd International Conference on Document Analysis and Recognition*, pages 278–282, Montreal, QC.

Yufang Hou. 2016a. Incremental fine-grained information status classification using attention-based LSTMs. In *Proceedings of COLING 2016, the 26th International Conference on Computational Linguistics: Technical Papers*, pages 1880–1890, Osaka, Japan.

Yufang Hou. 2016b. *Unrestricted Bridging Resolution*. Ph.D. thesis, Heidelberg University.

Yufang Hou, Katja Markert, and Michael Strube. 2013a. Cascading collective classification for bridging anaphora recognition using a rich linguistic feature set. In *Proceedings of the Conference on Empirical Methods in Natural Language Processing*, pages 814–820, Seattle, USA.

Yufang Hou, Katja Markert, and Michael Strube. 2013b. Global inference for bridging anaphora resolution. In *Proceedings of the 2013 Conference of the North American Chapter of the Association for Computational Linguistics: Human Language Technologies*, pages 907–917, Atlanta, USA.

Yufang Hou, Katja Markert, and Michael Strube. 2014. A rule-based system for unrestricted bridging resolution: Recognizing bridging anaphora and finding links to antecedents. In *Proceedings of the Conference on Empirical Methods in Natural Language Processing*, pages 2082–2093, Seattle, USA.

Katja Markert, Yufang Hou, and Michael Strube. 2012. Collective classification for fine-grained information status. In *Proceedings of the 50th Annual Meeting of the Association for Computational Linguistics: Long Papers-Volume 1*, pages 795–804. Association for Computational Linguistics.

Katja Markert, Michael Strube, and Udo Hahn. 1996. Inferential realization constraints on functional anaphora in the centering model. In *In Proc. of the 18 th Annual Conference of the Cognitive Science Society; La*, pages 609–614.

Altaf Rahman and Vincent Ng. 2012. Learning the fine-grained information status of discourse entities. In *Proceedings of the 13th Conference of the European Chapter of the Association for Computational Linguistics*, EACL '12, pages 798–807, Stroudsburg, PA, USA. Association for Computational Linguistics.

Marta Recasens and Eduard Hovy. 2010. A typology of near-identity relations for coreference (nident). In *LREC*.

Arndt Riester and Stefan Baumann. 2017. The RefLex Scheme – Annotation guidelines. SinSpeC. Working papers of the SFB 732 Vol. 14, University of Stuttgart.

Katrin Schweitzer, Kerstin Eckart, Markus Gärtner, Agnieszka Faleńska, Arndt Riester, Ina Rösiger, Antje Schweitzer, Sabrina Stehwien, and Jonas Kuhn. 2018. German radio interviews: The GRAIN release of the SFB732 Silver Standard Collection. In *Proceedings of the 11th International Conference on Language Resources and Evaluation*, LREC 2018.

Sidney Siegel and N. John Jr. Castellan. 1988. *Nonparametric Statistics for the Behavioral Sciences*, 2nd edition. McGraw-Hill, Berkeley, CA.

Detecting and Resolving Shell Nouns in German

Adam Roussel
Department of Linguistics
Ruhr-Universität Bochum
Bochum, Germany
`roussel@linguistics.rub.de`

Abstract

This paper describes the design and evaluation of a system for the automatic detection and resolution of shell nouns in German. Shell nouns are general nouns, such as *fact*, *question*, or *problem*, whose full interpretation relies on a content phrase located elsewhere in a text, which these nouns simultaneously serve to characterize and encapsulate. To accomplish this, the system uses a series of lexico-syntactic patterns in order to extract shell noun candidates and their content in parallel. Each pattern has its own classifier, which makes the final decision as to whether or not a link is to be established and the shell noun resolved. Overall, about 26.2% of the annotated shell noun instances were correctly identified by the system, and of these cases, about 72.5% are assigned the correct content phrase. Though it remains difficult to identify shell noun instances reliably (recall is accordingly low in this regard), this system usually assigns the right content to correctly classified cases.

1 Introduction

The term *shell noun* refers to the way in which particular general nouns are used to characterize and encapsulate a complex chunk of information for later reference, which might ordinarily be realized by a verb phrase or a sentence (Schmid, 2000). Example (1) below represents a typical shell noun instance.[1]

(1) Ich finde die **Tatsache**, <u>dass es keine Dinosaurier mehr gibt</u>, sehr traurig.
'I find the fact that there are no more dinosaurs very sad.'

As this encapsulation of information coincides with an ability to link information across sentences, shell nouns are an important means of text

---

[1] Shell nouns are in boldface, content phrases underlined.

or discourse coherence. They are also relatively common: Schmid (2000, p. 6) observes that many of the English nouns that can function as shell nouns are among the hundred most frequent nouns in the English language. However, the complete interpretation of a particular shell noun instance is only possible together with the complex content to which it, in one way or another, 'refers'. Shell nouns must be *resolved* to be properly interpreted. Thus, the resolution of shell nouns and their content forms an essential part of any NLP system for which a degree of natural language understanding is necessary, including summarization, question answering, and sentiment analysis.

This paper will describe a system that was implemented with the aim of identifying which nouns in a given text act as shell nouns and establishing a link between these instances and the content they refer to and serve to characterize.

In contrast to previous attempts to resolve shell nouns, in which it was known which noun instances were to be considered shell nouns, the current system does not know a priori which nouns may act as shell nouns, and it does not know which of these potential shell noun instances actually require resolution. The system therefore must simultaneously decide whether a given noun instance is acting as a shell noun and resolve it to its content.

2 The Algorithm

Extraction patterns One of the most salient aspects of the phenomenon of shell nouns is their tendency to be used in certain syntactic patterns (*the fact that ..., the question is whether ...,* etc.), such that these patterns are sometimes used to gather shell noun instances (Schmid, 2000; Simonjetz, 2015) and to resolve them (Kolhatkar and Hirst, 2014). I use this aspect of the phenomenon as a starting point, so that this linguistic knowl-

Proceedings of the Workshop on Computational Models of Reference, Anaphora and Coreference, pages 61–67
New Orleans, Louisiana, June 6, 2018. ©2018 Association for Computational Linguistics

edge ensures a basic level of functionality. The system as implemented uses an ordered sequence of nine extraction patterns, which are used to identify potential shell nouns along with their content phrase candidates. Capturing shell noun candidates together with potential content phrases has the additional benefit of reducing the range of candidates the system must consider—an important consideration, since content phrases can take on a variety of syntactic shapes and the system might otherwise be overwhelmed by candidates.

(2) Der Bildschirm geht nicht mehr an. Dieses **Problem** muss noch gelöst werden.
'The monitor won't turn on anymore. This problem must still be solved.'

The nine extraction patterns used here range from the *NN-dass* pattern, which would capture example (1), to the *PDAT-last-sent* pattern, which covers anaphoric shell nouns, i.e. cases in which the shell noun refers back to previous sentences, such as example (2) above. They are based in part on the patterns suggested in Simonjetz (2015), which are versions of Schmid's patterns adapted for use with German-language data and which have also been converted to dependency-based patterns in order to account for German's more flexible word order.

It is important to note that the patterns as used here are not intended primarily to filter noun instances or to discover shell noun instances by themselves, rather the extraction patterns serve mainly to select likely candidates for the shell noun content, based on what we know about the behavior of shell nouns. By adding more such patterns, the system can be extended to search more environments for content phrases.

Classifiers   However, though there is a close association between shell nouns and particular patterns, a noun that occurs in one of these patterns is not necessarily a shell noun usage. *Grund* in example (3) occurs in the *NN-zu* pattern, but the infinitive verb phrase does not contain the shell noun's content, as the pattern predicts. And even nouns that can and often do act as shell nouns will also occur in non–shell noun usages, as in example (4), in which the noun *Entscheidung* is not being used as a shell noun, though it is capable of fulfilling this function.

Name	Description
`NN-dass`	NN with a *dass*-phrase
`NN-ist-dass`	NN and *dass*-phrase connected by a form of *sein*
`NN-KOUS`	Like `NN-dass`, for other KOUS
`NN-zu`	NN with a dependent *zu*-form verb
`NN-ist-zu`	NN and *zu*-phrase connected by a form of *sein*
`NN-PP`	NN with dependent PP
`NN-NN`	NN with dependent NP in genitive case
`PDAT-last-sent`	NN with PDAT determiner, with previous sentence root as content phrase
`PDAT-last-verb`	NN with PDAT determiner, with last verbal element as root of content phrase

Table 1: Extraction patterns used in this system

(3) Das ist für mich ein **Grund**, jetzt abzustimmen.
'That is for me a reason to vote now.'

(4) Die Entscheidung der Kommission sollte das verhindern.
'The commission's decision should prevent that.'

In order to determine which of the extracted candidate pairs constitute actual shell noun instances, I use a series of Naive Bayes classifiers,[2] which make the final decisions as to whether or not a given noun is to be regarded as a shell noun and resolved to some content phrase. Naive Bayes were chosen for this application due to their effectiveness with small amounts of training data and imbalanced training data (Müller, 2008, p. 187), both of which are the case for this dataset.

Each pattern is associated with its own classifier, such that each classifier is free to focus on the features that are most important for that particular pattern. If a classifier approves a particular pattern match, then that instance is considered a positive instance. If a pattern match is classified as a negative instance, then the system will continue and try to apply the remaining patterns, testing various candidate shell noun–content pairs. This architecture means that the order in which patterns are applied is significant, and the patterns are roughly ordered with respect to the perceived probability that they will result in matches (cf. the ordering of sieves in Lee et al. (2013)).

---

[2]All classifiers, including the baseline classifiers, are from the `scikit-learn` package (Pedregosa et al., 2011).

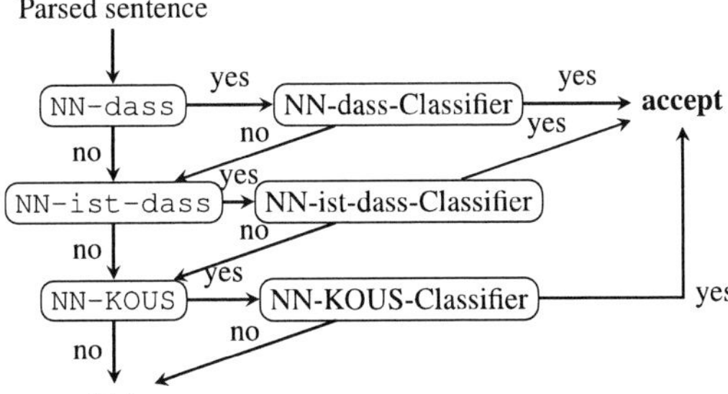

Figure 1: System architecture

Figure 1 illustrates graphically how the algorithm's various components interact.

Classification features The classifiers use a number of features[3] encompassing semantic, syntactic, and surface-level information to make its decisions regarding the status of a particular noun–content pair.

The lemma of the candidate shell noun is perhaps the most import feature, since individual shell nouns are known to prefer certain environments and disprefer others. *Tatsache* 'fact' is likely to occur often with *dass* 'that' clauses, since such clauses are associated with propositions and facts, to some degree, can be thought of as propositions that are true. *Frage* 'question', on the other hand, could conceivably be associated with *ob* 'whether' clauses.

In order to help recognize novel shell nouns and to operationalize some degree of 'abstractness', the system leverages the lexical database GermaNet (Hamp and Feldweg, 1997). Lexemes in the GermaNet database are organized hierarchically according to hypo-/hyperonomy relations, and at the top-level are a small number of semantic fields. On the hypothesis that certain of these semantic fields (e.g., 'cognition', 'communication') could correlate with whether or not a particular noun lemma might act as a shell noun, I include a noun's semantic field as a feature. GermaNet also includes subcategorization information, so I also include features indicating whether or not the verb, of which a particular noun is an argument, may ordinarily accept verbal or clausal complements (this being a rough approximation of Eckert and Strube (2000)'s I-incompatibility constraint).

The system also includes a number of syntactic or relational features, such as are also used in Müller (2007) and Jauhar et al. (2015). These include such things as the distance between the shell noun and the root node of its content phrase, the grammatical functions of shell noun and content and whether these match, and the type of determiner used with the candidate shell noun.

Finally, in order to help the system recognize nominalized content phrases (e.g. *die Möglichkeit der Aktualisierung der Software* 'the opportunity to update the software'), which are especially important for German-language data, I include a number of surface-level features, such as whether or not a lemma ends with *-ung*, *-keit*, or *-heit*, since these endings are typically associated with nominalized verbs or with more 'abstract' entities.

3 Data

I evaluated this approach using the German-language data from the German/English Parallel Shell Noun Corpus (Simonjetz and Roussel, 2016).[4] This corpus includes manually annotated shell noun complexes in 371 speaker turns from the Europarl corpus, which have been automatically tagged and parsed using Mate tools (Bohnet et al., 2013). The annotators in that study annotated shell nouns according to three main attributes:

1. "incompleteness": Shell nouns possess a semantic gap that is to be filled by a content phrase, which the shell noun also serves to characterize and describe.
2. "reference": Shell nouns refer to some content that occurs somewhere else in a discourse.
3. "abstractness": Shell nouns refer to entities, which are abstract and complex, such as facts, states-of-affairs, or propositions.

In the German-language data used here there are 1086 annotated noun instances, of which 466 are shell noun usages. Due to the small amount of manually annotated data available, all of the subsequent experiments described here have been performed using 5-fold cross validation.

Since only 50 nouns are completely annotated in this dataset, there remain a large number of nouns whose status is unclear. Disregarding these cases entirely would unfairly favor the baselines, which produce a large number of what are almost

---

[3]See Table 4 in the appendix for a summary of all of the features used here.

[4]Available at `https://github.com/ajroussel/shell-nouns-data`.

certainly false positives. However, always counting these as false positives would also be unfair, since some proportion are certainly actual shell noun instances. Therefore, in the following evaluation, I will assume that 61% of these unannotated cases are false positives, since this is the proportion of negative instances for the nouns in the corpus that are annotated.

4   Evaluation

In order to better understand the performance of this system, I will employ two baseline systems. The Constant baseline uses a classifier that always accepts any shell noun candidate that matches some pattern. It gives us an idea of what the maximum recall could be, given the current pattern set, and it also shows how far we can get using patterns alone. The Stratified baseline approves, at random, a number of candidate cases proportional to the frequency of positive instances in its training data. This baseline gives us an idea of the maximum precision and accuracy we can expect to achieve simply by choosing fewer positive cases.

Here I measure two main aspects of the system's performance: (1) To what degree are the noun instances classified correctly (regardless of the content assigned)? (2) Of the instances that are correctly classified, how many are also assigned the correct content phrase? Since the first question concerns classification performance, I use precision, recall, and F_1 score to answer this question. As for the second question, since the patterns always suggest a content phrase and this can only be correct or incorrect, I only measure accuracy with respect to content phrases ("Res" in Tables 2 and 3).

The performance of the Constant baseline shows that the patterns alone cover only about half of the cases in the test data. This system correctly classifies about half of the instances matched by some pattern, resulting in a recall of 24.2%. At the same time, the Naive Bayes classifier allows the system to produce significantly fewer false positives, and the resulting precision 56.4% is a significant improvement over both baselines.

The improvement in the system's accuracy over the baseline (72.5% vs. 57.7%) also shows that the correct pattern classifiers, rather than simply the first matching patterns, tend to approve each instance, suggesting that the system has some ability to handle such confusing cases as in example (3).

Name	P	R	F_1	Res
Constant	0.072	**0.494**	0.125	0.577
Stratified	0.178	0.060	0.090	**0.820**
This system	**0.564**	0.262	**0.356**	0.725

Table 2: Performance of the shell noun resolution algorithm (Res = resolution accuracy).

Name	P	R	F_1	Res
All	0.559	**0.277**	**0.367**	0.700
No lemmas	0.394	0.185	0.250	0.792
No GermaNet	0.682	0.251	0.366	0.736
Only lemmas	**0.741**	0.163	0.264	**0.799**

Table 3: Comparing various feature sets.

5   Related Work

Müller (2007) and Jauhar et al. (2015) attempt to automatically resolve instances of discourse deixis, specifically the anaphors *this*, *that*, and *it*, to their verbal antecedents. Using a maximum entropy classifier and a series of morphological and syntactic features, as well as some corpus-based features based on Eckert and Strube (2000)'s compatibility constraints, their algorithm achieves an F_1 score of 12.59 (P = 13.42, R = 11.84) for VP antecedents.

Jauhar et al. (2015) separates this task into two discrete stages, using a different classifier and different features for each stage. In the first stage 'classification', the classifier decides whether or not a particular pronominal instance refers to some verbal instance and thus requires resolution, and in the second stage 'resolution', their system selects the highest-scoring antecedent for this pronominal instance. For the classification stage their system has an F_1 score of 38.6 (P = 35.2, R = 42.9) and for the resolution stage, using the system classifications, 22.2 (P = 22.6, R = 21.8).

Kolhatkar and Hirst (2012) and Kolhatkar et al. (2013) use an SVM ranking algorithm to resolve instances of six anaphoric shell nouns, i.e. cases which refer back to content in previous sentences. The authors include a number of features similar to those used in Müller (2007) and Jauhar et al. (2015), such as antecedent length, syntactic type, and distance in tokens, as well as a few that are specific to the behavior of *issue* as a shell noun: use with a *whether* clause, antecedent is a question, etc. These systems had accuracies ranging from 35% to 72%, depending on the shell noun.

Kolhatkar and Hirst (2014) resolved instances of 12 English shell nouns using lexico-syntactic patterns and linguistic cues, as suggested by Schmid (2000), with the primarily goal of using this linguistic information to improve the resolution of shell nouns over the use of patterns alone. Their results (accuracy between 62% and 83%) show that this information is more useful for particular nouns whose requirements are very specific.

In order to resolve abstract anaphora (including shell nouns) Marasović et al. (2017) apply a Siamese LSTM neural network to the context of an anaphor and an antecedent candidate, thus training the network to recognize compatible anaphors and antecedents. The resulting model resolves 76.09% to 93.14% of the shell nouns in the Kolhatkar et al. (2013) dataset to the correct antecedent. On the ARRAU dataset (Poesio et al., 2013), for which Marasović et al. automatically generate training data, their system still resolves 51.89% of annotated shell noun instances correctly.

6 Discussion and Future Work

Though, in general, the implemented system has relatively high precision for the task and tends to link the identified shell nouns to the correct content, recall remains low. There are a number of potential explanations for this, each of which suggests a path along which future work could proceed.

Some of the errors the system produces appear to be related to parser errors, so one avenue could involve improving the syntactic information in the data or introducing new extraction patterns designed to capture instances that might otherwise be missed due to an erroneous parse.

Another difficulty is related to the logical structure of certain shell nouns themselves. *Reason*, for instance, (cf. example (3)) appears to actually refer to two content phrases: one denoting a cause and the other an effect. *Möglichkeit* 'opportunity' seems likewise to have two parts: something that can happen and the circumstance that makes it possible. This semantic structure complicates both the annotation and resolution of these particular nouns.

The most likely explanation for the system's low recall and the most important avenue of future

work relates to the lack of available training data for this task in general and for non-English languages in particular. If more data were available, a greater range of classification methods would become workable and significant performance improvements may be possible.

Alternatively, one could try to get more out of the existing data by allowing the classifiers to share certain information about the behavior of shell noun lemmas, in order to compensate for the fact that each lemma may only occur a handful of times in a particular pattern. Or one could use a lemma representation that better encodes semantic similarities, which might in turn help discover shell nouns that did not occur in the training data.

Most likely, improving the systems's performance will require both more annotated data and better use of the data that is available.

References

Bernd Bohnet, Joakim Nivre, Igor Boguslavsky, Richárd Farkas, Filip Ginter, and Jan Hajič. 2013. Joint morphological and syntactic analysis for richly inflected languages. *Transactions of the Association for Computational Linguistics*, 1:415–428.

Miriam Eckert and Michael Strube. 2000. Dialogue acts, synchronizing units, and anaphora resolution. *Journal of Semantics*, 17:51–89.

Birgit Hamp and Helmut Feldweg. 1997. GermaNet: A lexical-semantic net for German. In *Proceedings of the ACL workshop Automatic Information Extraction and Building of Lexical Semantic Resources for NLP Applications*, Madrid, Spain.

Sujay Kumar Jauhar, Raul D. Guerra, Edgar Gonzàlez, and Marta Recasens. 2015. Resolving discourse-deictic pronouns: A two-stage approach to do *it*. In *Proceedings of the Fourth Joint Conference on Lexical and Computational Semantics*, pages 299–308, Denver, CO, USA.

Varada Kolhatkar and Graeme Hirst. 2012. Resolving "this-issue" anaphora. In *Proceedings of the 2012 Conference on Empirical Methods in Natural Language Processing*, pages 1255–1265, Jeju Island, Korea.

Varada Kolhatkar and Graeme Hirst. 2014. Resolving shell nouns. In *Proceedings of the 2014 Conference on Empirical Methods in Natural Language Processing (EMNLP 2014)*, pages 499–510, Doha, Qatar.

Varada Kolhatkar, Heike Zinsmeister, and Graeme Hirst. 2013. Interpreting anaphoric shell nouns using antecedents of cataphoric shell nouns as training data. In *Proceedings of the 2013 Conference on*

Empirical Methods in Natural Language Processing, pages 300–310, Seattle, Washington, USA. Association for Computational Linguistics.

Heeyoung Lee, Angel Chang, Yves Peirsman, Nathanael Chambers, Mihai Surdeanu, and Dan Jurafsky. 2013. Deterministic coreference resolution based on entity-centric, precision-ranked rules. *Computational Linguistics*, 39(4):885–916.

Ana Marasović, Leo Born, Juri Opitz, and Anette Frank. 2017. A mention-ranking model for abstract anaphora resolution. In *Proceedings of the 2017 Conference on Empirical Methods in Natural Language Processing*, pages 221–232, Copenhagen, Denmark. Association for Computational Linguistics.

Christoph Müller. 2007. Resolving *it*, *this*, and *that* in unrestricted multi-party dialog. In *Proceedings of the 45th Annual Meeting of the Association of Computational Linguistics*, pages 816–823, Prague, Czechia.

Christoph Müller. 2008. *Fully Automatic Resolution of it, this and that in Unrestricted Multi-Party Dialog*. Ph.D. thesis, Universität Tübingen.

F. Pedregosa, G. Varoquaux, A. Gramfort, V. Michel, B. Thirion, O. Grisel, M. Blondel, P. Prettenhofer, R. Weiss, V. Dubourg, J. Vanderplas, A. Passos, D. Cournapeau, M. Brucher, M. Perrot, and E. Duchesnay. 2011. `scikit-learn`: Machine learning in Python. *Journal of Machine Learning Research*, 12:2825–2830.

Massimo Poesio, Ron Artstein, Olga Uryupina, Kepa Rodriguez, Francesca Delogu, Antonella Bristot, and Janet Hitzeman. 2013. *The ARRAU Corpus of Anaphoric Information LDC2013T22*, volume Web Download. Linguistic Data Consortium, Philadelphia, PA, USA.

Hans-Jörg Schmid. 2000. *English Abstract Nouns as Conceptual Shells: From Corpus to Cognition*. de Gruyter, Berlin, Germany.

Fabian Simonjetz. 2015. Retrieving German shell nouns using dependency patterns. `http://www.researchgate.net/publication/306020586_Retrieving_German_Shell_Nouns_Using_Dependency_Patterns`.

Fabian Simonjetz and Adam Roussel. 2016. Crosslinguistic annotation of German and English shell noun complexes. In *Proceedings of the 13th Conference on Natural Language Processing (KONVENS)*, pages 265–278, Bochum, Germany.

Appendix

Feature	Examples
Shell noun	
Lemma	*Tatsache, Umstand*
Number	Sing./Pl.
Grammatical function	*subj, obja*
Whether parent precedes shell noun	Yes/No
Whether parent is subjunctive	Yes/No
Whether parent is clausal verb	Yes/No
Semantic field	*Attribut, Kommunikation*
Parent semantic field	*Gefühl, Perzeption*
Semantic fields of dep. adjectives	*Bewegung, Menge*
Whether dep. article is definite or indefinite	Yes/No
Dep. determiners	*dieser, kein, beiden*
Content phrase	
Dependent preposition lemmas	*zu, für, nach*
Dependent complementizers	*dass, ob, weil*
Grammatical function	*root, objc*
Length	No. of tokens
Gender	*Masc, Fem, Neut*
Semantic field	*Attribut, Kommunikation*
Embedding depth	No. of deps. to sentence root
If nominal, ending	*-ung, -heit, -en*
Contains question mark	Yes/No
Relation	
Distance between shell noun and content phrase	No. of tokens
Whether shell noun precedes content phrase	Yes/No
Whether grammatical functions match	Yes/No
Whether colon between shell noun and content phrase	Yes/No

Table 4: Complete list of features.

PAWS: A Multi-lingual Parallel Treebank with Anaphoric Relations

Anna Nedoluzhko and **Michal Novák**
Charles University
Faculty of Mathematics and Physics
Prague, Czech Republic
{nedoluzko,mnovak}@ufal.mff.cuni.cz

Maciej Ogrodniczuk
Polish Academy of Sciences
Institute of Computer Science
Warsaw, Poland
maciej.ogrodniczuk@ipipan.waw.pl

Abstract

We present PAWS, a multi-lingual parallel treebank with coreference annotation. It consists of English texts from the Wall Street Journal translated into Czech, Russian and Polish. In addition, the texts are syntactically parsed and word-aligned. PAWS is based on PCEDT 2.0 and continues the tradition of multilingual treebanks with coreference annotation. The paper focuses on the coreference annotation in PAWS and its language-specific differences. PAWS offers linguistic material that can be further leveraged in cross-lingual studies, especially on coreference.

1 Introduction

In recent years, we have witnessed a rise in multilingual approaches to both theoretical and computational linguistics. Coreferential and anaphoric relations are no exception. For instance, the CoNLL 2012 Shared Task (Pradhan et al., 2012) has focused on modeling coreference in three different languages, making use of the data from the OntoNotes corpus (Weischedel et al., 2013). Since then, several other multilingual parallel corpora annotated with referential relations were produced (see Section 2). In this work, we go even further. We present the PAWS treebank, a multi-lingual parallel treebank annotated with full-fledged coreference relations. Its current release consists of texts in four languages: English, Czech, Russian and Polish.

A decision to build such treebank has multiple motivations, mostly related to cross-lingual studies of coreference relations.

First, construction of such corpus tests applicability of a particular annotation schema for other languages. The project of Universal Dependencies[1] has shown that efforts devoted to seeking

a language-universal syntactic and morphological representation may open up a space for novel research within the field. Concerning coreference, a single annotation schema has been applied to English, Chinese and Arabic already in OntoNotes 5.0 (Weischedel et al., 2013) and on parallel English-German-Russian texts by Grishina and Stede (2015).

Second, from a perspective of theoretical linguistics, a cross-lingual view on particular linguistic phenomena may give us more information than a monolingual view. The present work focuses on three Slavic languages, which despite their apparent closeness exhibit considerable differences in phenomena related to coreference, e.g. a degree of using pro-drops, or diverse usage of reflexive pronouns. With our corpus such phenomena can be directly compared across languages. This work thus follows on the comparative analysis that has been previously conducted on coreferential expressions in English and Czech (Novák and Nedoluzhko, 2015) and reflexive possessives in English, Czech and Russian (Nedoluzhko et al., 2016a).

Last but not least, a new coreference-annotated parallel corpus may drive a research on cross-lingual automatic approaches related to coreference. It includes coreference projection (Postolache et al., 2006; Grishina and Stede, 2017) and bilingually-informed coreference resolution (Mitkov and Barbu, 2003; Novák and Žabokrtský, 2014). Unlike ParCor 1.0 (Guillou et al., 2014), PAWS is not tailored to machine translation experiments. Nevertheless, its parallel nature suggests that it can also be leveraged for these purposes.

The main feature of PAWS is its manual annotation of coreferential relations in all included languages. As two of the languages extensively use zero subjects, we could miss a lot of valuable information if we annotated coreference only on sur-

---

[1] http://universaldependencies.org

68

Proceedings of the Workshop on Computational Models of Reference, Anaphora and Coreference, pages 68–76
New Orleans, Louisiana, June 6, 2018. ©2018 Association for Computational Linguistics

face. Therefore, we adopted the style based on the theory of Functional Generative Description (Sgall et al., 1986), first used for Czech in Prague Dependency Treebank 2.0 (Hajič et al., 2006) and for Czech and English in Prague Czech-English Dependency Treebank 2.0 (Hajič et al., 2012). In this style, coreference and other anaphoric relations are annotated on the layer of deep syntax called *tectogrammatical layer*. It consists of dependency trees containing both overt as well as important elided content words. Presence of elided words makes it possible to represent coreferential relations even for dropped pronouns.

To facilitate cross-lingual studies, we equip the treebank with word alignment links between all the language pairs. Since these links are annotated on the tectogrammatical layer, they also cover the reconstructed zeros. Most of the alignment links were collected automatically. However, for selected types of coreferential expressions, we labeled the alignment links also manually.

Figure 1 illustrates the annotation of a sample sentence in all languages, as visualized by the TrEd tool (Pajas and Štěpánek, 2008). Every sentence is represented as a dependency tree, with squared nodes representing the expressions elided on surface. Whereas the solid arrows correspond to coreferential links, word alignment is marked by dashed lines between the nodes in the trees (for clarity, the figure shows only alignment of coreferential expressions).

2 Related Corpora

Our work relates to all multilingual parallel corpora with linguistic annotation, especially those for Slavic languages. ParaSol: A Parallel Corpus of Slavic and other languages (Waldenfels, 2006) is an aligned corpus of translated and original belletristic texts featuring automatic morphosyntactic annotations. The latest version comprises more than 30 languages. InterCorp (Čermák and Rosen, 2012) is another large multi-lingual parallel synchronic corpus with Czech as a pivot language, i.e. every text has its Czech version. It features part-of-speech tagging and lemmatization. The Polish-Russian Parallel Corpus (Łaziński and Kuratczyk, 2016) features morphosyntactic description yet both sides differ as far as disambiguation is concerned (present in Polish, absent in Russian part). Paralela (Pęzik, 2016) is a translation-based Polish-English corpus based on publicly available

multilingual text collections and open-source parallel corpora featuring morphosyntactic annotation.

PAWS is also one of a few corpora annotated with coreference relations. Its English and Czech part directly corresponds to a subset of the Prague Czech-English Dependency Treebank 2.0 (Hajič et al., 2012, PCEDT) and its coreferential extension (Nedoluzhko et al., 2016b, PCEDT 2.0 Coref). ParCor 1.0 (Guillou et al., 2014) also belongs to this category. It is a German-English parallel corpus consisting of more than 8,000 sentences. Unlike PAWS, which has annotation of full coreference chains, only pronominal coreference is annotated in ParCor. On the other hand, texts in the corpus come from different genres, which is not the case in PAWS.

3 PAWS Data and Its Rich Annotation

This paper presents the PAWS treebank, which stands for *Parallel Anaphoric Wall Street* Journal. In its current version it comprises parallel texts in English, Czech, Russian, and Polish.

English texts with their Czech translations were extracted from Prague Czech-English Dependency Treebank 2.0 (Hajič et al., 2012). Namely, the data consist of 50 documents from sections `wsj1900-49`. The English texts originally come from the Wall Street Journal section of Penn Treebank (Marcus et al., 1999).

Russian and Polish texts were translated from English by one native speaker for each of the target languages. The translations were revised and corrected by the translators again, if necessary. Basic statistics of the collected texts is shown in the upper part of Table 1.

All the texts were annotated with rich linguistic information stratified into two layers of dependency trees – the surface and deep syntax (tectogrammatical) layer. Whereas the English and Czech annotation was copied from the PCEDT without any change, we produced the Russian and Polish annotation entirely within this project.

In PCEDT, English surface syntax trees had been built by transforming manually annotated constituency trees in Penn Treebank. On the other hand, Czech surface syntax trees had been created automatically by tools available in the multi-purpose NLP framework Treex (Popel and Žabokrtský, 2010). Both the English and Czech tectogrammatical layer had been annotated manu-

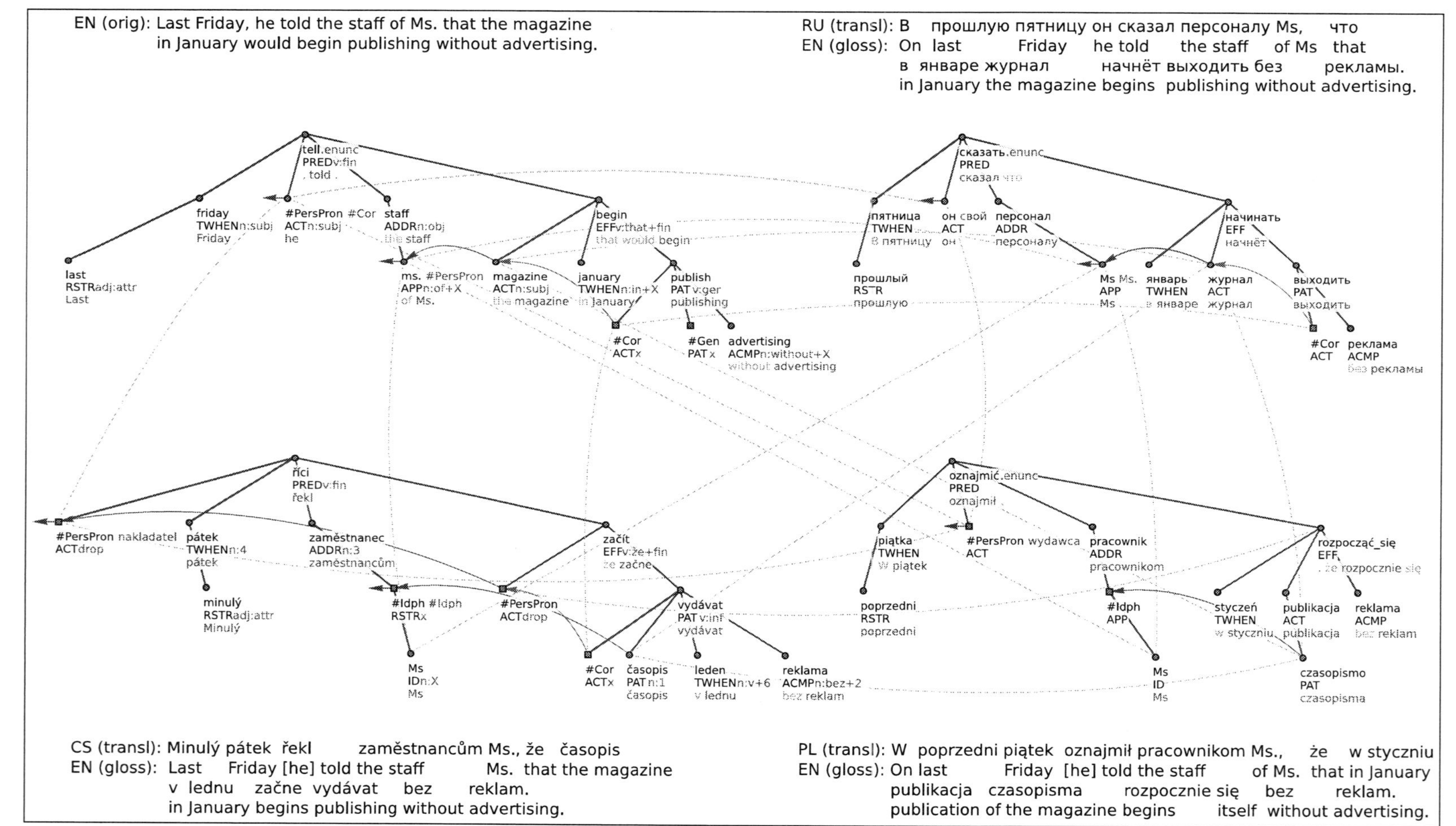

Figure 1: Tectogrammatical representation of a sample sentence in all four available languages, visualized by the TrEd tool. For clarity, we show alignments for coreferential nodes only.

ally from scratch.

The amount of automatic processing was even larger in the Russian and Polish annotations. Treex was employed to obtain both types of trees. Joint part-of-speech tagging, morphological analysis and dependency parsing provided by the UDPipe tool (Straka et al., 2016) were the key elements to build surface syntax trees. These trees were then transformed to tectogrammatical ones by a mostly generic sequence of rule-based modifications.

In other words, the final tectogrammatical trees are simplified and not always guaranteed to be correct, especially in the following aspects:

- Lemmata. Lemmata were set automatically for Russian and Polish and they have been corrected consistently only for expressions that take (or may take) part in coreference relations. The remaining nodes have been mostly corrected during the annotation of tectogrammatical structure and coreference, if annotators discovered a mistake, but no special check has been carried out.

- Obligatory valency positions of predicates. Unlike English and Czech, for which valency lexicons[2] had been used for consistent annotation of valency modifications, we used no such lexicons for Russian and Polish.

- Semantic roles. For Russian, we manually annotated semantic roles for arguments of a predicate, temporal, locative, and causal adjuncts etc. The annotation of semantic roles followed the guidelines for annotation on the tectogrammatical level in the Prague Dependency Treebank for Czech and English (Mikulová et al., 2007), but it was simplified in some respects. For example, instead of nine temporal roles, we used only three basic ones for Russian. As for Polish, semantic roles have not been annotated yet; we plan to add them in future development of the corpus.

- Ellipses. Whereas the English and Czech ellipses had been added by the rules used for the Prague Dependency Treebank[3], the inventory of reconstructed ellipsis types in Russian and Polish was narrowed. It includes

only the cases necessary for coreference annotation.

- Identification structures. For example, in the sample sentence in Figure 1, the name of the magazine (*Ms.*) is marked as an identification structure (with a special governing node *#Idph*) in English and Czech. However, this is not the case of Russian and Polish, where the tectogrammatical structure is more simple.

4 Annotation of Coreference in PAWS

The coreference annotation of PAWS has been conducted manually according to Prague coreference annotation style (Nedoluzhko et al., 2016b).[4] It takes place on the tectogrammatical layer to allow for marking zero anaphora. The annotation covers the cases of grammatical (syntactic) and textual coreference.

The **grammatical coreference** typically occurs within a single sentence, the antecedent is expected to be derived on the basis of grammar rules of a given language. These are the cases of relative and reflexive pronouns, verbs of control, coreference of arguments hidden in reciprocal constructions (***Peter**_i* and ***Mary**_j* kissed $\mathbf{\emptyset}_{i+j}$). and coreference with verbal modifications that have dual dependency (*John saw **Mary** [**∅** run around the lake]*). All the cases of grammatical coreference have been systematically annotated for English and Czech (Nedoluzhko et al., 2016b). For Russian and Polish, grammatical coreference annotation has been consistently provided for the cases of relative and reflexive pronouns. Coreference of arguments of verbs of control and coreference in reciprocal constructions have been manually annotated for Russian but only partly for Polish. However, this task is not especially urgent for our planned comparative analysis of coreferential expressions. In all four analyzed languages, the controllees of the arguments of control verbs, second arguments in reciprocal constructions and arguments in constructions with dual dependencies are unexpressed, thus the results of the comparison will be mostly trivial. For example in Figure 1, the unexpressed controllee is reconstructed as the first argument of the verb *publish* and its counterparts in Czech and Russian (see the dependent

---

[2]Lexicons PDT-Vallex (Hajič et al., 2003) and Engvallex (Urešová, 2012) for Czech and English, respectively.

[3]Described in more details in (Mikulová, 2014).

---

[4]This paper also describes comparative analysis of our approach with coreference annotation in the OntoNotes.

node with the lemma *#Cor* under the node *publish*).[5] It is controlled by the first argument of the verb *begin* (Czech: *začít*, Russian: начинать) and it cannot be explicitly expressed in either of the languages.

By **textual coreference**, arguments are not realized by grammatical means alone, but also via context. Within this type, we annotate the following relations:

- Pronominal coreference of personal, possessive and demonstrative pronouns (e.g., *Mary – she – her*).

- Coreference with textual ellipsis, for example coreference of zero subjects in pro-drop languages. This is the case of the unexpressed subject *he* in the Czech and Polish translations of the main clause *he told the staff of Ms.* in the running example (see Figure 1). In such cases, the special node *#PersPron* is added to the tectogrammatical tree and the coreference relation to the antecedent in the previous context is annotated (as shown in the figure). Interestingly, in the dependent clause of this sentence, the subject is dropped only in Czech and it is not cross-lingually coreferential with the expressions at the same position in the other languages (In Czech, it is coreferential with the subject of the main clause *he*; in English and Russian, this is the magazine; in Polish, this is the publication (*publikacja*)).

- Nominal textual coreference in case when the anaphoric expression is a full nominal group (noun with or without modifications) coreferring with an antecedent in the preceding context. In the running example, such relation is held between *magazine* (Polish: *czasopismo*, Czech: *časopis*, Russian: журнал), the name of this magazine *Ms.* in the same sentence and an antecedent in one of the previous sentences.

- Anaphoric reference of local and temporal adverbs (*there*, *then*, etc.).

- Textual reference to multiple antecedents (so-called *split antecedent*). In this case, there are (technically) two coreference links of a special type, pointing to the split parts of the antecedent.

In the same way as for the other coreference-annotated corpora with Prague-style annotation, the textual coreference is marked in case of anaphoric references to events (so-called *abstract anaphora*), i.e. anaphoric references to verbal groups, clauses, sentences and larger textual segments (Nedoluzhko and Lapshinova-Koltunski, 2016). If the antecedent does not exceed one sentence, it is annotated in the same way as other coreference types, the root of the verbal phrase being the antecedent of a pronominal element.

If an anaphoric expression refers endophorically to a *discourse segment* of more than one sentence, including the cases where the antecedent is understood by inference from a broader context, a special relation with no explicitly marked antecedent is annotated.

We also specifically mark presence of *exophora*, which denotes that the referent is "out" of the cotext, i.e. it is only known from the actual situation. Exophoric reference is annotated in cases of temporal and local deixis (*this year, this country*), deixis with pronominal adverbs (*here*), as well as exophoric reference to the whole text.

In accordance with the Prague coreference annotation tradition, textual coreference is marked up to the length of 20 sentences.

For more detailed description and examples of the applied coreference annotation scheme, see (Nedoluzhko et al., 2016b).

5 Statistics and Observations

The bottom part of Table 1 shows the statistics of coreference-related annotation in PAWS. Here are the main observations:

1. **The number of tectogrammatical nodes in Czech is larger** than in the three remaining languages. This could be caused either by the translator's style or by some language-specific features of Czech. The answer to this question requires further comparison (first of all to other translated and non-translated texts) but manual analysis of the texts shows a strong tendency in Czech to use finite subordinated clauses instead of non-finite infinitive or gerundial clauses in English, Polish and Russian. Finite constructions are naturally longer than infinite ones.

---

[5] In Polish, the sentence has a different syntactic structure, so the argument cannot be reconstructed.

	English	Czech	Russian	Polish
Sentences		1,078		
Tokens	26,149	25,697	25,704	25,763
Tectogrammatical nodes	18,611	20,696	18,874	18,541
Coreferring nodes	4,210	4,403	4,254	3,371
grammatical coreference	729	528	749	294
textual pron. coref. overt	544	213	493	206
textual pron. coref. elided	76	643	32	243
textual nominal coreference	1,361	1,496	1,610	1,568
first mentions	1,277	1,330	1,243	979
reference to split antecedents	149	149	91	65
reference to a segment	28	23	16	12
exophora	46	21	20	4

Table 1: Statistics of the data and its coreference-related annotation.

2. **The number of coreferring nodes in Polish is smaller** than in the three remaining languages. The explanation for this substantial difference is in the simplification of the tectogrammatical annotation for Polish. To keep the annotation consistency for different kind of complicated syntactic structures, the tectogrammatical annotation rules for Czech, English and Russian are very sophisticated. For example, for verbs of speech (e.g., *say*, *claim*, *contend*), the valency position of the verbal content has been reconstructed in the tectogrammatical tree (according to verbal valency lexicons for these languages), even if it is not explicitly expressed in the corresponding clause. See Figure 2, where two obligatory valencies are reconstructed for English, but not for Polish.

3. On the other hand, **the biggest number of coreferring nodes is in Czech**. This correlates with the greater amount of tectogrammatical nodes as well as to the fact that Czech uses personal constructions with overt and unexpressed pronouns more frequently. Besides, this high number reflects especially detailed manual annotation of tectogrammatical level, by which the omitted valency positions have been reconstructed also by a large part of deverbatives, which was not the case for other languages.

4. **The number of grammatical coreference relations is the largest in Russian**. In Polish, on the contrary, it is very small. The reason for the small number in Polish is the missing annotation of the control verbs coreference (see Section 4). As for the large number for Russian, it can be partially explained by a large number of infinitive constructions, where unexpressed subjects are controlled by the actants of their governing control verbs by means of grammatical coreference.

5. **Overt textual pronominal coreference**. This point is especially interesting, as it shows the different degree of pro-drop qualities of English, Czech, Polish and Russian. As observed from the table, overt textual pronominal coreference is most frequent in English. Indeed, in English, there is no possibility for subject omission, whereas for Slavic languages this often happens. However, the subject can be omitted in the analyzed languages to a different degree. Czech is a highly pro-drop language, where anaphoric use of personal pronouns in the subject position is untypical. On the other hand, Polish and Russian show substantially lower degree of pro-drop qualities, Polish being slightly more pro-drop than Russian (Kibrik, 2011).

6. Another observation supported by the brief inspection of Table 1 is that **coreference is more frequently realized by nominal groups in Russian** than in the other languages. This observation requires further analysis. This could be a translation effect that should be however proved by compar-

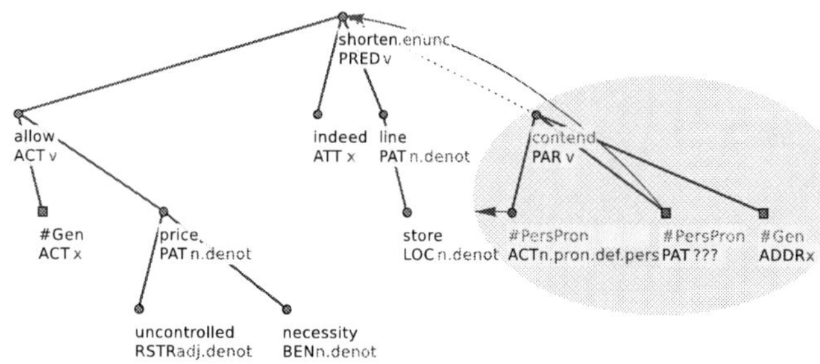
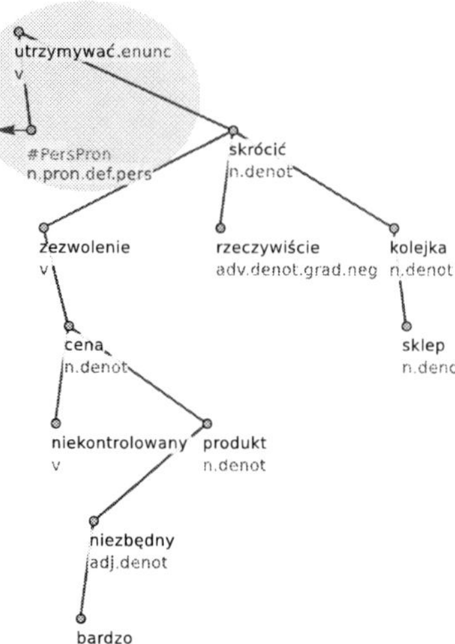

Figure 2: Different tectogrammatical representation of the English sentence and its Polish translation. The English sentence contains additional unexpressed coreferential node.

ison with other translations. On the other hand, the annotation effect is also possible. In some cases, especially in cases of nominal coreference, a coreference relation may be ambiguous (so-called near-identity (Recasens et al., 2011)) and it is up to the annotator, whether to annotate it or not. In such cases, the use of anaphoric markers can influence the annotator's decision: In case of explicit anaphoric reference, the relation is more likely to be annotated.

6 Word Alignment

The annotated texts are equipped with word alignment between each pair of the languages, both on the surface and deep syntax representations. Alignment links were collected by running GIZA++ (Och and Ney, 2000) on a union of the texts in question and a large number of additional parallel texts. The additional parallel texts were collected using the OPUS project (Tiedemann, 2012) and their size was roughly 15 million sentence pairs for each language pair. The word alignment was then projected to the tectogrammatical layer and complemented with alignment for reconstructed nodes using syntax-based heuristics.

For selected types of coreferential expressions, we annotated their cross-lingual counterparts also manually. Particularly, we marked alignment of English, Czech and Russian pronouns and zeros to their counterparts in each of these three lan-

guages.[6] Polish is not covered by manual alignment, yet.

7 Availability

PAWS is freely available for non-commercial research and educational purposes. It can be downloaded from the Lindat/Clarin repository.[7] The treebank is released in the following file formats:

Plain text format. The texts with inline annotation of coreferential mentions. This format also contains reconstructed ellipses, which can be easily removed by running a script that we provide in the release.

Treex XML format. The internal format of PAWS contains the entire annotation. Documents in this format can be viewed using the TrEd tool.

CoNLL 2012 format. This format was used for the CoNLL 2012 Shared Task in coreference resolution. As this format allows for representing surface words only, it does not include all annotated mentions and anaphoric links, especially for pro-drop languages.

8 Conclusion

In this work, we introduced the PAWS treebank: a multi-lingual parallel treebank with manual annotation of coreferential relations and cross-lingual

---

[6] It extends the annotation of English-Czech alignment already provided in PCEDT 2.0 Coref.

[7] http://hdl.handle.net/11234/1-2683

alignment between selected types of coreferential expressions. The treebank currently comprises English texts and its Czech, Russian and Polish translations.

We have primarily built PAWS for future analysis on difference between the languages in terms of how they express coreference. Nevertheless, due to its extensive annotation of syntax, semantic roles, coreference relations and alignment it may serve as a basis for many different linguistic studies. Cross-lingual analysis of any phenomena can bring a deeper insight and allow for its better understanding than if each of the languages was analyzed in isolation.

9 Acknowledgements

The authors gratefully acknowledge support from the Grant Agency of the Czech Republic (project GA16-05394S) and the Polish National Science Centre (contract number 2014/15/B/HS2/03435). The research reported in the present contribution has been using language resources developed, stored and distributed by the LINDAT/CLARIN project of the Ministry of Education, Youth and Sports of the Czech Republic (project LM2015071). We also thank three anonymous reviewers for their instructive comments.

References

Yulia Grishina and Manfred Stede. 2015. Knowledge-Lean Projection of Coreference Chains across Languages. In *Proceedings of the Eighth Workshop on Building and Using Comparable Corpora*, pages 14–22, Beijing, China. Association for Computational Linguistics.

Yulia Grishina and Manfred Stede. 2017. Multi-Source Annotation Projection of Coreference Chains: Assessing Strategies and Testing Opportunities. In *Proceedings of the 2nd Workshop on Coreference Resolution Beyond OntoNotes (CORBON 2017)*, pages 41–50, Valencia, Spain. Association for Computational Linguistics.

Liane Guillou, Christian Hardmeier, Aaron Smith, Jörg Tiedemann, and Bonnie Webber. 2014. ParCor 1.0: A Parallel Pronoun-Coreference Corpus to Support Statistical MT. In *Proceedings of the 9th International Conference on Language Resources and Evaluation (LREC 2014)*, pages 3191–3198, Reykjavik, Iceland. European Language Resources Association.

Jan Hajič, Eva Hajičová, Jarmila Panevová, Petr Sgall, Ondřej Bojar, Silvie Cinková, Eva Fučíková, Marie Mikulová, Petr Pajas, Jan Popelka, Jiří Semecký, Jana Šindlerová, Jan Štěpánek, Josef Toman, Zdeňka Urešová, and Zdeněk Žabokrtský. 2012. Announcing Prague Czech-English Dependency Treebank 2.0. In *Proceedings of the 8th International Conference on Language Resources and Evaluation (LREC 2012)*, pages 3153–3160, Istanbul, Turkey. European Language Resources Association.

Jan Hajič, Jarmila Panevová, Eva Hajičová, Petr Sgall, Petr Pajas, Jan Štěpánek, Jiří Havelka, Marie Mikulová, Zdeněk Žabokrtský, Magda Ševčíková-Razímová, and Zdeňka Urešová. 2006. Prague Dependency Treebank 2.0. Philadelphia, USA. Linguistic Data Consortium.

Jan Hajič, Jarmila Panevová, Zdeňka Urešová, Alevtina Bémová, Veronika Kolářová, and Petr Pajas. 2003. PDT-VALLEX: Creating a Large-coverage Valency Lexicon for Treebank Annotation. In *Proceedings of The Second Workshop on Treebanks and Linguistic Theories*, volume 9 of *Mathematical Modeling in Physics, Engineering and Cognitive Sciences*, pages 57–68, Vaxjo, Sweden. Vaxjo University Press.

Andrej A. Kibrik. 2011. *Reference in Discourse*. Oxford University Press, Oxford, United Kingdom.

Marek Laziński and Magdalena Kuratczyk. 2016. The University of Warsaw Polish-Russian Parallel Corpus. In *Polish-Language Parallel Corpora*, pages 83–95. Instytut Lingwistyki Stosowanej UW, Warsaw, Poland.

Mitchell Marcus, Beatrice Santorini, Mary Ann Marcinkiewicz, and Ann Taylor. 1999. Penn Treebank 3. Philadelphia, USA. Linguistic Data Consortium.

Marie Mikulová. 2014. Semantic Representation of Ellipsis in the Prague Dependency Treebanks. In *Proceedings of the Twenty-Sixth Conference on Computational Linguistics and Speech Processing ROCLING XXVI (2014)*, pages 125–138, Taipei, Taiwan. Association for Computational Linguistics and Chinese Language Processing (ACLCLP).

Marie Mikulová, Alevtina Bémová, Jan Hajič, Eva Hajičová, Jiří Havelka, Veronika Kolářová, Lucie Kučová, Markéta Lopatková, Petr Pajas, Jarmila Panevová, Magda Ševčíková, Petr Sgall, Jan Štěpánek, Zdeňka Urešová, Kateřina Veselá, and Zdeněk Žabokrtský. 2007. Annotation on the Tectogrammatical Level in the Prague Dependency Treebank. Technical Report 3.1. ÚFAL, Charles University. Prague, Czech Republic.

Ruslan Mitkov and Catalina Barbu. 2003. Using Bilingual Corpora to Improve Pronoun Resolution. *Languages in contrast*, 4(2).

Anna Nedoluzhko, Anna Schwarz (Khoroshkina), and Michal Novák. 2016a. Possessives in Parallel English-Czech-Russian Texts. *Computational Linguistics and Intellectual Technologies*, (15):483–497.

Anna Nedoluzhko and Ekaterina Lapshinova-Koltunski. 2016. Abstract Coreference in a Multilingual Perspective: A View on Czech and German. In *Proceedings of the Workshop on Coreference Resolution Beyond OntoNotes (COR-BON 2016)*, pages 47–52, Ann Arbor, Michigan. Association for Computational Linguistics.

Anna Nedoluzhko, Michal Novák, Silvie Cinková, Marie Mikulová, and Jiří Mírovský. 2016b. Coreference in Prague Czech-English Dependency Treebank. In *Proceedings of the 10th International Conference on Language Resources and Evaluation (LREC 2016)*, pages 169–176, Paris, France. European Language Resources Association.

Michal Novák and Anna Nedoluzhko. 2015. Correspondences between Czech and English Coreferential Expressions. *Discours: Revue de linguistique, psycholinguistique et informatique.*, 16:1–41.

Michal Novák and Zdeněk Žabokrtský. 2014. Cross-lingual Coreference Resolution of Pronouns. In *Proceedings of COLING 2014, the 25th International Conference on Computational Linguistics: Technical Papers*, Dublin, Ireland. Dublin City University and Association for Computational Linguistics.

Franz J. Och and Hermann Ney. 2000. Improved Statistical Alignment Models. In *Proceedings of the 38th Annual Meeting on Association for Computational Linguistics*, pages 440–447, Stroudsburg, PA, USA. Association for Computational Linguistics.

Petr Pajas and Jan Štěpánek. 2008. Recent Advances in a Feature-rich Framework for Treebank Annotation. In *Proceedings of the 22nd International Conference on Computational Linguistics - Volume 1*, Stroudsburg, PA, USA. Association for Computational Linguistics.

Piotr Pęzik. 2016. Exploring Phraseological Equivalence with Paralela. In *Polish-Language Parallel Corpora*, pages 67–81. Instytut Lingwistyki Stosowanej UW, Warsaw.

Martin Popel and Zdeněk Žabokrtský. 2010. TectoMT: Modular NLP Framework. In *Proceedings of the 7th International Conference on Advances in Natural Language Processing*, pages 293–304, Berlin, Heidelberg. Springer-Verlag.

Oana Postolache, Dan Cristea, and Constantin Orasan. 2006. Transferring Coreference Chains through Word Alignment. In *Proceedings of the Fifth International Conference on Language Resources and Evaluation*, Genoa, Italy. European Language Resources Association.

Sameer Pradhan, Alessandro Moschitti, Nianwen Xue, Olga Uryupina, and Yuchen Zhang. 2012. CoNLL-2012 Shared Task: Modeling Multilingual Unrestricted Coreference in OntoNotes. In *Joint Conference on EMNLP and CoNLL - Shared Task*, pages 1–40, Jeju Island, Korea. Association for Computational Linguistics.

Marta Recasens, Eduard Hovy, and M. Antònia Martí. 2011. Identity, Non-identity, and Near-identity: Addressing the Complexity of Coreference. *Lingua*, 121:1138–1152.

Petr Sgall, Eva Hajičová, and Jarmila Panevová. 1986. *The Meaning of the Sentence in Its Semantic and Pragmatic Aspects*. D. Reidel Publishing Company, Dordrecht, Netherlands.

Milan Straka, Jan Hajič, and Jana Straková. 2016. UD-Pipe: Trainable Pipeline for Processing CoNLL-U Files Performing Tokenization, Morphological Analysis, POS Tagging and Parsing. In *Proceedings of the Tenth International Conference on Language Resources and Evaluation (LREC 2016)*, pages 4290–4297, Paris, France. European Language Resources Association.

Jörg Tiedemann. 2012. Parallel Data, Tools and Interfaces in OPUS. In *Proceedings of the Eight International Conference on Language Resources and Evaluation (LREC 2012)*, pages 2214–2218, Paris, France. European Language Resources Association.

Zdeňka Urešová. 2012. Building the PDT-VALLEX Valency Lexicon. In *Proceedings of the fifth Corpus Linguistics Conference*, pages 1–18, Liverpool, UK. University of Liverpool.

František Čermák and Alexandr Rosen. 2012. The Case of InterCorp, a Multilingual Parallel Corpus. *International Journal of Corpus Linguistics*, 17(3):411–427.

Ruprecht von Waldenfels. 2006. Compiling a Parallel Corpus of Slavic Languages. Text Strategies, Tools and the Question of Lemmatization in Alignment. *Beiträge der Europäischen Slavistischen Linguistik (POLYSLAV)*, 9:123–138.

Ralph Weischedel, Martha Palmer, Mitchell Marcus, Eduard Hovy, Sameer Pradhan, Lance Ramshaw, Nianwen Xue, Ann Taylor, Jeff Kaufman, Michelle Franchini, Mohammed El-Bachouti, Robert Belvin, and Ann Houston. 2013. OntoNotes Release 5.0. Philadelphia, USA. Linguistic Data Consortium.

A Fine-grained Large-scale Analysis of Coreference Projection

Michal Novák

Charles University

Faculty of Mathematics and Physics

Prague, Czech Republic

{mnovak}@ufal.mff.cuni.cz

Abstract

We perform a fine-grained large-scale analysis of coreference projection. By projecting gold coreference from Czech to English and vice versa on Prague Czech-English Dependency Treebank 2.0 Coref, we set an upper bound of a proposed projection approach for these two languages. We undertake a detailed thorough analysis that combines the analysis of projection's subtasks with analysis of performance on individual mention types. The findings are accompanied with examples from the corpus.

1 Introduction

Projection has been for a long time seen as an alternative way to build a linguistic tool for resource-poor languages. Coreference projection has been no exception. Despite its mostly mediocre results, only some works perform a proper error analysis.

In this work, we conduct a fine-grained large-scale analysis of coreference projection. We adopt a corpus-based projection approach and apply it on Czech-English parallel texts in Prague Czech-English Dependency Treebank 2.0 Coref (Nedoluzhko et al., 2016) in both projection directions. We project manually annotated coreference links within texts enriched with mainly manually annotated linguistic annotation. Results obtained on manual (i.e. gold) annotation can be then considered as an upper bound for projection techniques where the gold annotation is replaced by the one obtained automatically.

We took inspiration from two works that have previously focused on projection of gold coreference. Even though both of them provided an analysis of collected projections, they treated it in a completely different way. Postolache et al. (2006) concentrated on factorized analysis. They split the task of projection into subtasks, such as mention matching, mention span overlapping and antecedent selection, and inspected their effect on the final result separately. Alternatively, in their multilingual projection approach Grishina and Stede (2017) carried out an analysis across mention types. They split all mentions to categories such as noun phrases, named entities and pronouns, and evaluated projection on these mention types separately.

Our work combines both these views on analysis, providing a factorized fine-grained analysis of projected coreference. In addition, we include new categories of mentions – zeros. These have been often neglected as they are not expressed on the surface. However, by ignoring them we would lose valuable information, especially in pro-drop language such as Czech and Spanish. Furthermore, our analysis is based on about 100-times bigger corpus than in the two related works, which makes the findings and conclusions more reliable.

The paper is structured as follows. In Section 2 we describe two main projection approaches with a special emphasis on corpus-based projection of gold coreference. Section 3 presents the corpus that we use for making projections and Section 4 describes the projection method we propose. The main projection experiments and its results are presented in Section 5 and analyzed in detail using a factorized view in Section 6. Finally, we conclude in Section 7.

2 Related Work

Approaches to cross-lingual projection are usually aimed to bridge the gap of missing resources in the target language. So far, they have been quite successfully applied to part-of-speech tagging (Täckström et al., 2013), syntactic parsing (Hwa et al., 2005), semantic role labeling (Padó and Lapata, 2009), opinion mining (Almeida et al.,

Proceedings of the Workshop on Computational Models of Reference, Anaphora and Coreference, pages 77–86

New Orleans, Louisiana, June 6, 2018. ©2018 Association for Computational Linguistics

2015), etc. Projection techniques are generally grouped into two types with respect to how they obtain the translation to the source language, which is usually a resource-rich language. *MT-based approaches* apply a machine-translation service to create synthetic data in source language. *Corpus-based approaches* take advantage of the human-translated parallel corpus of the two languages.

MT-based approaches. The workflow of these approaches is as follows. Starting with a text in the target language to be labeled with coreference, it first must be machine-translated to the source language. A coreference resolver for the source language is then applied on the translated text and, finally, the newly established coreference links are projected back to the target language. Flexibility of this approach lies in the fact that it can be applied in both train and test time, and no linguistic processing tools for the target language are required. To the best of our knowledge, this approach has been applied to coreference only twice, by Rahman and Ng (2012) on projection from English to Spanish and Italian, and by Ogrodniczuk (2013) on projection from English to Polish.

Corpus-based approaches. In these approaches, a human-translated parallel corpus of the two languages is available and the projection mechanism is applied within this corpus. Coreference annotation in the source-language side of the corpus may be both labeled by humans or a coreference system. The target-language side of the corpus then serves as a training dataset for a coreference resolver. This approach thus must be applied in train time and, moreover, it requires a coreference resolver trainable on the target-language data. As a consequence, linguistic processing tools should be available for the target language as most of the resolvers depend on some amount of additional linguistic information. On the other hand, human translation and gold coreference annotation, if available, should increase the quality of the projected coreference. This approach has been used to create a coreference resolver by multiple authors, e.g. de Souza and Orăsan (2011), Martins (2015), Wallin and Nugues (2017), and Novák et al. (2017). However, since the present work employs the corpus-based approach on gold annotations of coreference, we offer more details on works of Postolache et al.

(2006) and Grishina and Stede (2015, 2017).

Postolache et al. (2006) followed corpus-based approach using a small English-Romanian corpus of 638 sentence pairs in order to create a bilingually-annotated resource. They projected manually annotated coreference, which was then post-processed by linguists to acquire high quality annotation in Romanian. Based on the gold coreference annotation of the Romanian side of the corpus, they evaluated the F-scores of mention heads' matching, mention spans' overlapping, and coreference clusters on all as well as only correctly projected mentions. A factorized error analysis they carried out shows that the majority of errors in coreference projection stems from a lower recall (around 70%) caused by missing alignment due to alignment errors or language differences introduced in the translation.

Yulia Grishina with her colleagues also investigate possibilities of corpus-based coreference projection. In (Grishina and Stede, 2015), they introduced a "generalizable" annotation schema that they tested on parallel texts of three languages (English, Russian and German) and three genres (newswire articles, short stories, medical leaflets). Using this dataset consisting of less than 500 sentence triples, they conducted experiments on projection from English to the two other languages. In (Grishina and Stede, 2017), they pursue a goal of multi-source projection of manual coreference annotation. They propose several strategies of combining projections from multiple languages, with some of them slightly improving the F-score of the best-performing projection source. They also provide a qualitative analysis on individual mention types suggesting that pronouns have much higher projection accuracy[1] than nominal groups. They justify their unsatisfactory results especially for German nominal groups by problems with inclusion of an unaligned German determiner in definite descriptions.

3 Data Source

We employ a slightly modified version of the Prague Czech-English Dependency Treebank 2.0 Coref (Nedoluzhko et al., 2016, PCEDT 2.0

---

[1] As far as we are concerned, it is misleading to call their projection measure "accuracy". There is another measure that could be calculated as a proportion of target mentions covered by projection among all target mentions, i.e. "recall". Therefore, whenever we apply this measure in our experiments in Section 4, we rather denote it as "precision".

Coref) for our projection experiments.

PCEDT 2.0 Coref is a coreferential extension to the Prague Czech-English Dependency Treebank 2.0 (Hajič et al., 2012). It is a Czech-English parallel corpus, consisting of almost 50k sentence pairs (more on its basic statistics is shown in the upper part of the Table 1). The English part originally comes from the Wall Street Journal collected in the Penn Treebank (Marcus et al., 1999) and the Czech part was manually translated. It has been annotated at multiple layers of linguistic representation up to the layer of deep syntax (or *tectogrammatical layer*), based on the theory of Functional Generative Description (Sgall et al., 1986). The tectogrammatical representation of a sentence is a dependency tree with semantic labeling, coreference, and argument structure description based on a valency lexicon. The nodes of a tectogrammatical tree comprise merely auto-semantic words. Furthermore, some surface-elided expressions are reconstructed at this layer. They include anaphoric zeros (e.g. zero subjects in Czech, unexpressed arguments of non-finite clauses in both English and Czech) that are introduced in the tectogrammatical layer with a newly established node.

The coreference annotation of PCEDT 2.0 Coref takes place on the tectogrammatical layer to allow for marking zero anaphora. Coreference is technically annotated as links connecting two mentions: *the anaphor* (the referring expression) and *the antecedent* (the referred expression). The coreference links then form *chains*, which correspond to coreference entities. In tectogrammatics, the mention is determined only by its head. No mention boundaries are specified. Therefore, a coreference link always connects two nodes on a tectogrammatical layer.

In order to provide a fine-grained qualitative analysis, we divide mentions into multiple categories in this paper: (1) personal pronouns, (2) possessive pronouns, (3) reflexive possessive pronouns, (4) reflexive pronouns, all four types of pronouns in the 3rd or ambiguous person, (5) demonstrative pronouns, (6) zero subjects, (7) zeros in non-finite clauses, (8) relative pronouns, (9) the pronouns of types (1)-(4) in the 1st or 2nd person, (10) named entities, (11) common nominal groups, and (12) other expressions. Note that categories (3) and (6) are defined only in Czech. The last category contains coordination roots, verbs, adjectives, but the majority is formed by other

Mention type	Czech	English
Sentences	49,208	49,208
Tokens	1,151,150	1,173,766
Tecto. nodes	931,846	838,212
Mentions (total)	183,277	188,685
Personal pron.	3,038	14,887
Possessive pron.	3,777	9,186
Refl. poss. pron.	4,389	—
Reflexive pron.	1,272	484
Demonstr. pron.	3,429	1,492
Zero subject	16,875	—
Zero in nonfin. cl.	6,151	29,759
Relative pron.	15,198	8,170
1st/2nd pers. pron.	4,415	4,557
Named entities	18,874	36,833
Nominal group	80,124	68,866
Other	25,735	14,451

Table 1: Basic and coreferential statistics of PCEDT 2.0 Coref.

nodes restoring ellipsis, e.g. zeros in other than subject positions or missing arguments in reciprocal relation. We do not focus on this category in the rest of the paper. The statistics of coreferential mentions is collected in the bottom part of Table 1.

The treebank is aligned on the level of tectogrammatical nodes. The alignment is based on unsupervised word alignment by GIZA++ (Och and Ney, 2000), augmented with a supervised method (Novák and Žabokrtský, 2014) for selected coreferential expressions. The supervised alignment has been trained on a section of PCEDT 2.0 Coref comprising 1,078 sentence pairs with manual annotation of alignment. To ensure that the whole PCEDT 2.0 Coref is aligned in the same way for our experiments, we make a slight modification to it and replace the manual alignment in this particular section with the supervised one, obtained by 10-fold cross-validation.

4 Coreference Projection

Our approach to coreference projection belongs to the corpus-based methods as introduced in Section 2. We work with manually translated English-Czech parallel corpus with word alignment and project coreference from one language side to the other. In fact, our approach is similar to the one adopted by multiple previous works (Postolache et al., 2006; de Souza and Orăsan, 2011; Wallin and Nugues, 2017; Grishina, 2017, i.a.). Nevertheless, there is a substantial difference of our work compared to the others: our projection system operates on tectogrammatical representation. It leads to the two following consequences.

Firstly, our system is able to address zero anaphora. Thorough cross-lingual analysis by Novák and Nedoluzhko (2015) showed that many counterparts of Czech or English coreferential expressions are zeros. This likely holds for the other pro-drop languages, too. It is thus surprising that the previous work on projection to Spanish (Rahman and Ng, 2012; Martins, 2015) or Portuguese (de Souza and Orăsan, 2011; Martins, 2015) did not accent this problem at all. In tectogrammatics, generated nodes serve this purpose instead.

Secondly, mention spans are not specified in tectogrammatical trees, as mentioned in Section 3. Concerning projection, many of the previous works (Rahman and Ng, 2012; Postolache et al., 2006; Wallin and Nugues, 2017, i.a.) devote considerable space to answering the question of the proper strategy for determining boundaries of a projected mention. If a mention is solely defined by its head as in the present work, this question does not need to be answered.

The projection algorithm is schematized in Algorithm 1. An input of the algorithm are two aligned lists of tectogrammatical trees representing the same text in the source and the target language. First, a list of coreferential chains must be extracted from source trees (line 1). Every coreference chain is projected independently (lines 2-18) mention by mention, starting with the first one, the one that has no outcoming link. For each mention, at the moment viewed as an anaphor, its counterpart in the target language is returned using the alignment (line 5). In case there are several nodes aligned to the anaphor, those which do not yet participate in a different chain are interlinked and only the very last mention is returned by the function `GetAlignedAndInterlink`. If no aligned counterpart to the anaphor is found, the anaphor is skipped and its outgoing coreference link thus remains unprojected. Otherwise (lines 6-16), counterparts of anaphor's direct antecedents are retrieved (lines 7-8) and the algorithm adds a link between the anaphor's and antecedents' counterparts in the target language (line 10). If there

are no antecedents' counterparts, the last successfully projected anaphor from any of the previous iterations is used instead (line 13).

5 Experiments and Results

In the following experiment, we project gold coreference between gold trees in two directions: from English to Czech and vice versa. The experiment is carried out on the dataset presented in Section 3, PCEDT 2.0 Coref with supervised alignment in all its sections.

One of the objectives of this work is to analyze performance of coreference projection for individual mention types. Standard evaluation metrics (e.g. MUC (Vilain et al., 1995), B^3 (Bagga and Baldwin, 1998)) are not suitable for our purposes, though, since they do not allow for scoring only a subset of mentions. Instead, we use a measure similar to scores proposed by (Tuggener, 2014) that we denote as *anaphora score*.

Let $K = \{K_1, \ldots, K_m\}$ be the set of true and $S = \{S_1, \ldots, S_n\}$ the set of predicted coreferential chains. From K and S we derive sets of true anaphors $\text{ANAPH}(K)$ and predicted anaphors $\text{ANAPH}(S)$ using the following definition:

$$\text{ANAPH}(Z) = \{x | \exists i : x \in Z_i \text{ and } \exists y : y \in \text{ANTE}_{Z_i}(x)\}$$

where the set $\text{ANTE}_{Z_i}(x)$ contains all direct antecedents of x in chain Z_i. We also define an indicator function $both(a, K, S)$ as follows:

$$both(a, K, S) = \begin{cases} 1 & \begin{array}{l} \text{if } \exists i, j : a \in K_i \cap S_j \\ \text{and } \exists e \in K_i : e \in \text{ANTE}_{K_i}(a) \\ \text{and } \exists f \in \text{ANTE}_{S_j}(a) : f \in K_i \end{array} \\ 0 & \text{otherwise} \end{cases}$$

In other words, it fires only if a has an antecedent in both the truth and the prediction and the predicted antecedent of anaphor a belongs to a true coreferential chain associated with a. Precision (P), Recall (R) are then computed by averaging the function $both(a, K, S)$ over all predicted and true anaphors, respectively, and F-score (F) traditionally as a harmonic mean of P and R:

$$P = \frac{\sum\limits_{a \in \text{ANAPH}(S)} both(a, K, S)}{|\text{ANAPH}(S)|} \qquad R = \frac{\sum\limits_{a \in \text{ANAPH}(K)} both(a, K, S)}{|\text{ANAPH}(K)|}$$

$$F = \frac{2PR}{P + R}$$

To evaluate only a particular anaphor type, both sets $\text{ANAPH}(K)$ and $\text{ANAPH}(S)$ must be restricted only to anaphoric mentions of the given

```
   Input: SrcTrees = source language trees with coreference, TrgTrees = target language trees
   Output: TrgTrees = target language trees with projected coreference
 1 AllSrcChains ← GetCorefChains(SrcTrees);
 2 for SrcChain ∈ AllSrcChains do
 3     TrgLastAnte ← ∅;
 4     for SrcMention ∈ SrcChain do
 5         TrgMention ← GetAlignedAndInterlink(SrcMention, TrgTrees);
 6         if ∃TrgMention then
 7             SrcAntes ← GetCorefNodes(SrcMention);
 8             TrgAntes ← GetAligned(SrcAntes, TrgTrees);
 9             if TrgAntes ≠ ∅ then
10                 AddCorefNodes(TrgMention, TrgAntes);
11             end
12             else
13                 AddCorefNodes(TrgMention, TrgLastAnte);
14             end
15             TrgLastAnte ← TrgMention;
16         end
17     end
18 end
```

Algorithm 1: Algorithm for coreference projection

Mention type	EN→CS	CS→EN
Personal pron.	$^{81.92}_{52.05}$ 63.65	$^{86.52}_{67.45}$ 75.80
Possessive pron.	$^{72.85}_{59.87}$ 65.73	$^{89.33}_{60.88}$ 72.41
Refl. poss. pron.	$^{80.21}_{68.42}$ 73.85	—
Reflexive pron.	$^{87.36}_{11.96}$ 21.04	$^{89.17}_{22.20}$ 35.55
Demonstr. pron.	$^{57.43}_{35.19}$ 43.64	$^{55.81}_{42.73}$ 48.40
Zero subject	$^{78.71}_{59.06}$ 67.49	—
Zero in nonfin. cl.	$^{78.75}_{52.96}$ 63.33	$^{83.78}_{34.34}$ 48.71
Relative pron.	$^{74.71}_{51.18}$ 60.75	$^{85.02}_{70.00}$ 76.78
1st/2nd pers. pron.	$^{67.97}_{57.08}$ 62.05	$^{83.21}_{58.55}$ 68.73
Named entities	$^{38.04}_{62.07}$ 47.17	$^{80.29}_{39.04}$ 52.54
Nominal group	$^{50.15}_{37.80}$ 43.11	$^{61.70}_{47.27}$ 53.53
Other	$^{20.73}_{17.68}$ 19.09	$^{22.82}_{26.90}$ 24.69
Total	$^{53.86}_{44.86}$ 48.95	$^{71.31}_{46.47}$ 56.27

Table 2: Anaphora scores of gold coreference projected on PCEDT 2.0 Coref with thorough supervised alignment.

type. In the following tables, we use $^{P}_{R}$ F to format the three components of the anaphora score.

Table 2 shows results of gold coreference projection. The main observation is that with the overall F-scores around 50%, coreference projection between EN and CS seems to be a difficult problem. Moreover, let us emphasize that this experiment is supposed to set an upper bound for our projection approach since most of the annotation it exploits is manual. Comparing the two directions, the CS→EN projection appears to be a bit easier, yet still not reaching 60% F-score. Although precision rates are rather low, it is even lower recall rates that seem to have a more important effect on the weak performance of projection.

Note that our absolute projection scores are not easy to be directly compared with the numbers reported in other works performing projection of gold coreference (e.g. by Postolache et al. (2006) and Grishina and Stede (2017)). There are several factors affecting the score values, in which these experiments certainly differ: a target language, a range of expressions annotated with coreference, quality of alignment, evaluation measure, etc.

To slightly facilitate comparison, we can judge relative performance on individual mention types. In both languages, coreference information is obviously best preserved for central pronouns (except for basic reflexives). It agrees with findings by Grishina and Stede (2017), where they observed higher precision for pronouns than for nominal groups. They suggest that inferior performance for nominal groups may be a result of errors in mention matching. To find out if our results can be justified in this way, we undergo a detailed analysis of factors influencing the projection score.

6 Analysis of Factors

There are three main factors that contribute to the quality of coreference projection: quality of (1) alignment, (2) mention matching, and (3) antecedent selection. Every projection error can be associated with a factor that caused it. Table 3 shows the results of the analysis of factors that are elaborated in more details in the following paragraphs.

Proportion of aligned mentions. No coreference link can be projected to an unaligned mention. Missing alignment on target-language mentions thus causes errors of the first type. The left-hand side of Table 3 shows the proportion of aligned target-language mentions. Extremely low proportion of aligned mentions is observed for Czech basic reflexive pronouns. In the vast majority of cases, unaligned Czech basic reflexives are a result of not expressing the corresponding argument of the proposition in English. For instance, the Czech translation of the verb *to rent* in Example 1 requires explicit reflexive pronoun to signal the meaning that Exxon will pay for using the tower, not that Exxon will receive money as its owner.

(1) *Exxon* **si** *pronajme část výškové budovy.*
Exxon **[to it]** will rent part of a tower.
Do dokončení stavby si společnost Exxon pronajme část stávající kancelářské výškové budovy.
Until the building is completed, Exxon will rent part of an existing office tower.

Surprisingly, Czech personal pronouns are also less frequently aligned than the other mention types. Similarly to the previous case, the reason is often that some arguments of the English proposition are not explicitly mentioned (see Example 2). In general, missing English counterparts are a result of compact formulation of English sentences, like in Example 5. Compact language is, in our view, an inherent property of English as well as a feature of the specific journalistic style used in

Wall Street Journal (WSJ). Moreover, one should not neglect the factor of the so-called *Explicitation Hypothesis* as formulated by Blum-Kulka (1986): the redundancy expressed by a rise of cohesive explicitness in the target-language text might be caused by the nature of the translation process itself.

(2) *pocity,* **které je od práce odrazují.**
feelings **[which discourage them from working].**
Pro prodejce není úplně snadné vypořádat se s pocity, které je od práce odrazují.
It can be hard for a salesperson to fight off feelings **of discouragement.**

As for English, we can see lower scores for zeros in non-finite clauses and reflexive pronouns, again. The non-finite clauses mainly consist of past and present participles. All the missing Czech counterparts of zeros in the past participle are due to the participle being represented as an adjective in Czech, thus having no valency arguments annotated. The reasons behind a missing Czech counterpart of a zero in the present participle are more diverse. The counterpart is often missing even for the governing verb, not just for its zero argument (see Example 3). As opposed to the previous case of explicitation, this is an example of implicitation in the EN→CS translation.

(3) *Řada* *makléřských* *firem* *se vzdala*
A number of brokerage firms pulled back from
— *této strategie.*
using this strategy.
Program traders were publicly castigated following the 508-point crash Oct. 19, 1987, and a number of brokerage firms pulled back from using this strategy for a while.
Programoví obchodníci byli po propadu burzy o 508 bodů dne 19. října 1987 veřejně káráni a řada makléřských firem se načas této strategie vzdala.

Missing alignment for English reflexives stems from three prevailing reasons. In the first group, there is no counterpart at all. The second group has surface counterparts, however they are not represented in the tectogrammatical tree. This concerns Czech basic reflexive pronouns, which are often hard to distinguish whether they are tightly bound to a verb or they fill an argument of the verb. The last group are English reflexive pronoun in its emphatic use. As shown in Example 4, they are often translated as words *samotný* or *sám* (*alone*), for which the automatic alignment often fails.

(4) *the ringers* **themselves** *will be drawn into*
zvonící **samotní** budou vtaženi do
the life
života

Mention type	aligned (%)		ment. match. (P R)				ante. sel. (^P_R F)	
	CS	EN	CS		EN		CS	EN
Personal pron.	68.30	85.46	99.69	93.88	98.68	94.02	$^{95.34}_{93.92}$ 94.63	$^{95.20}_{90.59}$ 92.83
Possessive pron.	84.06	75.42	99.78	98.24	99.80	94.66	$^{95.64}_{94.76}$ 95.20	$^{95.45}_{90.61}$ 92.97
Refl. poss. pron.	87.08	—	100.00	98.56	—		$^{97.25}_{96.53}$ 96.89	—
Reflexive pron.	17.69	69.21	100.00	79.56	100.00	37.31	$^{95.60}_{92.68}$ 94.12	$^{93.86}_{89.92}$ 91.85
Demonstr. pron.	79.29	87.47	91.76	70.87	81.76	71.11	$^{84.79}_{82.40}$ 83.58	$^{91.41}_{88.25}$ 89.81
Zero subject	84.31	—	99.76	89.37	—		$^{95.71}_{94.78}$ 95.25	—
Zero in nonfin. cl.	80.15	49.90	100.00	85.07	99.84	85.06	$^{94.96}_{93.40}$ 94.17	$^{92.94}_{89.24}$ 91.05
Relative pron.	86.88	91.62	99.05	80.48	97.29	90.26	$^{95.43}_{91.95}$ 93.66	$^{97.35}_{93.80}$ 95.54
1st/2nd pers. pron.	85.14	84.46	88.42	88.53	94.20	79.73	$^{91.77}_{87.34}$ 89.50	$^{94.26}_{89.01}$ 91.56
Named entities	79.60	96.83	50.09	87.51	91.24	48.61	$^{95.82}_{94.15}$ 94.98	$^{95.03}_{91.88}$ 93.43
Nominal group	72.99	95.35	75.08	72.76	79.22	59.27	$^{90.52}_{87.46}$ 88.96	$^{90.60}_{84.37}$ 87.38
Other	53.43	73.54	32.90	54.14	41.81	53.24	$^{80.08}_{78.42}$ 79.24	$^{70.72}_{70.05}$ 70.38
Total	73.88	84.49	70.86	77.51	83.51	65.20	$^{92.91}_{90.69}$ 91.79	$^{92.73}_{88.31}$ 90.47

Table 3: Results of the analysis of the three factors directly affecting projection quality. The scores are always measured from a target-language perspective.

I live in hopes that the ringers themselves will be drawn into that fuller life.

Žiji v naději, že i samotní zvonící budou vtaženi do tohoto plnějšího života.

Mention matching. A coreference relation cannot be correctly projected unless both the anaphor and the antecedent match a mention in the target language. Not matching a target-language mention is an error of the second type. To check what is the impact of mention matching, we measure it solely on aligned target language mentions and show the results in the middle part of Table 3.

In agreement with findings of (Grishina and Stede, 2017), we observe that pronouns and zeros in the top part of the table clearly approach matching precision of 100% in both projection directions. At the same time, named entities, nominal and other coreferential expressions in the bottom part of the table exhibit drops in precision. We presume that the precision score grows with decreasing length of the mention span.[2]

An interesting behavior is displayed by named entities. Whereas in Czech their precision is much lower than recall, these rates are very similar but swapped in English. A closer insight to the data gives us a clear explanation illustrated in Example 5. A modifier, such as *společnost* (*company*), *firma* (*firm*), *trh* (*market*) etc., is added to many named entities in Czech. It sounds more natural

and is easier to comprehend, especially if you are not familiar with the WSJ domain. This modifier is in fact a head of the complete named entity and, more importantly, it is the node that may corefer with others. Since it has no counterpart in English, no coreference is transferred to English, which results in recall errors for corresponding named entities. In the opposite projection, the English coreference link that is connected directly to one of the words in a given named entity finds its Czech counterpart, which is not a head of the mention, though. Hence, the Czech counterpart is in fact not coreferential, which causes a precision error. And because the head of the mention, the true coreferential node, is a word like *společnost*, the recall error incurred by not covering it falls into the category of nominal groups, not named entities.

(5) stake   that   **Burmah**   announced
podílu, o kterém **společnost Burmah** prohlásila,
–[that it]   **SHV**   held
že ho   **společnost SHV** držela

The holding of 13.6 million shares is up from a 6.7% stake that Burmah announced SHV held as of last Monday.

Vlastnictví 13.6 milionu akcií je nárůst oproti 6.7% podílu, o kterém společnost Burmah prohlásila, že ho společnost SHV držela k minulému pondělí. (6)

Moreover, English reflexives see a dramatic fall in recall. These errors are again incurred for instances that translate to the Czech expressions *sám* or *samotný* (*alone*). Even if they are correctly aligned, these Czech expressions do not carry any

---

[2]Note that even if the tectogrammatical theory does not predetermine the mention span, it still exists.

coreference annotation. Therefore, no links can be projected.

Antecedent selection quality. If both the anaphor and the antecedent are correctly matched to some target-language mentions but these mentions belong to distinct chains, an error of the third type is incurred. The right-hand side of Table 3 shows the anaphora scores calculated on the same data as used until now, but only on correctly matched mentions. It accounts for around 49% of all coreferential links in Czech and 53% in English.

All F-scores move around 90% and more. The only exception is a category of Czech demonstrative pronouns. The reasons behind the errors related to them are various, including annotators' errors and alignment errors. But they are often caused by relatively free nature of demonstratives, which can refer to nominal groups, predicates, larger segments as well as entities outside the text. The free nature then allows the annotators to mark different (but somehow related) mentions as antecedents, especially when a different syntax structure of the languages encourages it. For instance, in Example 7 both expressions "the exchange" and "volume" are in some sense possible as the antecedent of "it". The same holds for the Czech translation.

(7)   ***the exchange***   *run up*   *volume*   *of X contracts.*
     burza   dosáhla   **objemu**   X smluv.
     later,   **it**   *was*   *Y.*
     později   **to**   bylo   Y.
      ...and the options exchange had run up volume of 1.1 million contracts. A year later, it was 5.7 million.
      ...a opční burza dosáhla objemu 1.1 milionu smluv. O rok později to bylo 5.7 milionu.

7 Conclusion

Coreference projection performs poorly in both investigated directions. And since the experiments were undertaken on gold data, it is doubtful that performance with automatic links would be better.

The analysis confirmed the conclusions drawn in the related literature. First, the bottleneck of coreference projections seems to be alignment and mention-matching, incurring mostly recall errors. Second, precision of projection on pronouns is much better than for nominal groups and named entities, which leads us to the belief that shorter mentions are easier to project. However, to confirm it we would need to define span boundaries for tectogrammatical mentions.

Our analysis revealed also some more detailed findings. Reflexive pronouns seem to be very problematic. Not only are they difficult to align, but they neither excel at mention matching. Surprisingly, a relatively high proportion of Czech personal pronouns remain unaligned. The reason for this cannot be clearly generalized from the current corpus and thus should be verified on data that consist of various domains and translation directions.

8 Acknowledgments

The authors gratefully acknowledge support from the Grant Agency of the Czech Republic (project GA16-05394S). The research reported in the present contribution has been using language resources developed, stored and distributed by the LINDAT/CLARIN project of the Ministry of Education, Youth and Sports of the Czech Republic (project LM2015071). We also thank three anonymous reviewers for their instructive comments.

References

Mariana S. C. Almeida, Cláudia Pinto, Helena Figueira, Pedro Mendes, and André F. T. Martins. 2015. Aligning Opinions: Cross-Lingual Opinion Mining with Dependencies. In *Proceedings of the 53rd Annual Meeting of the Association for Computational Linguistics and the 7th International Joint Conference on Natural Language Processing of the Asian Federation of Natural Language Processing, ACL 2015, Volume 1: Long Papers*, pages 408–418, Stroudsburg, PA, USA. The Association for Computer Linguistics.

Amit Bagga and Breck Baldwin. 1998. Algorithms for Scoring Coreference Chains. In *In The First International Conference on Language Resources and Evaluation Workshop on Linguistics Coreference*, pages 563–566.

Shoshana Blum-Kulka. 1986. Shifts of Cohesion and Coherence in Translation. In *Interlingual and intercultural communication*, pages 17–35, Tübingen, Germany. Gűnter Narr.

Yulia Grishina. 2017. Combining the Output of Two Coreference Resolution Systems for Two Source Languages to Improve Annotation Projection. In *Proceedings of the Third Workshop on Discourse in Machine Translation*, pages 67–72, Copenhagen, Denmark. Association for Computational Linguistics.

Yulia Grishina and Manfred Stede. 2015. Knowledge-Lean Projection of Coreference Chains across Languages. In *Proceedings of the Eighth Workshop on Building and Using Comparable Corpora*, pages 14–22, Beijing, China. Association for Computational Linguistics.

Yulia Grishina and Manfred Stede. 2017. Multi-Source Annotation Projection of Coreference Chains: Assessing Strategies and Testing Opportunities. In *Proceedings of the 2nd Workshop on Coreference Resolution Beyond OntoNotes (CORBON 2017)*, pages 41–50, Valencia, Spain. Association for Computational Linguistics.

Jan Hajič, Eva Hajičová, Jarmila Panevová, Petr Sgall, Ondřej Bojar, Silvie Cinková, Eva Fučíková, Marie Mikulová, Petr Pajas, Jan Popelka, Jiří Semecký, Jana Šindlerová, Jan Štěpánek, Josef Toman, Zdeňka Urešová, and Zdeněk Žabokrtský. 2012. Announcing Prague Czech-English Dependency Treebank 2.0. In *Proceedings of the 8th International Conference on Language Resources and Evaluation (LREC 2012)*, Istanbul, Turkey. European Language Resources Association.

Rebecca Hwa, Philip Resnik, Amy Weinberg, Clara Cabezas, and Okan Kolak. 2005. Bootstrapping Parsers via Syntactic Projection Across Parallel Texts. *Natural Language Engineering*, 11(3):311–325.

Mitchell Marcus, Beatrice Santorini, Mary Ann Marcinkiewicz, and Ann Taylor. 1999. Penn Treebank 3.

André F. T. Martins. 2015. Transferring Coreference Resolvers with Posterior Regularization. In *Proceedings of the 53rd Annual Meeting of the Association for Computational Linguistics and the 7th International Joint Conference on Natural Language Processing of the Asian Federation of Natural Language Processing, ACL 2015, Volume 1: Long Papers*, pages 1427–1437, Stroudsburg, PA, USA. Association for Computational Linguistics.

Anna Nedoluzhko, Michal Novák, Silvie Cinková, Marie Mikulová, and Jiří Mírovský. 2016. Coreference in Prague Czech-English Dependency Treebank. In *Proceedings of the 10th International Conference on Language Resources and Evaluation (LREC 2016)*, pages 169–176, Paris, France. European Language Resources Association.

Michal Novák and Anna Nedoluzhko. 2015. Correspondences between Czech and English Coreferential Expressions. *Discours: Revue de linguistique, psycholinguistique et informatique.*, 16:1–41.

Michal Novák, Anna Nedoluzhko, and Zdeněk Žabokrtský. 2017. Projection-based Coreference Resolution Using Deep Syntax. In *Proceedings of the 2nd Workshop on Coreference Resolution Beyond OntoNotes (CORBON 2017)*, pages 56–64, Stroudsburg, PA, USA. Association for Computational Linguistics.

Michal Novák and Zdeněk Žabokrtský. 2014. Cross-lingual Coreference Resolution of Pronouns. In *Proceedings of COLING 2014, the 25th International Conference on Computational Linguistics: Technical Papers*, Dublin, Ireland. Dublin City University and Association for Computational Linguistics.

Franz J. Och and Hermann Ney. 2000. Improved Statistical Alignment Models. In *Proceedings of the 38th Annual Meeting on Association for Computational Linguistics*, pages 440–447, Stroudsburg, PA, USA. Association for Computational Linguistics.

Maciej Ogrodniczuk. 2013. Translation- and Projection-Based Unsupervised Coreference Resolution for Polish. In *Language Processing and Intelligent Information Systems*, 7912, pages 125–130, Berlin / Heidelberg. Springer.

Sebastian Padó and Mirella Lapata. 2009. Cross-lingual Annotation Projection of Semantic Roles. *Journal of Artificial Intelligence Research*, 36(1):307–340.

Oana Postolache, Dan Cristea, and Constantin Orăsan. 2006. Transferring Coreference Chains through Word Alignment. In *Proceedings of the Fifth International Conference on Language Resources and Evaluation*, pages 889–892, Genoa, Italy. European Language Resources Association.

Altaf Rahman and Vincent Ng. 2012. Translation-based Projection for Multilingual Coreference Resolution. In *Proceedings of the 2012 Conference of the North American Chapter of the Association for Computational Linguistics: Human Language Technologies*, pages 968–977, Stroudsburg, PA, USA. Association for Computational Linguistics.

Petr Sgall, Eva Hajičová, and Jarmila Panevová. 1986. *The Meaning of the Sentence in Its Semantic and Pragmatic Aspects*. D. Reidel Publishing Company, Dordrecht, Netherlands.

José G. C. de Souza and Constantin Orăsan. 2011. Can Projected Chains in Parallel Corpora Help Coreference Resolution? In *Proceedings of the 8th International Conference on Anaphora Processing and Applications*, pages 59–69, Berlin, Heidelberg. Springer-Verlag.

Oscar Täckström, Dipanjan Das, Slav Petrov, Ryan T. McDonald, and Joakim Nivre. 2013. Token and Type Constraints for Cross-Lingual Part-of-Speech Tagging. *TACL*, 1:1–12.

Don Tuggener. 2014. Coreference Resolution Evaluation for Higher Level Applications. In *Proceedings of the 14th Conference of the European Chapter of the Association for Computational Linguistics, EACL 2014*, pages 231–235. The Association for Computer Linguistics.

Marc Vilain, John Burger, John Aberdeen, Dennis Connolly, and Lynette Hirschman. 1995. A Model-theoretic Coreference Scoring Scheme. In *Proceedings of the 6th Conference on Message Understanding*, pages 45–52, Stroudsburg, PA, USA. Association for Computational Linguistics.

Alexander Wallin and Pierre Nugues. 2017. Coreference Resolution for Swedish and German using Distant Supervision. In *Proceedings of the 21st Nordic Conference on Computational Linguistics*, pages 46–55, Gothenburg, Sweden. Association for Computational Linguistics.

Modeling Brain Activity Associated with Pronoun Resolution in English and Chinese

Jixing Li
Department of Linguistics
Cornell University
jl2939@cornell.edu

Murielle Fabre
Department of Linguistics
Cornell University
mf684@cornell.edu

Wen-Ming Luh
Cornell MRI Facility
Cornell University
wl358@cornell.edu

John Hale
Department of Linguistics
Cornell University
jthale@cornell.edu

Abstract

Typological differences between English and Chinese suggest stronger reliance on salience of the antecedent during pronoun resolution in Chinese. We examined this hypothesis by correlating a difficulty measure of pronoun resolution derived by the activation-based ACT-R model with the brain activity of English and Chinese participants listening to a same audiobook during fMRI recording. The ACT-R model predicts higher overall difficulty for English speakers, which is supported at the brain level in left Broca's area. More generally, it confirms that computational modeling approach is able to dissociate different dimensions that are involved in the complex process of pronoun resolution in the brain.

1 Introduction

Pronoun resolution has been suggested to be influenced by morpho-syntactic constraints such as gender/number/person agreement, and discourse factors such as salience of the antecedents (e.g., Grosz et al., 1995, for empircical evidence using eye tracking see Arnold, 2000). Yet, unlike English, Chinese pronouns in their spoken form lack morphosyntactic marking and can even be omitted. This leads to a general hypothesis that Chinese speakers may rely more on salience of the antecedent during pronoun resolution compared to English speakers, who have additional morphosyntactic cues to help resolve the referents.

The Adaptive Control of Thought-Rational (ACT-R) model of pronoun resolution (van Rij et al., 2013) offers a way to test this hypothesis. Built within the cognitive architecture of ACT-R (Anderson, 2007), this model represents pronoun resolution as the selection of a most-activated mention from a ranked list of candidates stored in declarative memory. As such, this model calculates the activation level for each mention and selects the most activated one as the antecedent. Given our hypothesis that Chinese has stronger reliance on salience of the antecedent during pronoun resolution in abscence of morphosyntactic cues for agreement, we predict that antecedents in Chinese have higher overall activation level than antecedents in English.

We compared the mean ACT-R activation level for each pronoun's antecedent in a same audiobook in English and Chinese translation, and confirmed higher activation level for antecedents in Chinese. We then took the negative of the antecedents' activation levels to represent "effort" during pronoun resolution, and correlated this difficulty measure with brain activity while both English and Chinese participants listened to the pronouns present in an audiobook during fMRI recoding. The results revealed different left-lateralized ACT-R difficulty effects for English and Chinese. Chinese specifically activates the Angular Gyrus where non-grammatical gender information processing was observed (Hammer et al., 2007), while English ACT-R effect encompasses left Broca's area.

This study builds upon the salience-based account of pronoun resolution, which has long been recognized both in computational linguistics (Kantor, 1977; Alshawi, 1987; Brennan et al., 1987; Lappin and Leass, 1994) and in psychology (Grosz et al., 1995; Gordon et al., 1993; Greene et al., 1992; Arnold, 2010; McElree, 2001). Our key contribution is in demonstrating different brain activation maps associated with measures of the ACT-R model in English and Chinese, suggesting that different factors are operative in the system of pronoun resolution in different languages.

In the following sections, we briefly review the typological differences linked to pronominal reference in English and Chinese, and describe the

Proceedings of the Workshop on Computational Models of Reference, Anaphora and Coreference, pages 87–96
New Orleans, Louisiana, June 6, 2018. ©2018 Association for Computational Linguistics

algorithm of the ACT-R model. We, then compare the model performance on our English and Chinese audiobook texts, and present the methods, results and discussion of the English and Chinese fMRI experiments.

2 English and Chinese Typological Differences in Pronominal Reference

In English, pronouns cannot be omitted in the subject or object position of a tensed clause, even though the referent of the omitted pronoun remains clear.On the contrary, Chinese can have null pronouns in subject or object position in tensed clauses under appropriate contextual licencing (see (1) and (2), data from Huang (1989)). This phenomenon is called *pro*-drop in generative syntax and has been considered a typological parameter that distinguishes *topic-prominent* languages like Chinese and *subject-prominent* languages like English (Li and Thompson, 1976; Xu, 2006).

(1) Speaker A: Did John see Bill yesterday?
    Speaker B: a. Yes, he saw him.
              b. *Yes, *e* saw him.
              c. *Yes, he saw *e*.
              d. *Yes, *e* saw *e*.
              e. *Yes, I guess *e* saw *e*.
              f. *Yes, John said *e* saw *e*.

(2) Speaker A: Zhangsan kanjian Lisi le ma?
                     Zhangsan see Lisi LE Q?
                     "Did Zhangsan see Lisi?"
    Speaker B: a. Ta kanjian ta le.
                  He see he LE.
                  "He saw him."
              b. *e* kanjian ta le.
                  "[He] saw him."
              c. Ta kanjian *e* le.
                  "He saw [him]."
              d. *e* kanjian *e* le.
                  "[He] saw [him]."
              e. Wo cai *e* kanjian *e* le.
                  I guess see LE.
                  "I guess [he] saw [him]."
              f. Zhangsan shuo *e* kanjian *e* le.
                  Zhangsan say see LE.
                   "Zhangsan said that [he] saw [him]."

Moreover, the spoken form of Chinese pronouns do not mark gender information. Therefore, Chinese pronouns in general provide fewer morpho-syntactic cues than English pronouns. This may additionally lead Chinese speakers to rely more on discourse information than English speakers when resolving the referencial linking of pronouns.

3 ACT-R Model for Pronoun Resolution

3.1 Salience-Based Account of Pronoun Resolution

According to the salience-based account on pronoun resolution, the antecedent of the pronoun is a highly prominent entity in the discourse context. The Centering Theory (Grosz et al., 1995), for example, refers to entities that link an utterance to another utterance as "centers". Each utterance (U) has a set of forward-looking centers (C_f(U); i.e., potential antecedents) and a single backward-looking center (C_b(U); i.e., the anaphoric expression). The backward-looking center of utterance U_{n+1} connects with one of the forward-looking center of utterance U_n. The elements of C_f are ordered to reflect their relative prominence in U_n, and the most highly ranked C_f is the C_b of U_{n+1}. The ranking of C_f is mainly determined by its grammatical role in U_n: SUBJECT > OBJECT > OTHERS. Thus the subject of the previous sentence is more likely to be the antecedent of the pronoun in the next sentence.

The Centering Theory has been tested by Gordon et al. (1993) in a number of self-paced reading experiments. They introduced a prominent entity (C_b) and a less prominent entity in a short passage and found that reading time significantly increased when the prominent entity is not pronominalized but repeated. They also showed the repeated-name penalty for C_b only in the grammatical subject position, confirmed the basic notion in the Centering Theory that there is only one C_b in an utterance, and that grammatical subject ranks the highest among the C_fs.

Arnold (2010) prosed a similar salience-based account for pronominalization. She referred to salience of the entity as "accessibility" and suggested that the more accessible entities tend to be pronominalized (see evidence from oral corpus analysis by Arnold et al. 2009). The accessibility of an entity is influenced by whether the entity has been mentioned before, how recent the entity occurs, and whether the entity is syntactically or thematically prominent. McElree (2001), from a memory decay point of view, also suggested that recency, together with frequency, i.e, how many times the entity occurs, contribute to the salience of the entity in the discourse context.

Based on the notion of salience, Greene et al. (1992) proposed a framework for pronouns resolution in which a pronoun is matched automatically against all the entities in the discourse model. The degree of match is determined by the accessibility of the entity, as well as the gender/number features. The entity is automatically identified as the antecedent of the pronoun if its degree of match to the pronoun is better than the match for other entities. If no match or more than one match is identified, the selection process is postponed for more discourse information, or strategic problem-solving can be attempted.

3.2 Salience-Based Computational Models for Pronoun Resolution

One early influential pronoun resolution model based on the Centering Theory is proposed by Brennan et al. (1987; henceforth BFP). The BFP algorithm computes the preferred antecedents from relations that hold between the forward and backward looking centers in adjacent sentences. The algorithm first generates all possible $C_b - C_f$ pairs for the pronoun in Utterance U_n. It then filters all pairs by constraints such as the Binding Theory (Chomsky, 1982) and Centering rules, For example, if C_b must be pronominalized if any C_f is pronominalized; C_b is the highest ranked elements in the list of C_fs, etc. Finally, the algorithm ranks the remaining pairs by transition orderings, where maintaining the same C_b (Continue) is preferred over maintaining the same C_b in U_{n+1} but not in U_{n+2} (Retain), which is preferred to changing C_b in U_{n+1} (Shift). The selected $C_b - C_f$ pair is the most preferred relation according to the transition order.

Another influential salience-based model for pronoun resolution is the RAP algorithm proposed by Lappin and Leass (1994). Unlike the BFP algorithm that compares a discrete number of centers, the RAP algorithm assumes a graded activation level for each entities. It also follows a generate-filter-rank procedure and takes as input the output of a full parser and filters entities according to binding constraints and gender/number agreement. It then assigns a salience weight to each entity depending on its recency, syntactic position, grammatical role, etc. The weights are halved for each sentence boundary in between the entity and the pronoun, and weights for all occurrence of the same entity are summed. The entity that receives the highest salience weight is the antecedent of the pronoun.

Both the BFP and the RAP algorithms incorporate claims from the Centering Theory, as well as binding constraints and gender/number agreements. The RAP algorithm is similar to the ACT-R model in that they both assume salience on a graded scale and compute the activation level for each entity. However, the ACT-R model for pronoun resolution is adapted from the cognitive architecture of ACT-R (Anderson, 2007), which is both a computational model and a theory of how different components of the mind worked to produce coherent cognition. ACT-R consists a set of modules, and the ACT-R model for pronoun resolution is adapted from its declarative module for retrieving information from memory. The elements in the ACT-R model for pronoun resolution include only the recency, frequency and grammatical role of the entity, with no syntactic and gender/number information. The following sections describes the formula of the ACT-R model in detail.

3.3 The ACT-R Model for Pronoun Resolution

Built within the cognitive architecture of ACT-R (Anderson, 2007), van Rij et al. (2013) proposed an ACT-R model of pronoun resolution which integrates the major factors that influences the salience of the antecedents – frequency, recency, and the grammatical role of the antecedent. The formula of for the activation level for the antecedent i of a pronoun is

$$A_i = ln(\sum_{k=1}^{n} t_k^{-0.5}) + \sum_j^m W_j \times 2$$

where the base-level activation $ln(\sum_{k=1}^{n} t_k^{-0.5})$ represents frequency and recency of each mention k of the antecedent i, and the associative activation $\sum_j^m W_j \times 2$ represents the influence of grammatical role of each mention k. If mention j is a subject, it has a weight (W) of 1; which is divided by the total number of mentions of this antecedent n ($W_j = W/n$), as the total value of associative activation cannot be infinite. W_j is then multiplied by 2, the default value of associative strength in ACT-R (see Anderson, 2007, p.110 for the ACT-R equations).

The effects of frequency and recency is folded into the calculation of the base activation for antecedent i, such that the more mentions it has, and the more recent the mentions occur, the higher the base activation. Conversely, if antecedent i has been mentioned only once, or if its last mention was a long time ago, its activation level will be low, and it will rank lower on the activation list for all the candidates antecedents. The subjecthood of the mentions of antecedent i gains a spreading activation in addition to the base activation. Overall, the amount of activation value of an antecedent is computed in an attempt to "abstract the impact of neural Hebbian-like learning and spread of activation among neurons" (Anderson, 2007, p.35).

To give a concrete example of how the activation level for each antecedent is calculated, in the English sentences in Figure 1, the immediate antecedent of the pronoun "they$_{16}$" is "they$_{15}$". The previous mentions of "they$_{15}$" are "their$_{13}$", "boa constrictors$_{12}$" and "boa constrictors$_8$". The time elapsed from these three previous mentions to "they$_{15}$" in the audio are 11.13 s, 3.68 s and 3.02 s respectively. Since "boa constrictor$_{12}$" is a subject of a subordinate clause, it gets an associative weighting W of 1. Therefore, the activation level for the antecedent of "they$_{15}$" is calculated as:

$$A_{they_{15}} = ln(11.13^{-0.5} + 3.68^{-0.5} + 3.02^{-0.5}) + 0/3 \times 2 + 1/3 \times 2 + 0/3 \times 2$$
$$\approx ln(0.3 + 0.52 + 0.58) + 0.67$$
$$\approx 1.01$$

Similarly, for the Chinese sentence in Figure 1, the antecedent of the last pronoun "它们$_{13}$ (tamen)" is "它们$_{11}$", and the the previous mentions of "它们$_{13}$" are "蟒蛇$_7$($mangshe$)" and "蟒蛇$_{10}$". The time elapsed from them to "它们$_{13}$" in the audio are 7.94s and 0.44 s, respectively. Therefore, its activation level is calculated as:

$$A_{它们_{11}} = ln(7.94^{-0.5} + 0.44^{-0.5}) + 1/2 \times 2 + 1/2 \times 2$$
$$\approx ln(1.51 + 0.35) + 2$$
$$\approx 2.62$$

4 Current Study

Given the typological difference of pronouns in English and Chinese, it is hypothesized that Chinese speakers rely more on salience of the antecedent to resolve pronouns as they do not have additional morpho-syntactic cues. The current study first tests this hypothesis by comparing the activation level of the antecedent for each pronoun in a same audiobook *The Little Prince* in English and Chinese translation. Our prediction is that antecedents in Chinese have higher overall activation levels than antecedents in English.

To explain how the theoretical predictions and the model performance are specifically brought to bear on brain activity, we further correlated the negative of the activation levels of the antecedents with fMRI time-courses when both English and Chinese participants listened to the pronouns in the audiobook in the scanner. We took the negative of the activation level to indicate difficulty during pronoun resolution: that lower the activation level of the antecedent, the more difficulty to successfully retrieve the antecedents, hence higher hemodynamic response.

Based on the elements in the ACT-R formula, we expected the difficulty of pronoun resolution modeled by activation spread to tease apart the brain areas whose activity is influenced by the frequency, recency and the grammatical role of the antecedent, and to highlight regions where the effort of pronoun resolution is stronger in English and Chinese respectively.

Previous neuroimgaing results on pronoun resolution have implicated the bilateral Inferior Frontal Gyrus (IFG), the left Medial Frontal Gyrus (MFG) and the bilateral Supramarginal/Angular Gyrus in gender mismatch between pronoun and antecedent (Hammer et al., 2007). We therefore expect associated activity in these regions for the ACT-R model of pronoun resolution. We also expect to see activity in the bilateral Superior Temporal Gyrus (STG) as they have been associated with long distance pronoun-antecedent linking (Matchin et al., 2014). The Precuneus cortex activity may also be activated as it has been suggested to track different sorts of story characters (Wehbe et al., 2014).

5 Model Performance on Text Data

Based on van Rij et al.'s (2013) formula, we calculated the activation level for each previously mentioned entities for each pronoun in the English and Chinese audiobook of Antoine de Saint-Exupéry's *The Little Prince*. Within the English audiobook text, 1755 pronouns (excluding possessives, reflexives and dummy pronoun "it") and 3127 nonpronominal entities (4882 mentions in total) are identified. Pronouns with sentential antecedents are removed. For example, in the conversation "That is funny where you live a day only last a minute." "It is not funny at all." "it" in the second sentence is removed from our pronoun set as it refers to the whole sentence "where you live a day

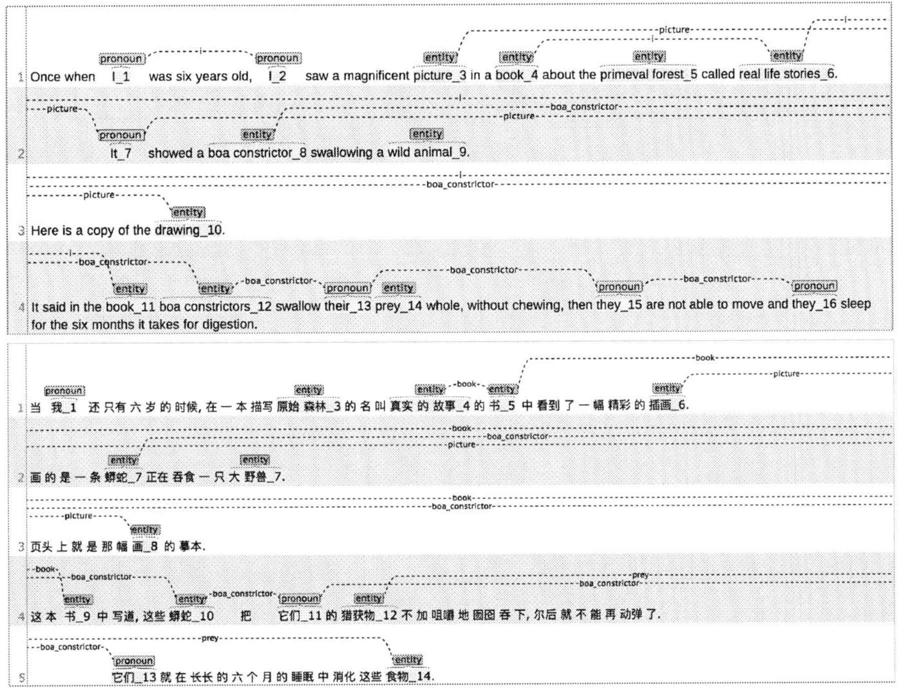

Figure 1: Sample annotations of pronouns and non-pronoun mentions in English and Chinese, visualized using the annotation tool brat (Stenetorp et al., 2012).

only last a minute". The resulting English data-set contains 645 1st person pronouns, 302 2nd person pronouns and 675 3rd person pronouns (see Table 1).

The Chinese audiobook text contains 1785 pronouns (excluding possessives and reflexives) and 2947 non-pronominal mentions (4732 mentions in total). We further pruned the pronoun set to exclude possessives, reflexives, and pronouns with sentential antecedents. Comparably to the English pronoun set, the resulting Chinese pronoun set contains 639 1st person pronouns, 298 2nd person pronouns and 529 3rd person pronouns (see Table 1). All pronouns and non-pronominal mentions in the English and Chinese texts were annotated using the annotation tool brat (Stenetorp et al., 2012; see Figure 1).

To evaluate the performance of the ACT-R model of pronoun resolution for the English and Chinese text, we ranked all the candidate antecedents for each pronoun according to their activation levels, such that the most activated antecedent has a rank of 1. We allow a certain level of ambiguity for cases where more than one antecedents can be linked to the pronoun, and decide that if the rank of the correct antecedent is

	English		Chinese		
1st	i	me	我(wo)		
	505	121	621		
	we	us	我们(women)		
	16	3	18		
2nd	you		你(ni)		
	302		261		
			你们(nimen)		
			37		
3rd	she	her	她(ta)		
	41	14	62		
	he	him	他(ta)		
	268	64	303		
	it		它(ta)		
	136		73		
	they	them	她们(tamen)	他们(tamen)	它们(tamen)
	94	58	2	74	15

Table 1: Attestations of each pronoun type in the English and Chinese texts. Note that Chinese 3rd person pronouns are homophones.

less or equal to 3 (top 3 on the ranking list), then the model is correct in predicting the antecedent for the pronoun.

Table 2 shows the accuracy of the model for each pronoun type in English and Chinese. As predicted, the model has higher overall accuracy for pronoun resolution in Chinese than in English. A further division of 1st, 2nd and 3rd person pronouns reveals a 78% accuracy for 1st person pronouns in both English and Chinese, yet 2nd and 3rd person pronouns in Chinese has $\sim$ 8% higher accuracy than 2nd and 3rd person pronouns in English.

	Pronoun Type	Accuracy (%)
English	1st person	0.78
	2nd person	0.62
	3rd person	**0.54**
	all pronoun	0.66
Chinese	1st person	0.78
	2nd person	0.71
	3rd person	**0.62**
	all pronoun	0.71

Table 2: *Accuracy of ACT-R model on pronoun resolution in English and Chinese.*

Direct comparison of the activation levels of the antecedents in the two groups by a two-sample t-test confirmed that the activation level for Chinese antecedents (M=3.07, SD=1.52) is significantly higher than that for English antecedents (M=2.86, SD=1.64; $t(3097) = 3.4$, $p < 0.001$). Taken together, the model performance suggests that salience-based pronoun resolution predicts antecedents better in Chinese than in English, confirming our hypothesis about the strong reliance of Chinese on discourse salience compared to English speakers.

6 Correlating ACT-R Measures with Brain Activity

6.1 Participants

English participants were 49 healthy, right-handed, young adults (30 female, mean age = 21.3, range = 18-37). They self-identified as native English speakers, and had no history of psychiatric, neurological or other medical illness that could compromise cognitive functions. All participants were paid for, and gave written informed consent prior to participation, in accordance with the guidelines of the Human Research Participant Protection Program at Cornell University.

Chinese participants were 35 healthy, right-handed, young adults (15 female, mean age=19.3, range = 18-25). They self-identified as native Chinese speakers, and had no history of psychiatric, neurological or other medical illness that could compromise cognitive functions. All participants were paid for, and gave written informed consent prior to participation, in accordance with the guidelines of the Ethics Committee at Jiangsu Normal University.

6.2 Stimuli

The English audio stimulus was an audiobook version of Antoine de Saint-Exupéry's *The Little Prince*, translated by David Wilkinson and read by Nadine Eckert-Boulet. This text contains 3127 non-pronominal mentions and 645 1st person pronouns, 302 2nd person pronouns and 675 3rd person pronouns (see Table 1).

The Chinese audio stimulus was a Chinese web version of *The Little Prince* [1], read by a professional female Chinese broadcaster. Within this text, 2947 non-pronominal mentions and 639 1st person pronouns, 298 2nd person pronouns and 529 3rd person pronouns are identified (see Table 1). The offset time of the pronouns and the non-pronominal mentions in the English and Chinese audiobook are marked as 1 and are entered as binary regressors into our GLM analysis.

6.3 Procedure

After giving their informed consent, participants were familiarized with the MRI facility and assumed a supine position on the scanner. The presentation script was written in PsychoPy (Peirce, 2007). Auditory stimuli were delivered through MRI-safe, high-fidelity headphones (English: Confon HP-VS01, MR Confon, Magdeburg, Germany; Chinese: Ear Bud Headset, Resonance Technology, Inc, California, USA) inside the head coil. The headphones were secured against the plastic frame of the coil using foam blocks. An experimenter increased the sound volume stepwise until the participants could hear clearly.

The English and Chinese audiobooks last for about 94 and 99 minutes, respectively. They were both divided into nine sections, each lasts for about ten minutes. Participants then listened passively to the nine sections and completed four quiz questions after each section (36 questions in total). These questions were used to confirm their comprehension and were viewed by the participants via a mirror attached to the head coil and they answered through a button box. The entire session lasted around 2.5 hours.

---

[1] http://www.xiaowangzi.org

6.4 MRI Data Collection and Preprocessing

Both English and Chinese brain imaging data were acquired with a 3T MRI GE Discovery MR750 scanner with a 32-channel head coil. Anatomical scans were acquired using a T1-weighted volumetric Magnetization Prepared RApid Gradient-Echo (MP-RAGE) pulse sequence. Blood-oxygen-level-dependent (BOLD) functional scans were acquired using a multi-echo planar imaging (ME-EPI) sequence with online reconstruction (TR=2000 ms; TE's=12.8, 27.5, 43 ms; FA=77°; matrix size=72 x 72; FOV=240.0 mm x 240.0 mm; 2 x image acceleration; 33 axial slices, voxel size=3.75 x 3.75 x 3.8 mm). Cushions and clamps were used to minimize head movement during scanning.

All fMRI data is preprocessed using AFNI version 16 (Cox, 1996). The first 4 volumes in each run were excluded from analyses to allow for T1-equilibration effects. Multi-echo independent components analysis (ME-ICA; Kundu et al.,2012) were used to denoise data for motion, physiology and scanner artifacts. Images were then spatially normalized to the standard space of the Montreal Neurological Institute (MNI) atlas, yielding a volumetric time series resampled at 2 mm cubic voxels.

6.5 Statistical Analysis

At the single subject level, the observed BOLD time course in each voxel were modeled by the difficulty of pronoun resolution derived by the ACT-R model for each 1st, 2nd and 3rd person pronoun time-locked at the offset of each pronoun in the audiobook. We also include a binary regressor for non-pronominal mentions time-locked at the its offset.

To further examine the status of ACT-R activation as a cognitive model for pronoun resolution, We did a second GLM analysis where we correlated only the binary regressors time-locked at the offset of each 1st, 2nd, 3rd person pronoun and each non-pronominal mention in the audiobook.

These two analyses both included three control variables of non-theoretical interest: *RMS intensity* at every 10 ms of the audio; *word rate* at the offset of each spoken word in time; *frequency* of the individual words in Google Book unigrams [2]. These regressors were added to ensure that any conclusions about pronoun resolution would be

specific to those processes, as opposed to more general aspects of speech perception.

At the group level, for each group, the activation maps for the ACT-R activation regressors and the binary regressors for 3rd person pronouns were computed using one sample t-test. The voxelwise threshold was set at $p \leq 0.05\ FWE$, with an extent threshold of 50 contiguous voxels ($k \geq 50$). Contrasts of the activation maps between the two groups were examined by a factorial design matrix, and statistical threshold was also set at $p \leq 0.05\ FWE$. The GLM analysis was performed using SPM12 (Penny et al., 2011).

We only focused on the results of 3rd person pronouns because they provide gender information in English but not Chinese, which points to potentially different brain activation maps. In addition, 3rd person pronouns have been suggested to differ from 1st and 2nd person pronouns in that 1st and 2nd person pronouns mark proximity in space and 3rd person pronouns are further away (Ariel, 1990).

7 fMRI Results

For English speakers, the largest clusters for 3rd person pronouns, which represents brain activity associated with the presence 3rd person pronouns were observed in the right Temporal Pole, and the left Middle Temporal Gyrus (MTG). For Chinese speakers, the presence of 3rd person pronouns is associated with increased activity in the left Middle Temporal Gyrus (MTG; $p < 0.001\ FWE$; see Figure 2a and Figure 2b). Direct comparison of the contrast maps between the English and Chinese group suggests stronger activity in the right Angular Gyrus, the right MTG and the right Precuneus for English speakers and stronger activity in the left Angular Fyrus for Chinese speakers ($p < 0.05\ FWE$).

Brain regions showing an increased activation for pronouns with higher processing difficulty predicted by our ACT-R measure (i.e., the negative of ACT-R activation level) include the left MTG and the left IFG and the left Superior Frontal Gyrus (SFG) for English speakers ($p < 0.001\ FWE$; see Figure 2c), whereas Chinese speakers has peak clusters in the left Angular Gyrus, the left SFG and the left MTG ($p < 0.05\ FWE$; see Figure 2d)).

The difference between the ACT-R difficulty measure for 3rd person pronoun resolution in Chinese and English is confirmed by the direct com-

---

[2] http://books.google.com/ngrams

parison reported in Table 3c ($p < 0.05\ FWE$). Although the cluster size is relatively small at the corrected threshold, Chinese ACT-R effect significantly differs form English in the Angular Gyrus, and English ACT-R effect shows a more right lateralized activation of the language network involving the Precuneus cortex. Table 3b lists of all the significant clusters using region names from the Harvard-Oxford Cortical Structure Atlas.

8 Discussion

ACT-R activation levels for 3rd person pronouns in Chinese are significantly higher than that in English (see Section 5), demonstrating as predicted a stronger reliance of Chinese on salience compared to English. It also relates to the rich linguistic literature on Chinese as a discourse-oriented language (Xu, 2006). When used as a regressor against hemodynamic responses to naturalistic text, ACT-R activation level reveals different left-lateralized activation patterns in English and Chinese, supporting different model performance on pronoun resolution in the two languages (cf. Table 2)

Only English shows a significant increased activation in the left Broca's area pars Triangularis, which has been recurrently reported as correlating with syntactic processing cost linked to antecedent pronoun (Santi and Grodzinsky, 2012), and particularly to the distance between the antecedent and the pronoun (Matchin et al., 2014; Santi and Grodzinsky, 2007).

Chinese, on the other hand, shows greater activation in the Angular Gyrus for the ACT-R difficulty measure compared to English. Notably, previous literature on German gender agreement in anaphoric reference reported increased activation in the Angular Gyrus (BA 39) for incongruent biological gender matching (Hammer et al., 2007). One interpretation of the result, therefore, is that the ACT-R model predicts processing effort when the antecedent is not salient or when there are equally salient competitors. In these cases, only English speakers could use morpho-syntactic cues such as gender to identify the correct antecedent, whereas Chinese speakers might have to work extra hard to accomplish gender matching using the discourse information.

The difference between the brain areas highlighted by the Chinese and English ACT-R results, is confirmed by the simpler GLM analysis that correlated brain activity with only the presence of pronouns in the text (cf. GLM Analysis 2 in Section 6.5). Whole-brain pronouns effects were observed with a temporally distributed response patterns (for backward anaphora see Matchin et al.; for intra-sentential co-referential link see Fabre), with the additional involvement of the right Broca's area for English.

In sum, this study highlighted brain areas involved in the discourse and syntactic dimension of pronoun-antecedent linking as modeled in the ACT-R activation level of pronoun resolution.

9 Conclusion

ACT-R activation levels of antecedents suggest interesting differences between the two languages, English appears to have significantly lower ACT-R activation levels, hence higher difficulty for salience-based pronoun resolution. This difficulty, as suggested in the fMRI results of the present study, is associated with activity in the left Broca's area.

Although the ACT-R model accuracy was higher for Chinese, the difficulty measure of pronoun resolution yields a greater activation in an area where non-grammatical gender information is processed. This suggests that the salience-based pronoun resolution model is more effortful when no gender information is encoded in the language.

The current study only compares pronoun resolution in speech, thus the conclusion may not hold for reading comprehension where pronouns with different gender have different forms in Chinese as well. Future directions may include comparing brain activity during pronoun resolution in both reading and listening comprehension. Overall, these results show that crossing computational approach and naturalistic ecologically valid linguistic stimuli to tease apart strongly interwoven cognitive processes is a promising perspective in neuroimaging. As such, they pave the way for increasing cross-fertilization between computational linguistics and the cognitive neuroscience of language.

10 Acknowledgments

This material is supported by Jeffrey Sean Lehman Fund for Scholarly Exchange with China, and is based upon work supported by the National Science Foundation under Grant No.1607441.

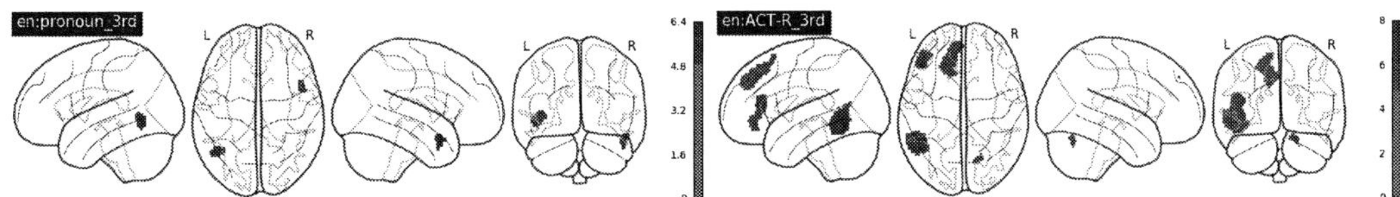

(a) T-score map for the binary 3rd person pronoun effect in English

(c) T-score map for the ACT-R difficulty measure for 3rd person pronouns in English

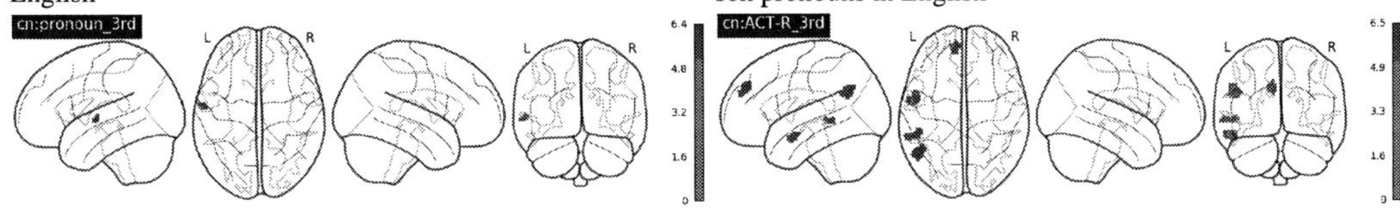

(b) T-score map for the binary 3rd person pronoun effect in Chinese

(d) T-score map for the ACT-R difficulty measure for 3rd person pronouns in Chinese

Figure 2: Whole-brain effect with significant clusters for (a) binary 3rd person pronouns effect in English, (b) binary 3rd person pronouns effect in Chinese, (c) ACT-R difficulty measure for 3rd person pronoun resolution in English and (d) ACT-R difficulty measure for 3rd person pronoun resolution in Chinese. All images underwent *FWE* voxel correction for multiple comparisons with $p < 0.05$.

3rd person pronoun effect	MNI coordinates			Region	p-value	k-size	t-score
	x	y	z		*FWE-corr*	*cluster*	*peak*
English	50	12	-26	right Temporal Pole	0.001	101	6.4
3rd pronoun	-46	-60	-8	left Inferior/Middle Temporal Gyrus	0.001	194	6.34
Chinese	-60	-10	0	left Superior//Middle Temporal Gyrus	0.003	57	6.36
3rd pronoun							

(a) Significantly activated clusters by the binary 3rd person pronoun effect in English and Chinese ($p < 0.05$ *FWE*)

ACT-R difficulty measure	MNI coordinates			Region	p-value	k-size	t-score
	x	y	z		*FWE-corr*	*cluster*	*peak*
English	-52	-58	-10	left Middle Temporal Gyrus	< 0.001	1074	7.96
ACT-R 3rd pronoun	-48	34	14	left Inferior Frontal Gyrus	< 0.001	494	7.20
	-12	40	40	left Superior Frontal Gyrus	0.001	724	6.36
	18	-68	-26	right Cerebellum	0.009	61	5.53
Chinese	-54	-62	28	left Angular Gyrus	0.002	217	6.51
ACT-R 3rd pronoun	-8	52	30	left Superior Frontal Gyrus	0.002	150	6.50
	-58	-4	-18	left anterior Middle Temporal Gyrus	0.006	167	4.95
	-50	-42	-4	left posterior Middle Temporal Gyrus	0.007	117	4.90

(b) Significantly activated clusters by the ACT-R difficulty measure for 3rd person pronouns in English and Chinese ($p < 0.05$ *FWE*)

Comparison of ACT-R difficulty measure	MNI coordinates			Region	p-value	k-size	t-score
	x	y	z		*FWE-corr*	*cluster*	*peak*
English > Chinese	4	-40	44	right Precuneus Cortex	0.008	55	5.23
ACT-R 3rd	68	-46	10	right Middle Temproal Gyrus	0.01	27	5.19
	64	-48	24	right Angular Gyrus	0.015	70	5.07
Chinese > English	-52	-62	28	left Angular Gyrus	0.033	6	4.82
ACT-R 3rd pronoun							

(c) Contrast between the ACT-R difficulty measure for 3rd person pronouns in English versus Chinese ($p < 0.05$ *FWE*)

Table 3: Significant clusters of BOLD activation for (a) 3rd person pronouns, (b) ACT-R difficulty measure on 3rd person pronoun in English and Chinese and (c) their contrast after FWE voxel correction for multiple comparisons with $p < 0.05$. Peak activations are given in MNI Coordinates.

References

Hiyan Alshawi. 1987. *Memory and context for language interpretation*. Cambridge University Press.

John R Anderson. 2007. *How can the human mind occur in the physical universe?* Oxford University Press, Oxford.

M. Ariel. 1990. *Accessing noun-phrase antecedents*. Routledge, London, UK.

Jennifer E. Arnold. 2010. How speakers refer: The role of accessibility. *Language and Linguistics Compass*, 4(4):187–203.

Susan E. Brennan, Marilyn W. Friedman, and Carl J. Pollard. 1987. A centering approach to pronouns. In *Proceedings of the 25th annual meeting on Association for Computational Linguistics*, pages 155–162. Association for Computational Linguistics.

Noam Chomsky. 1982. *Some concepts and consequences of the theory of government and binding*. MIT Press, Cambridge, Mass.

R. W. Cox. 1996. AFNI: software for analysis and visualization of functional magnetic resonance neuroimages. *Computers and Biomedical Research, an International Journal*, 29(3):162–173.

Murielle Fabre. 2017. *The sentence as cognitive object - The neural underpinnings of syntactic complexity in Chinese and French*. Ph.D. thesis, INALCO Paris.

P. C. Gordon, B. J. Grosz, and L. A. Gilliom. 1993. Pronouns, names, and the centering of attention in discourse. *Cognitive Science*, 17:311–47.

S. B. Greene, G. McKoon, and R. Ratcliff. 1992. Pronoun resolution and discourse models. *Journal of Experimental Psychology: Learning, Memory, & Cognition*, 18:266–83.

Barbara J. Grosz, Scott Weinstein, and Aravind K. Joshi. 1995. Centering: A framework for modeling the local coherence of discourse. *Computational linguistics*, 21(2):203–225.

Anke Hammer, Rainer Goebel, Jens Schwarzbach, Thomas F. Münte, and Bernadette M. Jansma. 2007. When sex meets syntactic gender on a neural basis during pronoun processing. *Brain Research*, 1146:185–198.

C.-T. James Huang. 1989. Pro-drop in Chinese: A generalized control theory. In Osvaldo Jaeggli and Kenneth Safir, editors, *The null subject parameter*, pages 185–214. Springer.

Robert Kantor. 1977. *The management and comprehension of discourse connection by pronouns in English*. Ph.D. thesis, Ohio State University.

Prantik Kundu, Souheil J. Inati, Jennifer W. Evans, Wen-Ming Luh, and Peter A. Bandettini. 2012. Differentiating BOLD and non-BOLD signals in fMRI time series using multi-echo EPI. *NeuroImage*, 60(3):1759–1770.

Shalom Lappin and Herbert J. Leass. 1994. An algorithm for pronominal anaphora resolution. *Computational linguistics*, 20(4):535–561.

Charles N. Li and Sandra A. Thompson. 1976. Subject and topic: A new typology. In Charles N. Li, editor, *Subject and topic*, pages 457–89. Academic Press, New York.

William Matchin, Jon Sprouse, and Gregory Hickok. 2014. A structural distance effect for backward anaphora in Broca's area: An fMRI study. *Brain and Language*, 138:1–11.

Brian McElree. 2001. Working memory and focal attention. *Journal of experimental psychology. Learning, memory, and cognition*, 27(3):817–835.

Jonathan W. Peirce. 2007. PsychoPy—Psychophysics software in Python. *Journal of Neuroscience Methods*, 162(1-2):8–13.

William Penny, Karl Friston, John Ashburner, Stefan Kiebel, and Thomas Nichols. 2011. *Statistical parametric mapping: The analysis of functional brain images*. Academic Press.

Jacolien van Rij, Hedderik van Rijn, and Petra Hendriks. 2013. How WM load influences linguistic processing in adults: A computational model of pronoun interpretation in discourse. *Topics in Cognitive Science*, 5(3):564–580.

Andrea Santi and Yosef Grodzinsky. 2007. Taxing working memory with syntax: Bihemispheric modulations. *Human Brain Mapping*, 28(11):1089–1097.

Andrea Santi and Yosef Grodzinsky. 2012. Broca's area and sentence comprehension: A relationship parasitic on dependency, displacement or predictability? *Neuropsychologia*, 50(5):821–832.

Pontus Stenetorp, Sampo Pyysalo, Goran Topić, Tomoko Ohta, Sophia Ananiadou, and Jun'ichi Tsujii. 2012. BRAT: a web-based tool for NLP-assisted text annotation. In *Proceedings of the Demonstrations at the 13th Conference of the European Chapter of the Association for Computational Linguistics*, pages 102–107. Association for Computational Linguistics.

Leila Wehbe, Ashish Vaswani, Kevin Knight, and Tom M. Mitchell. 2014. Aligning context-based statistical models of language with brain activity during reading. In *EMNLP*, pages 233–243.

Liejion Xu. 2006. Topicalization in asian languages. In Marting Everaert and Henk van Riemsdijk, editors, *The Wiley Blackwell Companion to Syntax, 2nd Edition*, pages 137–174. Hoboken, NJ: Blackwell Publishing, Hoboken, NJ.

Event versus entity co-reference:
Effects of context and form of referring expression

Sharid Loáiciga[1]   **Luca Bevacqua**[2]   **Hannah Rohde**[2]   **Christian Hardmeier**[3]

[1]CLASP, University of Gothenburg
[2]Department of Linguistics and English Language, University of Edinburgh
[3]Department of Linguistics and Philology, Uppsala University

`sharid.loaiciga@gu.se`   `lbevacqu@ed.ac.uk`
`hannah.rohde@ed.ac.uk`   `christian.hardmeier@lingfil.uu.se`

Abstract

Anaphora resolution systems require both an enumeration of possible candidate antecedents and an identification process of the antecedent. This paper focuses on (i) the impact of the form of referring expression on entity-vs-event preferences and (ii) how properties of the passage interact with referential form. Two crowd-sourced story-continuation experiments were conducted, using constructed and naturally-occurring passages, to see how participants interpret *It* and *This* pronouns following a context sentence that makes available event and entity referents. Our participants show a strong, but not categorical, bias to use *This* to refer to events and *It* to refer to entities. However, these preferences vary with passage characteristics such as verb class (a proxy in our constructed examples for the number of explicit and implicit entities) and more subtle author intentions regarding subsequent re-mention (the original event-vs-entity re-mention of our corpus items).

1 Introduction

A challenge in discourse interpretation is the resolution of referring expressions, particularly those whose meaning is compatible with many potential antecedents. To take an example like (1), a passage may introduce a number of entities and situations that a subsequent sentence might refer to.

(1) Everybody who is involved with this debate has been struggling over me and my personality. [ParCorFull]

For a sentence following (1), certain expressions would be resolved unambiguously to a unique entity (e.g., to the speaker for a 1st person singular pronoun *I*) or would easily be linked to the only compatible referent in the context (e.g., to the group of relevant individuals described as *Everybody* for a 3rd person plural pronoun *They*). Other expressions are compatible with more than one entity (e.g., the debate or the personality for a pronoun *It*) and therefore create potential ambiguity. Making matters worse, the antecedent of some expressions can be either an entity or something more abstract: an event or situation or idea. Such expressions include personal pronouns like *It* and demonstrative pronouns like *This/That*.

Given the complexity of identifying a set of candidate abstract antecedents in a given context and then determining whether a particular expression is re-mentioning one of those abstract antecedents or a more concrete entity, many co-reference systems focus only on nominal antecedents (e.g., BART, Stanford's sieve-based, HOTCoref (Versley and Björkelund, 2015)). However, event instances are also referential.[1]

This paper asks when and to what degree event instances serve as antecedents when a competing entity referent is also available. The goal is to model human choices as a baseline to inform co-reference systems. We report two psycholinguistic studies that use a story-continuation task to measure participants' resolution of pronouns *It* and *This*.

Improving our understanding of the interpretation of the "difficult" anaphoric cases is a step towards better anaphora and co-reference systems. It has been noted that current systems struggle to identify this type of reference and that anaphoricity determiners have poor performance (Heinzerling et al., 2017). *It*, *This* and *That* are also frequent in dialogue data for which co-reference sys-

---

[1] Here we call *event* what is more commonly known as *abstract anaphora* (cf. Dipper and Zinsmeister (2010); Nedoluzhko and Lapshinova-Koltunski (2016)). We take as an *event* any non-nominal relationship for the pronouns *It* and *This* and a *textual* antecedent in the form of a text span of variable length (e.g., a word, a clause, several sentences). *Textual* means that anaphoric relations for which some type of inference is necessary are not included, e.g., bridging or extra-textual reference. The term *event reference* is founded upon Webber (1986), and we set on the name *event* for the sake of consistency with the annotation in the corpus used in the second study presented here.

97

Proceedings of the Workshop on Computational Models of Reference, Anaphora and Coreference, pages 97–103
New Orleans, Louisiana, June 6, 2018. ©2018 Association for Computational Linguistics

tems' performance is particularly low (Eckert and Strube, 2000; Müller, 2007). In addition, pronoun function is relevant to the evaluation of machine translation systems since different functions entail different translations according to the constraints of the language pair and can thus affect performance (Guillou, 2016).

2   Related Work

Both corpus-based and psycholinguistics works on the interpretation of anaphoric expressions concentrate on the identification of the antecedents of nominal expressions.   Abstract anaphora—anaphora that involve reference to abstract entities such as events or states (Asher, 1993)—is much less studied from both fields, as evidenced by the little amount of annotated data available (Dipper and Zinsmeister, 2010; Poesio, 2015).

Corpus-based studies of pronouns are often done in relationship to the texts on which co-reference resolution systems will be trained and tested.   With the clear aim to improve precision, the authors of these systems have an interest in quantifying "non-anaphoric" pronouns for preventing their resolution. We know for instance, that about 5% of referential pronouns and 71% of demonstratives in dialogue data refer to events (Müller, 2007; Poesio, 2015), whereas about 3% of referential *it* pronouns in written text of various genres refer to events (Evans, 2001).

In psycholinguistic research, on the other hand, the focus has been on using theoretical constructs of complexity, salience, and focus to capture co-reference patterns. The demonstratives *This* and *That* have been grouped together, assuming that they behave in the same manner, but potentially differently from *It*. Brown-Schmidt et al. (2005) analyze *It* vs *That* and report a preference for *That* if what is referred to is a composite (e.g., *I'll have the hamburger and fries. I'll have that, too.*), independent of other metrics of the salience of the referent. Building on the Centering co-reference model (Grosz et al., 1995), Passonneau (1989) analyzes intra-sentential instances of *It* vs *That* with an explicit NP antecedent. She reports that *It* is used to refer to the center (most often the subject), whereas *That* favors non-centers.

Corpus-based studies offer insights about language use, since the written texts they are based on are, after all, natural passages. They offer better estimates for building systems that will be used

on those texts. Corpus-based studies, on the other hand, do not offer any explanation as to why a particular item follows a certain distribution, and they grant little control over the confounding variables responsible for that distribution. In this respect, psycholinguistics studies provide more suitable methods for capturing the cognitive processes behind naturally occurring phenomena. We therefore start the next section with a study using constructed passages to allow for careful control over format and content.

3   Study 1: Constructed passages

A story-continuation experiment was conducted to establish a baseline rate at which participants assign *It/This* pronouns to entity vs event antecedents.   By varying a property of the context sentence, we test how malleable the two pronouns' respective co-reference preferences are. A 2x2 design manipulated the context sentence (alternating/non-alternating verb) and the pronoun prompt (*It/This*, as in (2)-(3)).

(2)   The   train   from   the   Highlands   arrived promptly. It/This ____

(3)   The balloon with the red hearts popped noiselessly. It/This ____

The availability of entities for anaphoric resolution is dependent on the argument structure of the previous predicates. Alternating verbs can have an intransitive as well as a transitive use: the first usually describes a change of state (4-a), and the latter specifics, in subject position, which entity brought on the change (4-b). Conversely, non-alternating verbs do not allow a transitive use (5).[2]

(4)   a. The snow melted.
      b. The heat melted the snow.

(5)   a. The battery died.
      b. * The heat died the battery.

Manipulating the verb in the context sentence affects the argument realization options associated with the predicate: Non-alternating verbs like *arrive* permit only a single realization with the entity that arrives always in subject position; alternating verbs like *pop* are compatible with realizations

---

[2] Jespersen (1927) collects verbs undergoing alternation in a "move and change class". They have also been referred to as respectively *causative* and *anticausative* (or *inchoative*) verbs (Schäfer, 2009); the phenomenon has also been studied as "causative-inchoative alternation" (Haspelmath, 1993).

where the entity that pops appears in subject position or object position. For alternating verbs, an explicit agent entity can be introduced (*I popped the balloon*) or left implicit, as in (3).

One hypothesis is that alternating verbs could make available an additional (implicit) agent who might provide more entity co-reference opportunities and thereby increase entity co-reference and reduce event co-reference. Another hypothesis is that non-alternating verbs may make salient one single (explicit) entity by eliminating competition from other (implicit) entities and thereby yield more entity co-reference and less event co-reference. The existence of an external, unspecified argument in the syntax of alternating verbs is still controversial (Embick, 2004; Schäfer, 2009), but the cognitive accessibility of a possible agentive entity arises from the very fact that the causative alternation exists.

Although differences have been observed between the use of proximal and distal demonstratives *this* and *that* (Çokal et al., 2014), we targeted only one demonstrative pronoun in order to simplify the design. This is in keeping with observations about the functional grouping of a number of pronouns (zeros, demonstratives, and personal pronouns) when used deictically (Webber, 1990).

3.1 Materials

The 24 experimental items consisted of a context sentence and a pronoun prompt, as in (2)-(3). Participants saw all items, with either *It* or *This*. Subject NPs were modified (8 nouns with pre-nominal adjectives, 8 nouns with post-nominal prepositional phrases, 8 nouns with post-nominal relative clauses). The verb used an adverbial or particle predicate (roughly half alternating, half non-alternating). The head of the subject NP was always the only singular entity, with any other mentioned entities being incompatible with 3rd person singular co-reference (e.g., *we* or *the red hearts*).[3]

The 24 experimental items were interleaved with 40 filler items. These included 20 passages with a context sentence mentioning one or two entities, followed by a discourse adverbial prompt (e.g., *As a result*, *Then*), 16 passages for an unrelated experiment involving mentions of companies and other organisations, and 4 catch trials with an obvious correct response (e.g., *Caleb did all the*

cooking for the BBQ even though he hates BBQ. He prefers mac 'n ____).

3.2 Participants

Twenty-seven monolingual English-speaking participants aged 19-63 (mean age 36, σ=11.2; 15 male) were recruited from Amazon's Mechanical Turk (Munro et al., 2010; Gibson et al., 2011) and received \$4 for an estimated 30-minute task.

3.3 Procedure

Continuations were collected via a web-based interface that participants could access from their own computer. Each item was presented on a page by itself with a text box for participants to use for writing their continuation.

3.4 Annotation and analysis

Continuations for experimental items were annotated for type of co-reference (entity vs event). The four authors of this paper shared the annotation such that all target continuations were coded by two annotators. To be conservative, annotators were blind to the *It/This* prompt condition and agreed to err on the side of annotating a pronoun as ambiguous if the pronoun could be interpreted plausibly as coreferential with an event or an entity (e.g., *The brand new siren sounded loud.* [omitted *pronoun*] *startled some people*).

Using mixed-effects logistic regression, we modeled the binary outcome of entity or event co-reference with fixed effects for prompt type, verb class, and their interaction, with maximal random effects structure when supported by the data (Barr et al., 2013). Where a model did not converge, we removed random correlations. All factors were centered. Reported p-values are from glmer model output using the lme4 package (Bates et al., 2015) in R (R Development Core Team, 2008).

3.5 Results

Of the 626 total continuations, we excluded 128 that were judged by one or more annotators to be ambiguous (or for which the annotators gave conflicting annotations) as well as 55 that used the prompt in another way (e.g., *This noun*). This left 443 continuations with either entity or event co-reference. Note that at the analysis stage, 2 of the 24 verbs were re-classified as alternating verbs, shifting the original even split between alternating/non-alternating verbs. However,

---

[3] The data to reproduce our experiments and the full models can be found on `https://github.com/sharidloaiciga/event_vs_entity`.

glmer models are understood to be robust against datasets that are not perfectly balanced.

The results (see Figure 1) show a strong, but not categorical, bias to use *It* to refer to entities and *This* to refer to events. In addition, verb type impacts co-reference, whereby verbs that permit alternations yield more event co-reference than non-alternating verbs. This is in keeping with our second hypothesis that the salience of the single argument of non-alternating verbs may have attracted more entity co-reference.

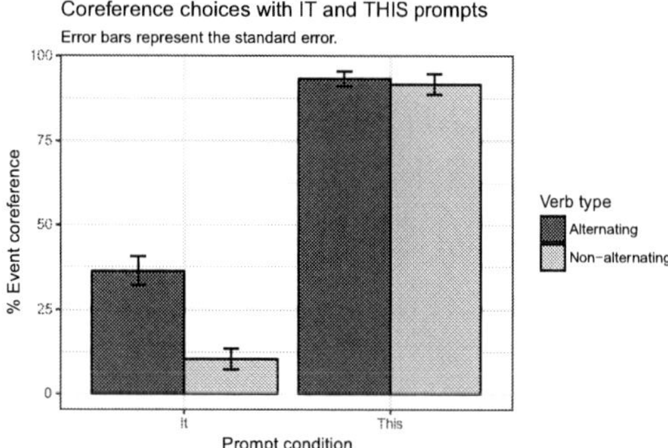

Figure 1: Study 1 results by prompt and verb type.

The prompt type $\times$ verb type model of co-reference choice confirms a main effect of prompt type (β=5.100, p<0.001) and a main effect of verb type (β=1.437, p<0.05). There was no prompt $\times$ verb type interaction (β=-1.350, p=0.22).[4]

4 Study 2: Corpus passages

4.1 Materials

The 48 target passages are minimally edited sentences extracted from the ParCorFull corpus (Lapshinova-Koltunski et al., 2018). This is a German-English parallel corpus annotated with full co-reference. Although the corpus is designed for nominal co-reference, it includes annotations of two types of antecedents: entities and events. Entities can be either pronouns or NPs, whereas events can be VPs, clauses or a set of clauses.

ParCorFull includes texts from TED talks transcripts and also newswire data.[5] Since pronouns are generally more frequent in the TED talks genre than news, we concentrated on this portion of the corpus only. Twelve examples of each *It-entity*, *It-event*, *This-entity*, and *This-event* were selected. In comparison to the sentences from Study 1, the corpus sentences were relatively long; therefore, simplified or shortened versions were used.

Additionally, the target passages were interleaved with 52 filler items. From these, 24 were extracted from ParCorFull sentences with no annotation and a continuation starting with an adverbial expression was prompted (e.g., *The encyclopedia business in the days of leatherbound books was basically a distribution business. Eventually, ____*). 24 other fillers were extracted from the OntoNotes corpus (Pradhan et al., 2013) for a dataset for an unrelated experiment involving mentions of companies and other organisations, as in Study 1. A final 4 fillers repeated the catch trials from Study 1.

4.2 Participants

Nineteen monolingual English-speaking participants aged 23-44 (mean age 30, σ=6.5; 13 male) were recruited from Amazon's Mechanical Turk and received $7 for an estimated 50-minute task.

4.3 Procedure, annotation, and analysis

The procedure was identical to that in Study 1. The annotation followed that described for Study 1. As an illustration, example (6) shows a passage whose original co-reference relation was one between an *it* pronoun and an entity antecedent. The continuations in (7) were annotated as event co-reference (7-a), entity co-reference (7-b), and no co-reference when the *It* prompt was classed as being used pleonastically (7-c).

(6) You carry a phone. It knows where you are.
     [original co-reference: entity~*it*]

(7) a. You carry a phone. This is something that just about everyone does these days.
     b. You carry a phone. It is capable of connecting you to others and the world around you.
     c. You carry a phone. It wouldn't hurt you to call once in a while.

The binary outcome of entity/event co-reference

---

[4] Inspection of Figure 1 suggests a possible interaction whereby the effect of verb type looks stronger in the *It* condition than in the *This* condition. The lack of a significant interaction in the model may reflect the fact that the co-reference rate for non-alternating verbs in the *This* condition is already near ceiling and there may be little room for (measuring) a further increase.

[5] Specifically, the ParCorFull corpus includes the datasets used in the ParCor corpus (Guillou et al., 2014), the DiscoMT workshop (Hardmeier et al., 2016) and the test sets from the WMT 2017 shared task (Bojar et al., 2017).

was again modeled with a logistic regression. We included fixed effects for prompt type, original passage co-reference (entity/event), original passage referring expression (*it/this*), and the 2-way and 3-way interactions. All factors were centered.

4.4 Results

Of the 788 total continuations, we excluded 94 that were judged by one or more annotators to be ambiguous (or for which the annotators gave conflicting annotations) as well as 98 that used the prompt in another way (e.g., *This noun*). This left 596 continuations with either entity or event co-reference.

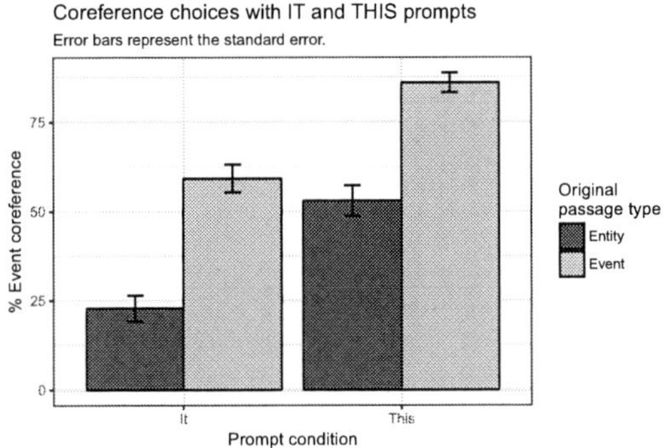

Figure 2: Study 2 results by prompt and original co-reference (collapsing over original *it/this* pronoun type)

The results (see Figure 2) follow those of Study 1 for the prompt manipulation: Event co-reference is higher with *This* than *It*. Event co-reference further increases when the original passage contained event co-reference. The model (prompt type × original passage type × original passage pronoun) confirms a main effect of prompt type (β=2.529, p<0.001) and a main effect of original passage type (β=3.053, p<0.001), with no effect of original pronoun or any significant interactions.

5   Discussion

The two studies show divergent co-reference distributions for the personal pronoun *It* and the demonstrative *This*: a bias towards entity co-reference for *It* and a bias for event co-reference for *This*. As far as we know, this pattern has been proposed (Dipper and Zinsmeister, 2010), but not properly measured. Given the oft-assumed division of labor between these two pronouns, what is notable is their flexibility. Neither form was found to be used categorically in Study 1 or Study 2.

Interestingly, the study with the constructed passages showed that verbs which permit an agent alternation as either an implicit or explicit argument are more prone to trigger an event co-referent than an entity one. This finding is potentially useful as an additional feature for anaphoricity detection or event mention identification in co-reference resolution systems.

Furthermore, we saw a bias towards event co-reference for the corpus passages in Study 2 that were known to have yielded event co-reference in their original passages. This suggests that there are properties of the context sentence that may make salient an event over an entity. If there are event-favoring properties of the context sentence that human participants are sensitive to, it is a tractable task to build automatic classifiers that learn to recognize such properties. This supports the idea that the task of differentiating anaphoric and pleonastic instances of *It* (Evans, 2001; Boyd et al., 2005; Bergsma and Yarowsky, 2011; Lee et al., 2016; Loáiciga et al., 2017) could potentially improve performance.

Although presumably (machine) learnable, the question of what exactly constitutes an event remains unanswered. A number of ambiguous examples which were excluded from our analysis included entities that are close to their entailed event (e.g., *The bomb that the arsonists had planted exploded violently*) or that were very abstract (e.g., *The greatest opportunity materialized unexpectedly. It/This was almost like magic.*).

6   Conclusions and Future Work

This paper reports an investigation on abstract anaphora. Specifically, two studies targeted the ambiguity that occurs when entity and event antecedents are available for the pronouns *It* and *This*. A clear pattern emerged whereby *It* favors entity co-reference and *This* favors event co-reference. This pattern is also affected by the number of arguments that the main verb can take. Although further investigation is needed regarding the properties of events, their salience, and the gray area between events and entities, our results take a first step towards disentangling the behavior of less well-understood anaphoric relations.

Acknowledgments

Christian Hardmeier was supported by the Swedish Research Council under grant 2017-930, *Neural Pronoun Models for Machine Translation*.

References

Nicholas Asher. 1993. *Reference to Abstract Objects in Discourse*. Springer, Netherlands.

Dale J. Barr, Roger Levy, Christoph Scheepers, and Harry J. Tily. 2013. Random effects structure for confirmatory hypothesis testing: Keep it maximal. *Journal of memory and language*, 68(3):255–278.

Douglas Bates, Martin Mächler, Ben Bolker, and Steve Walker. 2015. Fitting linear mixed-effects models using lme4. *Journal of Statistical Software*, 67(1):1–48.

Shane Bergsma and David Yarowsky. 2011. NADA: A robust system for non - referential pronoun detection. In Iris Hendrickx, Sobha Lalitha Devi, António Branco, and Ruslan Mitkov, editors, *Anaphora Processing and Applications: 8th Discourse Anaphora and Anaphor Resolution Colloquium (DAARC)*, Lecture Notes in Artificial Intelligence, pages 12–23. Springer, Faro, Portugal.

Ondřej Bojar, Rajen Chatterjee, Christian Federmann, Yvette Graham, Barry Haddow, Shujian Huang, Matthias Huck, Philipp Koehn, Qun Liu, Varvara Logacheva, Christof Monz, Matteo Negri, Matt Post, Raphael Rubino, Lucia Specia, and Marco Turchi. 2017. Findings of the 2017 conference on machine translation (wmt17). In *Proceedings of the Second Conference on Machine Translation, Volume 2: Shared Task Papers*, pages 169–214, Copenhagen, Denmark. Association for Computational Linguistics.

Adriane Boyd, Whitney Gegg-Harrison, and Donna K. Byron. 2005. Identifying non-referential *it*: a machine learning approach incorporating linguistically motivated patterns. In *Proceedings of the ACL Workshop on Feature Engineering for Machine Learning in Natural Language Processing*, pages 40–47, Ann Arbor, Michigan. Association for Computational Linguistics.

Sarah Brown-Schmidt, Donna K. Byron, and Michael K. Tanenhaus. 2005. Beyond salience: Interpretation of personal and demonstrative pronouns. *Journal of Memory and Language*, 53(2):292–313.

Derya Çokal, Patrick Sturt, and Fernanda Ferreira. 2014. Deixis: *This* and *That* in written narrative discourse. *Discourse Processes*, 51(3):201–229.

Stefanie Dipper and Heike Zinsmeister. 2010. Towards a standard for annotating abstract anaphora. In *Proceedings of the LREC Workshop on Language Resource and Language Technology Standards state of the art, emerging needs, and future developments*, LREC10-W4, pages 54–59, Valleta, Malta. European Language Resources Association (ELRA).

Miriam Eckert and Michael Strube. 2000. Dialogue acts, synchronising units and anaphora resolution. *Journal of Semantics*, 17(1):51–89.

David Embick. 2004. Unaccusative syntax and verbal alternations. In Artemis Alexiadou, Elena Anagnostopoulou, and Martin Everaert, editors, *The Unaccusativity Puzzle: Explorations of the Syntax-Lexicon Interface*, pages 137–158. Oxford University Press, Oxford, New York.

Richard Evans. 2001. Applying machine learning toward an automatic classification of it. *Literary and Linguistic Computing*, 16(1):45–57.

Edward Gibson, Steve Piantadosi, and Kristina Fedorenko. 2011. Using mechanichal turk to obtain and analyze english acceptability judgments. *Language and Linguistics Compass*, 5(8):509–524.

Barbara J. Grosz, Aravind K. Joshi, and Scott Weinstein. 1995. Centering: A framework for modelling the local coherence of discourse. *Computational Linguistics*, 21(2):203–225.

Liane Guillou. 2016. *Incorporating Pronoun Function into Statistical Machine Translation*. Ph.D. thesis, University of Edinburgh, Scotland, UK.

Liane Guillou, Christian Hardmeier, Aaron Smith, Jörg Tiedemann, and Bonnie Webber. 2014. ParCor 1.0: A parallel pronoun-coreference corpus to support statistical MT. In *Proceedings of the 9th International Conference on Language Resources and Evaluation*, LREC 2014, pages 3191–3198, Reykjavik, Iceland. European Language Resources Association (ELRA).

Christian Hardmeier, Jörg Tiedemann, Preslav Nakov, Sara Stymne, and Yannick Versely. 2016. DiscoMT 2015 Shared Task on Pronoun Translation. LINDAT/CLARIN digital library at Institute of Formal and Applied Linguistics, Charles University in Prague. http://hdl.handle.net/11372/LRT-1611.

Martin Haspelmath. 1993. More on the typology of inchoative/causative verb alternations. In Bernard Comrie and Maria Polinsky, editors, *Causatives and transitivity*, pages 87–120. John Benjamins, Amsterdam.

Benjamin Heinzerling, Nafise Sadat Moosavi, and Michael Strube. 2017. Revisiting selectional preferences for coreference resolution. In *Proceedings of the 2017 Conference on Empirical Methods in Natural Language Processing*, pages 1332–1339, Copenhagen, Denmark. Association for Computational Linguistics.

Otto Jespersen. 1927. *Modern English grammar on historical principles, Part III: Syntax (Second Volume)*. Allen and Unwin, London.

Ekaterina Lapshinova-Koltunski, Christian Hardmeier, and Pauline Krielke. 2018. ParCorFull: a parallel corpus annotated with full coreference. In *Proceedings of 11th Language Resources and Evaluation Conference*, pages 00–00, Miyazaki, Japan. European Language Resources Association (ELRA). To appear.

Timothy Lee, Alex Lutz, and Jinho D. Choi. 2016. QA-It: classifying non-referential it for question answer pairs. In *Proceedings of the ACL 2016 Student Research Workshop*, pages 132–137, Berlin, Germany. Association for Computational Linguistics.

Sharid Loáiciga, Liane Guillou, and Christian Hardmeier. 2017. What is it? disambiguating the different readings of the pronoun "it". In *Proceedings of the 2017 Conference on Empirical Methods in Natural Language Processing*, pages 1325–1331, Copenhagen, Denmark. Association for Computational Linguistics.

Christoph Müller. 2007. Resolving *It*, *This*, and *That* in unrestricted multi-party dialog. In *Proceedings of the 45th Annual Meeting of the Association for Computational Linguistics*, ACL07, pages 816–823, Prague, Czech Republic. Association for Computational Linguistics (ACL).

Robert Munro, Steven Bethard, Victor Kuperman, Vicky T. Lai, Robin Melnick, Christopher Potts, Tyler Schnoebelen, and Harry Tily. 2010. Crowdsourcing and language studies: the new generation of linguistic data. In *Proceedings of the NAACL HLT 2010 Workshop on Creating Speech and Language Data with Amazon's Mechanical Turk*, pages 122–130. Association for Computational Linguistics.

Anna Nedoluzhko and Ekaterina Lapshinova-Koltunski. 2016. Abstract coreference in a multilingual perspective: a view on czech and german. In *Proceedings of the Workshop on Coreference Resolution Beyond OntoNotes*, CORBON 2016, pages 47–52, Ann Arbor, Michigan. Association for Computational Linguistics.

Rebecca J. Passonneau. 1989. Getting at discourse referents. In *Proceedings of the 27th Annual Meeting of the Association for Computational Linguistics*, pages 51–59, Vancouver, British Columbia, Canada. Association for Computational Linguistics.

Massimo Poesio. 2015. Linguistic and cognitive evidence about anaphora. In Massimo Poesio, Roland Stuckardt, and Yannick Versley, editors, *Anaphora Resolution: Algorithms, Resources and Application*, pages 23–54. Springer-Verlag, Berlin Heidelberg.

Sameer Pradhan, Alessandro Moschitti, Nianwen Xue, Hwee Tou Ng, Anders Björkelund, Olga Uryupina, Yuchen Zhang, and Zhi Zhong. 2013. Towards robust linguistic analysis using OntoNotes. In *Proceedings of the Seventeenth Conference on Computational Natural Language Learning*, pages 143–152, Sofia, Bulgaria. Association for Computational Linguistics.

R Development Core Team. 2008. *R: A Language and Environment for Statistical Computing*. R Foundation for Statistical Computing, Vienna, Austria. ISBN 3-900051-07-0.

Florian Schäfer. 2009. The causative alternation. *Language and Linguistics Compass*, 3(2):641–681.

Yannick Versley and Anders Björkelund. 2015. Off-the-shelf tools. In Massimo Poesio, Roland Stuckardt, and Yannick Versley, editors, *Anaphora Resolution: Algorithms, Resources and Applications*, pages 237–266. Springer-Verlag, Berlin Heidelberg.

Bonnie Webber. 1986. Findings of the 2016 WMT shared task on cross-lingual pronoun prediction. In *Theoretical Issues in Natural Language Processing*, TINLAP-3, pages 158–163, Las Cruces, New Mexico. Association for Computational Linguistics.

Bonnie L. Webber. 1990. Structure and ostension in the interpretation of discourse deixis. Technical Report MS-CIS-90-58, University of Pennsylvania, Department of Computer and Information Science.

Author Index